Western European Communists and the Collapse of Communism

Western European Communists and the Collapse of Communism

Edited by

David S. Bell

BERG

Oxford/Providence

First published in 1993 by
Berg Publishers Limited
Editorial offices:
221 Waterman Street, Providence, RI 02906, USA
150 Cowley Road, Oxford, OX4 1JJ. UK

Library of Congress Cataloging-in-Publication Data
Western European Communists and the collapse of communism / edited by
David S. Bell.
    p.   cm.
    Includes index.
    ISBN 0–85496–806–7
    1. Communist parties—Europe.   2. Post-communism—Europe,
Eastern.   I. Bell, David Scott.
    HX239.W47   1993
324.2'175'094—dc20   92–12214
                                                CIP

British Library Cataloguing in Publication Data
A CIP catalogue record for this book is available from the British Library

Printed in the United States by Edwards Brothers, Ann Arbor, MI.

Contents

Preface

This book examines the predicament of Western Communist Parties faced with the impact of the reforms in the Soviet Union initiated by Gorbachev, the collapse of the Eastern bloc and the end of 'really existing sicialism' in the USSR itself. The Western European parties we have chosen are the big (sometimes called 'mass' parties – the Italian, French, Finnish, Spanish and Portuguese – plus the British and German parties which illustrate particular aspects of the decline of the movement.

The revolutions in the East caught the Communist movement in terminal decline and in a degree of dismay at its prospects. Many took the obvious course and wound up their affairs, others transformed their appeal (some laying claim to 'social democracy'), but a few (and those not insignificant) chose to behave as if nothing had happened. The denial that the 'Socialist ideal' had been damaged carried some credibility when it was the Eastern satellites which were being freed, but when the Soviet Union disintegrated it was clear that Leninist systems were unreformable – the moment there is a departure from the model they collapse. However, Communism as a movement no longer exists and this book is an epitaph to a monument to an unsuccessful protest in Western Europe. It is a small irony that Communist history has, until now, been impossible to research, but the opening of archives may mean that Communists and historians will be able to disentangle the affairs of the Third International.

As this book goes to press the red flag is being replaced on the Kremlin with the Russian Tricolour. We hope to continue to contribute to Communist studies even if the world movement itself no longer exists.

David S. Bell
Leeds University

Abbreviations

AKEL *Anorthotikon Komma Ergazomenou Laou* (Progressive Party of the Working People) Cyprus

CC Central Committee

CGIL *Confederazione Generale del Lavoro* (Union Confederation Italy)

CGT *Confédération Général du Travail* (France)

CGTP *Confederação Geral de Trabalhadores Portugueses* – *Intersindical Nacional* (General Confederation of Portuguese Workers)

CPB Communist Party of Britain

CPN *Communistische Partij van Nederland* (Communist Party of the Netherlands)

CPSU Communist Party of the Soviet Union

DC *Deamocrazia Cristiana* (Christian Democrats Italy)

DEVA *Demokraattinen Vaihtoehto* (Democratic Alternative) Finland

DKP *Deutsche Komunistische Partei* (German Communist Party)

DKP Danish Communist Party

EVP *Evangelische Volkspartij* (Evangelical People's Party) Netherlands

FP *Federacion Progresista* (Progressive Federation) Spain

FRG Federal Republic of Germany

GDR German Democratic Republic

IU *Izquierda Unida* (United Left) Spain

KKE *Kommounistiko Komma Elladas* Spain (Greek Communist Party) (Exterior)

KOMEP *Kommunistiki Epiteoris* (Communist Review) Greek

KPD *Kommunistische Partei Deutschlands*I (German Communist Party)

KTP *Kommunistinen Tyoekansan Puolue* (Communist Workers' Party) Finland

LA *Vasemnistoliitto* (Leftist Alliance) Finland

MFA *Movimento das Forcas Armadas* (Armed Forces Movement) Portugal

NCP New Communist Party (UK)

NKP Norges Kommunistiske Parti (Norwegian Communist Party)

PA *Altydubandalagid* (People's Alliance) Iceland

PASOC *Partido de Acción Socialista* (Socialist Action Party)

PaSoK *Panellino Sociaistiko Kinima* (Panhellenic Socialist Movement) Greece

PCE *Partido Comunista de España* (Spanish Communist Party)

PCF *Parti Communiste Français* (French Communist Party)

PCI *Partito Communista Italiano* (Italian Communist Party)

PCP *Partido Communista Português* (Portuguese Communist Party)

PCPE *Partido Comunista de los Pueblos de España* (Communist Party of the Peoples of Spain)

PDS *Partei des Demokratischen Sozialismus* (Party of Democratic Socialism) Germany

PDUP *Partito d'Unità Proletaria* (Party of Proletarian Unity) Italy

PPR *Politieke Partij Radikalen* (Radical Party) Netherlands

PS *Parti Socialiste* (Socialist Party) France

PS *Partido Socialista* (Socialist Party) Portugal

PSD *Partito Democratico della Sinistra* (Democratic Party of the Left) Italy

PSD *Partido Social Democràtico* (Social Democratic Party) Portugal

PSI *Partito Socialista Italiano* (Italian Socialist Party)

PSOE *Partido Socialista Obrero Español* (Spanish Socialist Workers Party)

PSP *Pacifistische Socialistische Partij* (Pacifist-Socialist Party) Netherlands

PSUC *Partit Socialista Unificat de Catalunya* (Unified Socialist Party of Catalonia)

PTE *Partido del Trabajo de España* (Spanish Labour Party)

RAF *Rote Armee Fraktion* (Red Army Faction) Germany

SED *Sozialistische Einheitspartei Deutschland* (Socialist Unity Party) Germany

SF *Socialstisk Folkeparti* (Socialist People's Party) Denmark

SFIO *Section Française de l'International Ouvrière* (French Section of the Workers' International)

SI Socialist Initiative (Berlin)

SKDL *Suomen Kansan Demokraatinen Liiito*, (Finnish People's Democratic League)

SKP *Suomen Kommunistien Puolue*, (Finnish Communist Party)

SKP-y *Suomen Kommunistinen Puolue – Yhtenäisyys* (Finnish Communist Party Unity)

KPD *Sozialdemokratische Partei Deutschlands* (Social Democratic Party) Germany

SV *Socialistisk Venstreparti* (Socialist Left Party) Norway

UGT *União Geral dos Trabalhadores* (General Union of Workers) Portugal

UGT *Uniòn General de Trabajadores* (General Union of Workers) Spain

VCN Verbond ran Communisten in Nederland (Netherlands Communist Party) (hard-line)

VKP *Vönsterpartiet Kommunisterna* (Swedish Communist Party

VPK *Vänsterpartiet* (Left Party) Sweden

WFTU World Federation of Trade Unions (Communist)

Introduction

The ascent of Mikhail Gorbachev to power in March 1985 as General Secretary of the Communist Party of the Soviet Union (CPSU) was initially welcomed by all sections of Western Communist opinion. However, the pace of the reform movements initiated and the subsequent fall of the Eastern bloc regimes, followed by the disintegration of the Soviet Union, have been shattering for the Western Communists even if the impact has been uneven. In fact, the Western Communists were moving in different directions already in the 1980s. The dramatic collapse of the Eastern bloc in 1989, followed by the August 'coup' in 1991, revealed to western parties how out of contact the Eastern Comunists were with the societies they had ruled for forty-five years or more, and then how much of a minority the Communist Party was in the 'fatherland' of socialism itself. The setting of the sun on the Soviet empire removed any residual illusions about the 'future which works' – or 'real existing socialism' as Communists called it – and touched off a further wave of dissidence inside the orthodox Western Parties.

This book looks at the state of Western Communism after the impact of these extraordinary events, but it may be useful to paint in some background because Western Communists were by the 1980s (with only a few exceptions) already marginal forces in a continent dominated by conservatives (mainly Christian Democrats) and Socialists of the Second International stamp.

Communist Parties (with the exception of the Netherlands party) were formed in 1920 and usually from the left wings, union militants and pacifist sections of the Social Democratic parties. These new parties were then 'Bolshevised' – that is given the Leninist bureaucracy and run on totalitarian democratic centralist lines. When Stalin took over there was a further change in the top leadership to remove those Communists who had been recruited by the pre-Stalinist International and replace them with Stalinists. During the 1920s the sectarian strategies of the Communists – mainly aimed at undercutting the Socialist Parties by revolutionary action on the Left – directly caused the rise of Mussolini and Hitler. The brief respite from the sectarian 'class against class' strategy (the Popular Fronts) had some success in France, where it enabled the French party to rise from 8.3 per cent to 15.3 per cent but these gains were probably all destroyed by the impact of the Nazi/Soviet pact and the Communists' subsequent opposition to the 'imperialist' war and – in some countries – collaboration.

However, this is a soufflé which rose twice. The Communists participation in the Resistance – and in some cases they were the principal component – their association with the Red Army (then a 'victorious ally') and the general appeal of the Left and discredit of the Right at the Liberation led to respectable votes for Communists in most Western European countries. The Liberation was, in general, the time when the Communists gained their greatest electoral support, and they participated in numerous governments. It is one of the many ironies of the 'revolutionary' movement that the parties had their most successful mass votes when they were following governmental moderate reformist strategies. They were not, however, reformist Social Democrats ('reformism' being a choice term of Communist contempt) but revolutionary Leninist Parties loyal to the Soviet Union and to the Soviet Leninist – version of socialism. The Social Democratic approach reforms which have characterised Western European government since the Second World War (health and welfare, demand management, state intervention, tripartite social consensus) did not have a Communist origin. Communists fought reforms, for example ridiculing 'fascist social security laws', because they postponed the necessary revolution.

At the end of the war Communists participated in numerous Western governments: these included the Italian Communist leader Togliatti (Vice-President of the Italian government in 1944), Maurice Thorez (who narrowly missed being voted French Prime Minister in December 1946), Johann Koplenig (Vice-Chancellor of the Austrian government), Edgar Lallmond (a Belgian minister) and Dominique Urbani (a Luxembourg minister).

Western Communist commitment to Soviet socialism lessened when the Cold War started and the Communist vote fell across the board. The receding tide did leave a few isolated pools but for the most part it went out in the early 1950s as can be seen from Table 1.

Table 1 Maximum Communist Votes in Western Europe

San Marino	42.3%	(1949)
Italy	34.4%	(1976)
Cyprus	30.0%	(1991)
France	28.6%	(1946)
Greece	24.4%	(1958)
Finland	23.5%	(1945)
Iceland	19.5%	(1945)
Luxembourg	15.9%	(1948)
West Berlin	14.7%	(1946)
Belgium	12.7%	(1946)

Denmark	12.5%	(1945)
Norway	11.9%	(1945)
Netherlands	10.5%	(1946)
Sweden	10.3%	(1944)
Switzerland	5.0%	(1947)
West Germany	5.7%	(1949)
Austria	5.4%	(1945)
United Kingdom	0.4%	(1945)
Eire	0.0%	(1965)

In the 1950s and 1960s the Communists Parties failed to get elected representatives in many parliaments. The last Communist representative in West Berlin was in 1948, in the UK in 1950, in West Germany in 1953, in Austria in 1957, in Denmark in 1960, and in Norway in 1961. The Communist Parties which survived the onset of the Cold War and which were able to retain over 10 per cent of the vote in 1972 were in Italy (28 per cent), France (22 per cent), Finland (18 per cent) and Iceland (11 per cent), although they were joined later in the 1970s by the parties which had organised resistance movements to the southern European dictatorships – the Portuguese, Spanish and Greek parties. (By the end of the 1980s only the Italian and Cypriot parties were regularly polling over 10 per cent, and only the Cypriot party vote was rising).

Before Stalin's death there were signs that the sectarian and Cold War strategy which caused the electoral disaster was about to be changed, but it was left to Khruschev when he had firmly established power to inaugurate another co-operative phase – the so-called 'peaceful road to power' or parliamentary strategy. Communist revolutionary aspirations (with the significant exception of Portugal in the mid-1970s) were transferred to the Third World. The division between Eastern and Western Europe had seemingly hardened and left the big 'Latin parties' isolated behind enemy capitalist lines – *in partibus infidelium* Western Communists were enjoined to seek alliances which would enable them to move into power as they had done at the Liberation and this meant, for the most part, looking first to the Social Democratic Parties (who were understandably suspicious). The road to power through elections posed the problem (which was never resolved) of how parties could both seek votes and remain loyal to Moscow. This dilemma had not been a problem in 1945 because no clash had been perceived, but in the new climate Communists were faced with the need to disavow the USSR in order to demonstrate their credentials as potential governing parties. The first example of dissidence came not over the Hungarian revolution (which the parties supported but weathered badly) but over elections. In 1958 the Danish party under its leader Axel Larsen was the first to break ranks to declare its independence from Moscow. It was split at the cost of its effectiveness and taken over by Knud Jespersen's pro-Moscow hard-liners (at a Congress supervised by Piotr Pospolov of the CPSU Central Committee).

In the 1970s there had been dramatic modernisation movements in Western Communism and some public relations successes around the vague but promising 'Eurocommunism'. The 1970s were a period in which the parties staved off decline to some extent. The Communist Parties in Spain, Portugal and Greece had emerged from the dictatorships as the best organised forces in their respective societies, the Spanish party was thought by many to be a potential government partner, the Portuguese party participated in government and then sponsored a military coup and the Greek party kept up a constant pressure on the Greek PaSoK Socialists whilst maintaining a hard line. In Italy the Communists polled the figure of 34.4 per cent (the highest by a CP in free elections), becoming the largest party in Italy. The French Communist Party, polling well in the 20 to 22 per cent range, also appeared to be on the verge of government and, with the Italians and Spanish, conducted an intermittent polemic with the CPSU.

It was this tension between the strategy of electoral vote-seeking and loyalty to Moscow which lay behind the 'Eurocommunist' interlude in the 1970s, but the problem was not manifest in the same way in all parties. The quasi-Communist Icelandic Popular Alliance was in centre-left alliances from 1956 to 1958, from 1971 to 1974 and then again from 1978 to 1983, but this eccentric party is probably best regarded as having been outside the Communist movement proper. The first governmental partner amongst major parties was the Finnish Communist Party which, from May 1966 to December 1982, participated in seven coalition cabinets. The French Communist Party participated in government from 1981 to 1984 but very much as a junior partner after an election setback which underscored its continuing decline. The Portuguese party was in government from 25 April 1974 (its leader Cuhnal was a Minister of State, but it was ousted in August 1975, supported a coup in November and has been in opposition since that time. The Communists supported 'bourgeois' governments in Sweden and in Cyprus, but the great Communist hopes of the 1970s – the Italian 'Historic Compromise', the Spanish party and the French left alliance – came to nothing. The Communists had very little to show for their twenty or so years of endeavours to enter government.

Hence these Western Communist *coups de théâtre* were without electoral effect and in retrospect the 1970s look less like a resurgence than a last feverish rally before setting into terminal decline. The Italian case is in this respect misleading because, if a few Western parties only maintained their low electoral support but were incapable of increasing it, decline was in fact the overall trend. But the Communists made an impact because of the residue from the radicalism of the 1960s (they recruited well from student radicals) and the lingering anti-Americanism of the Vietnam War as well as the impact of the oil crises and spiralling inflation in the West.

From the Communist point of view the position was that the sixties, with their non-inflationary boom, were the best years to have been in government and the 1970s would have enabled progress, but the stagflation of the 1980s, with their growing unemployment and painful industrial restructuring, meant bad years in which to take responsibility. The Finnish party, when it went into government in 1966, had been informed that the coalition was no new Popular Front but a co-operation to ensure a stable parliamentary majority. But inflation and unemployment became problems which demanded wage restraint – hitting at the Left's own constituencies – and there were doubts within the parties about whether these austerities could be accepted. The Finnish party, which had held ministerial portfolios almost constantly since 1966, voted against defence estimates being increased in December 1982 and was evicted (in Iceland the party entered opposition after April 1983).

In the late 1970s the Soviet line had changed from the simple search for *détente* to the manichaean confrontational theory of the 'two camps', Socialist and capitalist, between which a choice had to be made. Revolutionary ardour in the West was to be rekindled ('We live in the epoch of revolutions,' proclaimed the French party). But the invasion of Afghanistan in 1979 revealed a reluctance by many Western parties to loyally second Soviet policy even greater than the invasion of Czechoslovakia had done ten years previously in 1968. It is tempting to see pressure from Moscow behind the domestic realignments (such as the ending of the 'Historic Compromise') because of the coincidence with the Soviet foreign policy offensive in Western Europe in the late 1970s which encouraged Communist Parties to use the new 'social movements' against the 'bourgeois capitalist systems'.

Yet after the feverish Communism of the seventies the 1980s came as a confirmation of decline. The impact of the Soviet invasion of Afghanistan and the Polish crisis showed with clarity what the Communists of the 1970s had promised to do but had not done – that is to free themselves from the Soviet Union and the Leninist model. The parties' continuing inability to modernise and adapt to contemporary

Western society became strikingly evident in the 1980s. There were issues which the parties could have used and which they did try to use, such as peace movements, ecology and the like ('post-industrial' issues), but their position as outriders of the Communist system and their inflexible structures as Leninist Parties made the exploitation of discontent impossible.

By the 1980s the 'typical' Communist Parties were in fact more like the British party – the CPGB – than like the Italian party or the French. That is they were small formations of activists with relatively large bureaucracies struggling to make an electoral impact of any sort – though perhaps winning the odd local or parliamentary seat (often as a result of personal influence). They usually ran a press and by dint of professional bureaucracy had power in a few front organisations or non-Communist movements (like the 'peace movements') which had the same aims and sometimes had a disproportionate influence in unions. These attributes were not negligible, and through the discipline on which the parties were based (democratic centralism and a professional bureaucracy), they made contributions to the international movement by promoting Soviet 'socialism', defending the Eastern regimes (asserting the legitimacy of the regimes installed by force, circulating glowing reports about them) and promoting Soviet causes – but they were marginal to mainstream politics.

Hence when Gorbachev came to power in 1985 the situation was already one of disarray in the Western Communist movement and of a split between the pro-Moscow hard-liners and the modernisers (the Italians being the best known of the latter). Gorbachev was genuinely popular in Western Europe and his popularity increased as the westernising impetus of the reform movement in the USSR became prominent, but although the parties tried to use this appeal it did not transfer to them. At first the vigour and dynamism of Gorbachev's foreign policies were welcomed by the parties as a change from the torpor of the inter-regnum between Brezhnev and Gorbachev. Communists in Western Europe saw Gorbachev's offensives against President Reagan's SDI and 'Euromissiles' as popular themes around which they could mobilise opinion, and the 'disarmament' initiatives (taken with a subtle understanding of the Western media) were also welcomed. Gorbachev also tried to revitalise the international movement – by for example trying to resolve some splits – but this was not effective. It soon became clear that Gorbachev intended another change of line which involved the Western Communists in a search for rapprochement with the Second International Socialist Parties and a move away from the frontal assault on the West: in short a move back to a *détente* rather than Cold War strategy. Moreover, Gorbachev's reforms of the Communist system itself were not to the liking of hard-liners. The implications of the reforms became increasingly clear to them and were symbolised by a rapprochement between the CPSU and the Italian party to the detriment of the Portuguese and the French (who declared that *perestroika* and *glasnost* were not compulsory).

It is not easy to generalise about the electoral performance of such small parties, but even so there is little exception to the rule that all Communist Parties experienced the 1980s decline of Communism. Parties which were prepared to be pro-Gorbachev – within the limits of the Leninist corset – and which tried to modernise under the impact of the events of 1989, did not thrive. The Italian Communists fell to 26.6 per cent in the legislative elections of 1987, and in the local elections of May 1991 (the first under the new name), they fell from 25 per cent to 17 per cent and the Socialists were ahead for the first time since the Liberation. (*Rifondazione*, the 'orthodox' Communist Party, had no success.)

The Netherlands Communist Party, one of the oldest (founded in 1918 before the Bolsheviks became a Communist Party), had a seat in the Parliament for about sixty-eight years, and as one component of the Green Left which took six seats in 1989, became the first party to dissolve itself on 15 June 1991. In Sweden the Communist Party polled 10.3 per cent in 1944 but only 4.5 per cent in 1991 and the Icelandic party – which broke links with Moscow after 1968 and which has been absent from international movement events since then – reached its high point in the 1960s but in 1984 polled 18.8 per cent and in 1987 13.2 per cent. The Finnish party, one of the giants, which polled 23.5 per cent in 1945 (coming just one seat behind the Socialists with forty-nine MPs) and which participated in government in 1966, suffered a massive desertion by voters in the 1980s. It polled 19 per cent in 1975, but in 1983 it collapsed to 13.5 per cent. By 1987 it had split into 'modernisers' and hard-liners and its vote fell to 9.4 per cent although in 1991, by virtue of a precarious unity, it took 10.1 per cent (well down on the combined vote of the two wings in 1987).

The stitching together of an eclectic coaltion also explains how the Spanish Communist front *Izquierda Unida* became the third electoral force in Spain, although at 9.05 per cent in the 1989 election it is below the PCE's first election result after the dictatorship (not in coalition) of 9.4 per cent. The Spanish Communist Party may yet dissolve into *Izquierda Unida* as a result of the divisions sparked off by the events of August 1991 in the Soviet Union.

It is curious that the hard-line parties held out rather better than the modernisers. For example the peculiar Cypriot party (AKEL), despite a quarrel which led to the formation of a 'modernist' Communist Party

(Adisok), has withstood the trend to Communist decline – its vote increased to 30 per cent in May 1991. This might be because the 'modernised' Communists are competing for an electoral space on the left of the Socialist Parties which is either very small or already occupied. If voters feel strongly about ecological and 'new Left' issues, then they may prefer the original Greens to a carbon copy of 'red-green' alternative. The 'modernist' parties also fell prey to factional in-fighting and splits which further debilitated parties used to being able to rely on iron discipline.

However, hard-line parties also declined. The Portuguese party, which has made as few concessions as the French party to the collapse of 'socialism', took 11 per cent as the dominant part of a coalition in the elections of 1987, down o its 14.6 per cent in April 1976. The Greek Communist Party, which has been similarly hard-line (but with considerably more internal dissent), is the rare example of a Western party that attempted both an insurrection and the parliamentary road to power. In 1958, before the military government, it had polled 24.4 per cent and the Left coalition (of which it is the dominant part) polled 10.9 per cent in November 1989. The Greek Communist Party, inspired by its dislike of the Socialists (PaSoK) then briefly participated with the Right in an anti-PaSoK coalition government. The French party virtually disappeared as a political force in the 1980s despite having participated in government for three years from 1981 to 1984. In 1978 the French Communists polled 20.6 per cent in March 1978 but in 1981 this fell to 16.1 per cent and in 1986 to 9.7 per cent. In the presidential election of 1988 the French party's candidate polled only 6.7 per cent, but although the poor turn-out and the effective mobilisation of its vote by the party machine gave it 11.3 per cent in the subsequent legislatives, there is every reason to believe (based on opinion polls, by-elections and local elections) that the vote hovered around 7 per cent in 1991.

Other tiny orthodox parties fared no better. In Luxembourg the party had polled 13.5 per cent in 1945 but took only 3.6 per cent in 1989; the Swiss party polled 5.1 per cent in 1947 but only 0.8 per cent in 1987 (it went out of existence in 1991); the Austrian Communist Party took 5.4 per cent in 1945 but only 0.7 per cent in 1986; the Belgian party took 12.6 per cent in 1946 and 0.8 per cent in 1987; and the Danish Communist Party took 12.5 per cent in 1945 as compared with 0.8 per cent in 1988. In West Germany the Communists polled 5.7 per cent in 1949 but this fell to 2.2 per cent in 1953 and thereafter they struggled to maintain a presence despite substantial aid from the East, and in 1989 polled a mere 0.5 per cent.

The Western Communist Parties had established themselves in rural and heavy industry sectors of their respective economies. They developed intense and well-structured 'eco-systems' (to use Courtois' term) which imitated the 'womb to tomb' institutions of the early social democratic parties. These communities were stable and, like the mining villages in the UK, had a strong sense of their own identity. However, they were located in 'historically doomed' parts of the economy not, as was often assumed, in the newer advanced sectors where the Communists made little impact. The same is true of the rural areas where the Communists gained support from the small farming peasantry – another diminishing class in post-war Europe. Communist Parties are now confined to the European periphery and to the 'sunset' or 'smokestack' industries and backward uncompetitive agricultural areas, (an irony given what Marx had to say about the 'idiocy of rural life'). There is no reason why the original social base of a party cannot be transcended (if the social origin of a party were determinative the Tory Party would have gone out of existence at least a century ago and the Social Democrats would be struggling), but the Communists have not been able to do so. The Communist Parties, when it came to it, were too determined by their Leninist structure and convictions to be able to adapt.

The reaction the the coup of August 1991, which was intended to depose Gorbachev, revealed the Western Communists' conservatism very clearly. The hard-line parties which either did not condemn the coup or were slow in doing so faced dissident opposition internally, and they were deprived of their last line of defence. Hard-liners had asserted that if 'socialism' had collapsed in Eastern Europe the CPSU was innovative enough and dynamic enough to slove the problems of the USSR. It became clear after the August 1991 coup that this was not so and that the USSR was going to be dissolved into a loose comonwealth of non-Communist states. Far from being the outposts of the 'Socialist' system and the victorious revolution the Greek, French and Portuguese Parties became the world's last Communists. The Italian party, which made an outspoken, clear and forthright response to the massacre of protestors against the Chinese Communist regime in Tiananmen Square, did condemn the 'coup' against Gorbachev in 1991 and at least avoided that trap. The ex-Communist Parties were not directly affected by the events in the USSR in August 1991, and they reacted in much the same way as other Western parties. (If they had reacted in that way in 1956 they would have been given credit, but in 1991 it was too late.)

Hence it must be remembered that communism was on the decline (most were micro-parties) well before the coup, but the two intellectual thrusts of communism, democratic centralism and state planning, had also been discredited. Nearly all parties retained democratic centralism (including the Italian party but not the eccentric Netherlands party), and all of them retained a belief that the Eastern totalitarian regimes were 'Socialist'. Yet it was clear that the political superstructure of modern totalitarian communism was incompatible with humane politics. The system of co-option into the élite (despite purely formal elections), the stifling of dissent and a carefully guarded lack of responsiveness (communism's 'vanguard' nature) comprised a transplantation of the Eastern systems into a Western environment. Western Communist Parties which experimented with *glasnost* and *perestroika* before Gorbachev – like the Italians – did not touch these two features: the machine at the core of the party and the commitment to totalitarian 'socialism'. The Communist Parties were unable to reform because, as in the Eastern bloc, to reform was to fatally weaken the system, and this explains in large part they were unable to profit from the new 1980s 'post-industrial' issues.

Try as they might to disguise it now, and they tried to disguise it at the time, for the Western Communists all roads led to Moscow. There were different national roads, people started from different origins, but the destination was the same: the Soviet-style system. It was clear that the intellectual project was a failure and it had few takers on the political market by the 1980s, but the events in Eastern Europe and in the Soviet Union made its practical bankruptcy inescapable. Although the failure of totalitarian communism to reform itself should not have been unexpected. Western Communists could not credibly say – as they did of the Khruschev report – 'nobody told us it was that bad'. They should have known what was happening. Communist denials have been rightly treated with scepticism, but with the collapse of the Eastern bloc, the evidence of social and ecological ruin and the hostility of the populations have forced the Communists to react with an unparalled defensiveness.

The collapse of Eastern Europe, the reunification of Germany and the end of the Soviet Union came with a speed and unexpectedness which caught everybody by surprise (including the Soviet leadership, which may have expected a steady drift towards Western type systems via a reform communism of some sort). The reactions of the Western Communists to that movement from the core of this volume and they fall broadly into three categories. In the first category are the hard-liners who retain a faith in the 'Communist ideal' (to use the Portuguese party's term), and who have either delayed addressing the changes or denied their import (in Cuhnal's words, 'there is nothing to discuss'). They say that the 'Socialist' model remains untarnished because it has yet to be properly implemented and that the leaders of the Eastern bloc had become separated from the real base of their societies. These hard-liners formed an opposition to Gorbachev within the remaining institutions of the international movement in 1990 and retain contacts with the Communist regimes of the periphery (Cuba and North Korea). Secondly, there are some parties which have reacted by dissolving themselves or merging into wider radical movements: these include the Swiss party and the Netherlands party and the Spanish party hovered on the brink of dissolving itself). And then, thirdly, there are the parties which have broken with the old Soviet socialism and set out in search of a 'Third Way' independent of the 'state Socialist' model but based on a reovated Marxism of some sort. That means mainly the Italians although the Finnish Party takes a simiar view. For all of them time is short and there is no evidence that they will fare better than the old CPs. For the hard-liners the devasting reality of the Socialist model – even in the USSR – is now inescapable. The 'Third Way' has been the Holy Grail of the non-Communist Marxist Left since Lenin, but the route has never been convincingly specified. Nor is there any evidence of a 'space' for a party between the Social Democrats and the revolutionary Left that can be exploited by the ex-Communists (though many have tried).

The irony is that as the Soviet empire dissolved the Communists become viable electoral partners, but their tiny size meant that they were no longer relevant. The Leninist model spawned numerous progeny and Western Communist Parties now find themselves on the margins of rational politics amongst a myriad of Leninist sects.

The various contributors to this collaborative volume are researchers and experts on the Communist Parties of their respective countries. To the extent that they were successful, Communist Parties were sustained by local factors and their social support was based on national rather than international politics. However, the collapse of communism makes its international dimension inescapable, and that is what the studies analyse. What is the position of each party, how do they see themselves and where can they go from here?

The first five chapters are about the big 'mass Communist Parties' which survived as electoral and political forces into the 1980s but which have gone in very different directions since 1989. In the first chapter Stephen Gundle writes about the former Italian Communist Party and its transformation (in February 1991) into the Democratic Left. This party, perhaps because of its attention to intellectual debate combined with its persistent voting strength, has attracted a good deal of attention from researchers but Chapter 1 looks at its persistently weak position and its inability to cast off its old handicaps.

In the Nordic region communism was a force mainly in Finland, although it had its impact – through a parliamentary presence – in

Sweden and Iceland. In Denmark and Norway the ex-Communist Parties are marginal minorities despite several attempts at renovation. The Left in the Nordic countries, as David Arter points out in Chapter 2, has tried to reform its appeal through a 'red-greenery', and he examines this process and its likely outcome given the continuing problems of the ex-Communist Parties.

In Chapter 3, on the French Communist Party, the strange career of the French party is examined. It started the 1970s as an orthodox pro-Soviet party, wobbled from this course in the mid-1970s (espousing the so-called 'Eurocommunism') and then returned to a hard-line in the late 1970s. Its incapacity to modrnise and free itself from the Soviet model were contributory factors in the decline of the party, but the main cause was its inability to compete with the rising force of the new French Socialist Party.

The Portuguese Communist Party, like the French, has resisted attempts to modernise and retains a faith in the 'Communist ideal'. Unlike the other big parties it was untouched by the Hitler/Stalin pact and has a record of almost constant opposition to the dictatorship – its leader Cuhnal is a representative of that fight. In Chapter 4, Maria Teresa Patricio and Alan Stoleroff examine the sources of Portuguese Communist continuity and the roots of its continuing domestic support. The party suffered from internal dissidence as a result of its support for the coup, but the leadership easily defeated the opposition and continued its course.

The Greek Communist Party, which is discussed by Ole Smith in Chapter 5, is also an orthodox party and one which – like the Portuguese – initially welcomed the coup against Gorbachev. However, the party has suffered from greater internal dissidence than the Portuguese even if the leadership has been able to maintain its control of the party. Ole Smith discusses the efforts of this orthodox party to come to terms with changes in the former Eastern bloc and the ex-USSR but within a constricting Communist orthodoxy in a party led by veterans of the guerilla struggle and the resistance to the dictatorships.

In Chapter 6 José Amodia looks at the Spanish Communist Party which, as the main part of the coalition 'United Left' (*Izquierda Unida*), has been on a rising curve. The Spanish Communist Party played a big role in the transition to Spanish democracy and in the 'Eurocommunist' polemics with the CPSU in the mid-1970s. However, it was sidelined by the success of the Spanish Socialist Party, which won the elections in 1982 (and was confirmed in office in 1986 and 1989) and by its own internal splits. The anti-NATO referendum provided a focus for anti-Socialist groups on the Left, and out of the campaign (which the Socialist government almost lost) grew the

'United Left' which has had some success. However, many on the Spanish Left and in the party itself feel that there is no longer any room for a Communist Party – although its professional full-time apparatus does not hold this view. Santiago Carrillo, the former Secretary General, drew the obvious conclusion from the fall of the USSR and decided that the party was over.

Chapters 7 and 8 deal with the minor parties – the CPGB and the German Communists. In Chapter 7 John Callaghan looks at the curious history of British communism which, although a small party, was a curiously lively performer in the 1980s through its *Marxism Today* journal, which promoted eclectic debate. Like *Marxism Today*, the CPGB has gone out of existence, although the successor 'Democratic Left' survives. However, the New Communist Party – backing the *Morning Star* – still survives as do other orthodox splinters. German communism was crucial at the heart of the Cold War tempest in a divided Germany, and Chapter 8, by Heinrich Bortfeldt and Wayne C. Thompson, examines the condition of the German Communist movement (which retains a toehold). Their survey and prognosis is not optimistic and the parties show all the signs of an inability to come to terms with their own past. The Netherlands Communist Party (CPN), one of the oldest and one which tried to 'moderise', also concluded that a line had to be drawn through the past and it dissolved itself in 1991. In chapter 9 Gerrit Voerman looks at the struggle the CPN had to adapt to changing society, to Gorbachev's policies and with the new movements in the Netherlands and concludes that it was already moribund though the collapse of the Eastern bloc hastened its demise. The Conclusion looks at what remained of the international Communist movement under Gorbachev and its subsequent slow disintegration. There is little left of what was once a coherent and well-funded movement with branches in every country in Western Europe.

The Italian Communist Party: Gorbachev and the End of 'Really Existing Socialism'

Stephen Gundle

(handwritten: Conclusion πρωτυς (ρωτι 6us)

Of all Communist Parties perhaps the Italian Communist Party (PCI) had least to fear from the reforming drive of Mikhail Gorbachev. It had a distinctive political tradition of its own and not since the far-off days of the 1950s had it relied heavily on the external sponsorship of the Soviet Union for its legitimation and internal cohesion. Following the Warsaw Pact's suppression of the Prague Spring in 1968, the party had become increasingly critical of Soviet Policy and Soviet society itself. In the mid-seventies it explicitly embraced political pluralism as a universal value. Finally, an open breach in relations with the USSR occurred following the declaration of a state of seige in Poland in 1981. Yet even the PCI was shaken by the revelations of the *glasnost* era and the pitiless light that was shed on the past and present of the USSR. The rapid dissolution of 'really existing socialism' in Eastern Europe in 1989 undermined the party's claim to originality and made it seem backward with respect to parties such as the Hungarian Communist Party in reassessing its own traditions and identity.

To save the best elements of its heritage and distinguish itself radically from 'totalitarian states' that had 'usurped the name of socialism', the party leader Achille Occhetto announced, just four days after the fall of the Berlin Wall in November 1989, his intention to refound the PCI on new bases, with a new name and new symbol.[1] With this gesture he opened a process that led, fourteen months later, following two party congresses, unprecedented internal acrimony and much collective heart-searching, to the foundation of a new left-wing party, the Democratic Party of the Left (PDS). If the reasons for this decision are to be understood and the causes of the internal divisions it

1. 'La relazione di Achille Occhetto', in *Documenti per il congresso straordinario del PCI*, vol. 1, Rome, *L'Unità*, 1989.

provoked explained, particular attention must be paid to both ambiguities in the PCI's tradition of autonomy and the increasing difficulties the party faced in the late eighties as its attempts to reverse its declining fortunes failed to produce the desired results.

The 1980s: A Decade of Uncertainty and Setbacks

Writing in the mid-1980s, Gianfranco Pasquino argued that the PCI could not be correctly described as a party in crisis. In particular by comparison with other Communist Parties its situation was remarkably healthy. It was regularly polling around 30 per cent of the vote, counted a membership of 1.6 million and governed a significant slice of Italian territory. It possessed a widely-read press, influence in many quarters of society, a following among opinion leaders and a good international reputation.[2] Yet the party was indisputably beset by problems. Both its membership and leadership were aging, recruitment was sluggish and difficult especially among the young, there was a lack of dynamism in local government and a widely-shared political culture was undergoing erosion. In addition the PCI's strategy of social and political alliances was in need of reformulation.

The poor results obtained in the June 1987 election threw these difficulties into sharp relief. After a long period of continuous electoral expansion, which saw the party reach a peak of 34.4 per cent in 1976, it entered a phase of stagnation in the 1980s which by the 1987 election had turned unequivocally into decline. Its total of 26.6 per cent represented a three-point drop on the 1983 result of 29.9 per cent, which itself barely maintained the 30.4 per cent obtained in 1979. In the course of the decade the PCI suffered a series of political defeats. Having failed to bring to fruition a coalition with the Christian Democrats and Socialists (the 'Historic Compromise') in the 1970s, it found itself lacking credibility as a potential force of government while the renewed collaboration between the DC and the PSI meant that stable coalitions could be formed without its support. At the same time it found it difficult to re-establish a clear oppositional profile after having lent its approval to economic sacrifices and stern law and order measures in the late seventies. In 1985 it was ousted from most of the city and regional administrations it had dominated since 1975 and in the same year the party was roundly defeated in the referendum it

2. B. Pasquino, 'Mid-stream and under Stress: the Italian Communist Party', in M. Waller and F. Fennema (eds.), *Communist Parties in Western Europe: Decline or Adaptation?* Oxford, Basil Blackwell, 1988, pp. 26–7.

promoted against the Craxi government's cutback of index-linked wage rises. At the polls it lost support among middle-class floating voters, in the big cities and, most sharply, among young people.[3]

The PCI's difficulties went deep and renewal was complex because many of its characteristics remained distinctively Communist. Organisational problems were often paramount in party discussions and fundamental differences between the left and right wings were invariably fudged rather than resolved because of the need to preserve internal unity and strategic continuity. Formulating a clear and up-to-date programme, which in any case was a complex exercise for a party so long consigned to opposition, became even more difficult in these circumstances. Real renovation was also rendered problematic by disagreement over how far the party should remain anchored to its original roots. For the right wing the time had come, as Giorgio Napolitano put it, 'to move decisively beyond the confines of tradition and of the Communist movement'.[4] This was not a view that the PCI's cautious leader, Alessandro Natta, was willing to endorse, even though he talked of the need for 'a genuine act of refoundation' in the wake of the 1987 election result. For his part the leading pro-Soviet hard-liner, Armando Cossutta, threatened to set up a separate party if the PCI renounced its ideological heritage or applied to join the Socialist International. (He carried out this threat in January 1991.)

The Gorbachev Challenge

Despite the leadership's repeated insistence on the PCI's pro-Western alignment, the past and present nature of the party's link to the Soviet Union remained fairly central to its identity in the second half of the 1980s. Gorbachev's concerted attempts to revive a relationship that by the early 1980s seemed to have reached a point of no return were important here. But so too were historical factors. Although the party developed distinctive traits from 1944 it also remained loyal to Moscow throughout the tensest Cold War years, uncritically approving the 'excommunication' of Tito's Yugoslavia from the Communist movement in 1948 and the invasion of Hungary in 1956. Members were fed small doses of Gramsci but their main diet consisted of orthodox Marxist-Leninism. Consequently the idea of the Soviet Union as a superior civilisation, fairer and more technologically advanced

3. See S. Gundle, 'On the Brink of Decline? The PCI and the Italian Elections of June 1987', *Journal of Communist Studies*, vol. III, no. 4, 1987, pp. 159–66.
4. *L'Unità*, 27 June 1987.

than Western capitalism, and as a vital bulwark of the cause of world peace and social progress, was deeply entrenched in the party. From 1956 national objectives were given systematic priority over international ones, but even beyond the Czech crisis of 1968 the USSR continued to be seen as a vital reference point in world politics. In the eyes of many Italian Communists any negative image deriving from its repression of dissent in Eastern Europe was counterbalanced by the wars of liberation that were fought in the Third World from the sixties on under the banner of communism. Even in the 1970s one of the attractions of being a Communist was still the feeling of belonging to an international movement, albeit one without any precise confines or organisational expression.

Only at the start of the 1980s did the PCI begin to shift from dissent within a Moscow-aligned Communist movement to disengagement from it. In the wake of the Soviet invasion of Afghanistan in December 1979 formal links were re-established with China. After the imposition of martial law in Poland, the revolutionary credentials of the Soviet Union were openly disputed and the vanguard role of the Communist movement itself deemed to be exhausted. Appearing on television on 15 December 1981, three days after Jaruzelski's seizure of power, Berlinguer proclaimed that 'the propulsive force that began with the October Revolution has come to an end'.[5] The seriousness of the *strappo* (tear) in relations was confirmed by Moscow's furious response and the PCI's subsequent stance on disarmament. While it opposed the installation of Cruise and Pershing missiles the party's parallel condemnation of the USSR's role in triggering the arms race and its active independent efforts to further *détente* meant that, by the time Berlinguer died in 1984, it appeared there was little the two sides had left to say to each other. Changes in the Soviet leadership, however, brought a change of attitude. From the very moment of his accession to power Gorbachev strove to re-establish good relations with the PCI, receiving the new leader Alessandro Natta and his colleagues for over an hour before other party delegations at Chernenko's funeral in March 1985.

Gorbachev's motives were eminently political. As Joan Barth Urban has argued, he wished both to 'normalise' relations with the Chinese regime and enlist the support of centrist and left-wing forces in Western Europe for his arms control initiatives and more general policy of *détente*. Given the strong ties that had existed between Beijing and the Italian Communists since 1980 he could hardly hope to achieve the former objective without first establishing a rapport with the PCI.

5. *L'Unità*, 16 December 1981.

Similarly, the Soviet leadership could not project a credible image in Europe without some evidence that it respected Western sovereignty, and it could not achieve that if it refused to respect the autonomy of the largest non-ruling Communist Party.[6] As early as October 1985 Gorbachev revised the hitherto prevailing conception of the international Communist movement using words that Palmiro Togliatti had first employed in the early 1960s: 'a dialectical unity of diversity'. This view was confirmed in his report to the twenty-seventh CPSU Congress, where it was announced that the 'unity of Communists has nothing to do with uniformity and hierarchy'. For Urban, this was 'tantamount to a public show of deference towards the very Party the CPSU had accused of undermining Socialism during the celebrated *strappo* of early 1982'.[7]

Gorbachev accompanied these substantial consessions with a variety of courtesies. At the first formal summit meeting with Natta in Moscow in January 1986, a banquet was held for the PCI delegation, an honour that was normally reserved for state visits. The PCI's Seventeenth Congress in 1986 was attended by a high-level Soviet team headed by Lev Zaikov. Later the same year the Soviet leader kept a promise that his first Italian newspaper interview would be for the Communist daily *L'Unità*. Still more significantly, he let it be known that he felt a special affinity for the PCI, a force whose dissent from official Soviet policy had been consistently and coherently sustained over the years. These dissenting ideas probably contributed to the process of reflection which found an outlet in the new course.[8]

This sort of attention was immensely flattering. Yet the PCI leadership remained cautious in its reaction to Gorbachev. Having received internal reports detailing the Soviet Union's economic problems in the early 1980s, it was sceptical over how far the verbal radicalism of the Soviet leader was sufficient to deal with what was seen as a profound structural crisis. While they welcomed the setting aside of the sort of doctrinal examinations and remonstration that once characterised Soviet-PCI bilateral meetings, PCI leaders also jealously guarded their party's hard-won autonomy. Whereas Gorbachev seemed to see the PCI as still 'Eurocommunist', a force in other words that remained essentially a variant of the Communist movement, PCI leaders took the view that it belonged to the family of the West

6. J. Barth Urban, 'The PCI's 17th Congress: a triumph of the "new internationalism"', in P. Corbetta, R. Leonardi and R. Nanetti (eds.), *Italian Politics – a Review*, vol. 2, London, Pinter Publishers, 1988, p. 49.

7. Urban, 'The PCI's 17th Congress', p. 48.

8. A. Rubbi, *Incontri con Gorbachev: i colloqui di Natta e Occhetto con il leader sovietico-giugno 1984* – November 1989, Rome, Editori Riuniti, 1990, pp. 26–7.

European Left, to an alignment of forces that had no affiliation at all with Moscow.[9] Thus they resented Soviet press releases and official toasts in which the PCI was described as a 'fraternal party'. On the same grounds the party resisted all Gorbachev's attempts to gain support for renewed multilateral meetings between Communist parties. The importance of the PCI can be measured by the fact that its veto was sufficient to force the Soviet leader eventually to abandon any idea of reuniting the international Communist movement by spring 1988.

To counter any impression that the party was being reabsorbed within the Soviet orbit, the PCI accompanied its obvious sympathy for Gorbachev with steps designed to clarify and formalise its Western and European alignment. At the Seventeenth PCI Congress it proclaimed itself to be 'an integral part of the European Left' and in the successive year or so Natta travelled extensively, building links with European Social Democrats in meetings with Willy Brandt, Felipe González, Mário Soares and Ingvar Carlsson.

From the PCI's point of view there were no legitimate grounds for confusion. If it found areas of agreement with Moscow then it was because there were objective concordances on policy, not because there was any organic link. Yet in fact matters were not so simple. It might have been expected that hostile journalists and politicians in Italy would accuse the party of 'restitching' the *strappo* of the early eighties. But Gorbachev too was evidently under the impression long after the PCI's Congress that a closer formal bond might in some way be re-established. There were several reasons for this. In the first place the party itself seemed reluctant to carry through the logic of its position. In a singularly ill-judged remark to journalists in January 1986, Natta undermined the credibility of his party's position by denying that a 'tear' with the USSR had ever occurred. Moreover, he managed to visit Hungary close to the thirtieth anniversary of the Soviet invasion without issuing any comment, critical or otherwise, on that event or the PCI's approval of it.

The PCI also retained links with international Communist organisations. It remained a member of the Communist group in the European parliament until after the European elections of June 1980, and it only severed its association with the *World Marxist Review* in 1986. In other ways too the PCI continued to act in a manner that recalled its past affiliations more than its present vocation. It used its privileged relationship with the Soviet leadership under *perestroika* to advance the request of Alexander Dubček, with whom it had maintained close contact since the 1968 'Prague Spring,' for a recognition that the Czech invasion of 1968 had been an error. At the same time it

9. Rubbi, *Incontri con Gorbachev*, pp. 74–5.

urged Gorbachev to restore political honour to Dubček and the 478,000 Communists who were expelled from the Czech party in 1970. In a bizarre acceptance of the post-Stalinist logic of rehabilitation, which allowed the Soviet authorities to conserve the role of moral arbiters over the whole history of the Communist movement, it even took pride in the attention accorded to Berlinguer in January 1989. Official recognition of the justice of the former PCI secretary's positions on the Soviet Union and 'really existing socialism', including the famous judgement on the 'exhaustion of the propulsive force of the October Revolution', took the form of an article published in *Kommunist*. That the PCI agreed with this procedure or at any rate was informed of it in advance is borne out by the fact that the article was published simultaneously in its weekly journal *Rinascita*.[10]

As time went on Gorbachev increasingly accepted PCI positions. Against a backdrop of worsening social and economic conditions he acknowledged that democracy was the most appropriate route to socialism, showed interest in Italian and Swedish forms of co-operative enterprise and even considered the merits of social democracy. In consequence the international prestige of the PCI was enhanced. But ambiguities in its stance and its leaders' reluctance to critically examine its own history exposed it to unforeseen challenges as the difficulties of the Soviet renewal programme became apparent and Gorbachev himself lurched unpredictably between the defence of tradition and dramatic, wide-ranging attacks on the Soviet past.

Skeletons in the Cupboard

The Soviet rehabilitation of Bukharin, Kamenev, Rykov, Radek and Zinoviev, all of whom were declared in February 1988 to have been unjustly condemned to death during the great purges, should not have created particular difficulties for the PCI. Widely regarded as the least Stalinist of Communist Parties, it had long distanced itself in practice from the methods of the Third International. In the 1960s and 1970s Italian Communist historians such as Paolo Spriano and Giuseppe Boffa contributed to the development of a critical historiography of the Communist movement which in a small way informed the revisionism of the *glasnost* era. Despite this record of analysis of the alternatives to Stalinism the PCI found itself being criticised almost incessantly in the late 1980s for allegedly failing to review its own history and ideology.

10. Rubbi, *Incontri con Gorbachev*, pp. 227.

While Gorbachev was revealing the truth about the past, it was argued, the PCI preferred to keep silent about its own complicity with the crimes of the Stalin era.

At the centre of all debate about the heritage of the PCI was the role of Palmiro Togliatti, its leader from 1926 until his death in 1964. Togliatti had slavishly accepted Soviet propaganda between 1944 and 1956, he continued to take the international Communist movement as his reference point in the post-Stalin period and his own view of socialism and style of leadership were neither liberal nor democratic. Yet Togliatti remained a popular myth and in *L'Unità* in 1984 on the twentieth anniversary of his death there was scarcely a single contribution which suggested his achievement was incomplete.[11] The rehabilitation of Bukharin, however, threw into sharp relief the negative dimension of Togliatti: his close collaboration with Stalin and complicity in the horrors of his rule. On the day of the announcement the Socialist Party newspaper *L'Avanti* took the lead in asserting that a 'Togliatti-problem' existed for the PCI since its leader, as Vice-Secretary of the Komintern, had supported Bukharin's trial and execution. Moreover, he had continued to refer to Bukharin as a 'traitor' and 'double-agent' well into the 1950s, even though he had initially taken his side in the inner-party struggles of the 1920s. Between 1988 and 1989 Togliatti's alleged role in the elimination of Trotskyists and anarchists in Spain, his approval of the execution of the Polish Communist Party leaders in 1939 and his indifference to the fate of Italians caught in the infernal mechanisms of the terror were all the subject of public polemic. In the most bitter moment of the dispute the Socialist deputy leader Claudio Martelli dubbed Togliatti 'a stalinist accomplice and executioner in Italy and Europe'.[12] In response, the PCI did not attempt a blanket defence. Such a line would not in any case have been plausible since even the director of the CPSU Institute of Marxism-Leninism, interviewed in the Italian press, confirmed that the moral responsibilities of Togliatti were beyond dispute.[13] Rather its spokesmen sought to situate the role of Togliatti in a historical context and direct attention back to his positive, national side.

The PCI was caught in a bind. The row produced no revelations that had not already been discussed in the works of Communist historians. Yet the long debate on Stalin, Togliatti and Gramsci was politically significant. By raising and insisting on the question of Togliatti's historical and moral responsibilities the PSI challenged the democratic

---

11. 'Togliatti: che cosa ci la lasciato', supplement to *L'Unità*, 14 October 1984.
12. A. Stabile, 'Perché Togliatti fu colpevole', *La Repubblica*, 1 March 1988.
13. E. Mauro, "Per la Storia Togliatti è colpevole", *La Repubblica*, 26 July 1988.

legitimacy of the PCI. In consequence the party ran the risk of making itself appear Stalinist if it refused to abjure Togliatti. But, if it did so, it could not avoid undermining the value of its own past achievements. In either case, as Piero Ostellino noted, Craxi emerged as the rightful leader of the democratic Left.[14]

In fact the PCI tried to steer a middle course. It responded to suggestions of secrecy by selectively opening its archives for the period 1944-58 in March 1988 and challenging other parties to do likewise. It insisted that Togliatti could not simply be written off, for he had helped turn the PCI into an authentic, mass and democratic force, profoundly rooted in the life of the country. To reduce him to Stalinism was to deny the role of the Left in founding the democratic state, and this benefited only the DC. In an article published in *La Repubblica*, Occhetto argued that it was more important to look forward than back. The October Revolution, he said, had been important, it had opened the way to liberation movements worldwide, but it could not provide models for the future. The PCI's view of the world and of social transformation was not reducible to the Bolshevik revolution in the way that it had been in 1921, not just because the methods were different but because it now upheld non-violence and full respect for democratic liberties.[15] The problem was that in openly breaking with a tradition that in the functioning of the party had largely been overcome anyway, the PCI would be left with no choice but to reconcile itself to a limited, social democratic role – something that neither pride nor politics would really allow it to do.

Occhetto's 'New PCI'

The extent of the resistances within the PCI to social democratisation would be fully revealed under Occhetto's tumultuous secretaryship. In the run-up to the Nineteenth Party Congress in March 1989, at which he won the approval of all but a small group of hard-liners, Occhetto launched a campaign to reassert the PCI as a dynamic actor capable of promoting the interests of the weak in society. At the same time he recognised the value of discontinuity with respect to the party's traditional approaches and made ever more frequent references in his speeches to such prominent exponents of progressive liberal democratic thought as Ralf Dahrendorf, Norberto Bobbio, Maurice

14. P. Ostellino, 'Un cadavere ideologico così utile a Craxi', *Il Corriere della Sera*, 1 March 1988.

15. A. Occhetto, '"Caro Craxi, il passato è già sepolto"', *La Repubblica*, 10 March 1988.

Duverger and Robert Dahl, all of whom were interviewed periodically in *L'Unità* and actively canvassed for support. In conjunction with this new departure, an effort was made to pack environmentalism, feminism and pacifism into the party's baggage. External to the mainstream Communist tradition and to the workers' movement in general, these currents had long enjoyed support in some sections of the PCI but had never been taken very seriously by the leadership. Now they were regarded not as secondary matters but as the source of a renewed critique of the failings of capitalist society.

How far did the Congress signal the final evolution of the PCI into a force no different from some of the more radical and intellectually flexible components of European social democracy? Broadly this had been Occhetto's objective yet the actual results fell short of his desired goal. Although international social democracy was explicitly regarded as providing an essential compass for the new course, the party was drawn into an ever closer identification with Gorbachev's reform programme. Not only did the magnetism of the Soviet leader have a great personal effect on Occhetto, but he was persuaded to postpone the PCI's application for membership of the Socialist International until such time as a larger restructuring of the European Left could permit the definitive overcoming of divisions between the parties of East and West. This was a dangerous position to occupy. Yet support for reform and democratisation in Eastern Europe was a necessary condition of the Left's support for the new course. Wary of being absorbed into the mainstream of social democracy, Ingrao, Magri and Cossutta, albeit with important shades of difference between their views, all looked optimistically to the potential for reformed socialism.

In other areas Occhetto found it impossible to proceed as far or as fast as he would have wished. It was initially intended that the party's symbol and possibly its name would be changed by the Congress. Yet an attempt to alter the former was rejected while all that was said on the latter was that it might be subject to change if domestic events evolved in the direction of a left-wing coalition. Similar difficulties obstructed the leadership's aim to dethrone Togliatti and consign him firmly to the past. To clear the way for the new course Occhetto denounced Togliatti as 'sharing inevitable co-responsibility for Stalinism' in his first public engagement as Secretary (which, ironically, was the unveiling of a statue of the former leader at Civitavecchia). However, the consternation this statement caused within the party was surpassed only by reactions to an article by the Neapolitan intellectual and noted revisionist Biagio De Giovanni, published a year later by *L'Unità* to mark the twenty-fifth anniversary of Togliatti's death. Entitled, 'Once upon a Time There Was Togliatti and "Real Communism"', it identified

Togliatti 'above all as a man of the Communist International' profoundly associated with a Soviet-style socialism that was nearing the end of its lifespan. 'We reject all that is involved with the heritage of Stalin not in a defensive spirit but out of a sense of moral and political responsibility towards Italian society and ourselves,' De Giovanni wrote.[16] The outrage these views provoked was unprecedented. In a protracted row almost all leading members of the older generation in the leadership took up positions hostile to De Giovanni. To calm the situation Occhetto was compelled to intervene to say that discontinuity, which he regarded as necessary and positive, should not involve a demolition of the past.[17] This was a substantial step backwards, an admission almost that at a time when the whole history of Stalinism and even Lenin was being subjected to criticism in the Soviet Union, the PCI could not come to terms with the dark zones of its own history.

The inability to make progress in this area illustrated how far continuity persisted even under the new course. Despite his personal triumph at the Congress in March 1989, Occhetto was still a prisoner of a pre-existing balance of power within the party. It was for this reason that he continually sought to go outside existing structures in his effort to propel the new course forward, for example by creating a 'shadow cabinet' based on the Westminister model, giving many interviews to the press and television, appointing an intellectual (Alberto Asor Rosa) rather than a functionary to the editorship of the weekly *Rinascita* and promoting new forms of participation in grass-roots activities. However, the degree of real innovation that could be achieved without fundamentally polarising the party or radically reforming its slow-moving organisational machine was limited. Despite attempts to reduce the number of full-time officials and attract new energies to the party, old structures proved to be remarkably resilient.

In the months between June and October 1989 the party faced a series of crucial electoral tests. A round of local elections (mostly in the south), and the regional election in Sardinia in June offered small comfort. Despite the innovations, both signalled further erosions in Communist support. Only the European elections produced a more hopeful outcome. Despite fears that the repression of the Chinese student protest in Tiananmen Square might damage the party (despite its swift condemnation of these events and decision to break off relations with the Chinese party), it in fact polled reasonably well. Although its vote of 27.6 per cent marked a decline from the 33.3 per

16. B. De Giovanni, 'C'era una volta Togliatti e il comunismo reale', *L'Unità*, 20 August 1989.

17. A. Occhetto, 'Il nuovo corso è demolizione del passato', *L'Unità*, 14 September 1989.

cent obtained shortly after Berlinguer's death in 1984, it signalled growth of 1 per cent on the 26.6 per cent obtained in 1987. Given that they said they would be satisfied with 25 per cent, PCI leaders made a point of celebrating the result as a great victory.[18] However, Occhetto's standing was not automatically strengthened. Content with the vote the PCI had obtained in its conventional guise, a number of left-wingers made it plain they saw no need for renewal to be pursued further and set about undermining the Secretary's position.

At virtually the same time events began to precipitate in Eastern Europe. Ostensibly the PCI's position on developments in the Eastern bloc was clear. Any residual suspicion that it sympathised with the model of social and economic organisation practised by state Socialist regimes had been eradicated at the Eighteenth Congress in 1989, when a document was approved accepting the market economy and profit as a legitimate stimulus to efficiency. On the political level it had long denounced the identification of party and state and offered its support to reform movements that surfaced. This continued after Gorbachev withdrew the Soviet guarantee early in 1989. At a Budapest funeral ceremony in June 1989 which marked the political rehabilitation of the Hungarian revolt of 1956 and its leader Nagy, Occhetto was the only foreign Communist leader present. But the events of the summer and autumn, from the bloody crackdown in Tiananmen Square to the fall of the Berlin Wall and finally the makeshift trial and execution of the Ceausescus in Romania, signalled not the reform of state socialism but its decisive rejection. The PCI suffered in two ways. First, the equilibrium it had sought to maintain between support for Gorbachev and collaboration with social democracy was dramatically upset by the course of events. Second, the Hungarian Communist Party's decision to cast off its Communist heritage and seek membership of the Socialist International contrasted sharply with the PCI's attachment to its name and tradition. Having championed the cause of slow reform in the hope of avoiding destabilisation, it was made to appear backward and conservative as Eastern parties and peoples rushed to embrace Western values and institutions.

It was against this background that Occhetto decided to force the hand of his opponents in the party. In a speech delivered on 12 November 1989 to a Sunday morning gathering of former Resistance partisans near Bologna, he fiercely denounced the record of 'really existing socialism', which he claimed had nothing to do with the PCI . The role of intermediary between the parties of East and West which it

18. There was no real inversion of the downward tendency: R. Mannheimer, 'Il PCI alle europee: non minimizzo ma insisto – prudenza', *L'Unità*, 14 July 1989.

had conserved in order to promote debate and reform, even at a cost to itself, was now over.[19] With the end of bloc politics the party had to find a new form in which the best of its ideals and tradition could find expression. Occhetto proposed the dissolution of the PCI and the opening of a 'constituent phase' that he hoped would lead to the foundation of a new party comprising all the genuinely progressive currents of the Italian Left. The new party would not be Communist but 'socialist', 'popular' (i.e. less class-oriented), 'democratic' and 'progressive'. It would be committed to the realisation of a left-wing alternative and would hope to be not only an integral part of the European Left but also a full member of the Socialist International.

The Crisis of 1989–91

Far from being a relatively simple and straightforward process, Occhetto's proposed modifications plunged the party into turmoil. Objections were raised on various grounds. First, there was enormous resentment that Occhetto had acted without consultation or prior discussion. This turned to anger, when he insisted on a simple Yes or No vote, eschewing the compromises that were customary in internal debates.[20] Second, the proposal was unclear as to the identity of the allies that Occhetto proposed to draw into the new party as co-founders. After the speedy refusal of Greens and radical Catholics there was a risk of absorption by the PSI, a force considered by many on the left of the PCI to be right-wing in everything but name. Third, the circumstances of Occhetto's decision risked confusing the trajectory of the PCI with the discredited ruling parties of Eastern Europe. Ingrao, for example, while he recognised that the PCI had been slow to grasp the rotten nature of the regimes of 'really existing socialism' and personally regretted not having done more to support dissidents, rejected utterly any suggestion that the ideal of communism could be equated with one-party dictatorships.[21] Opponents of the proposal argued that communism was an essential part of any movement committed to the defence of the exploited, liberation from oppression, resistance to the market and to money values, and participatory

19. 'La relazione di Achille Occhetto'.

20. G. Chiaromonte, *Col senno di poi: autocritica e no di un uomo politico*, Rome, Editori Riuniti, 1990, p. 217.

21. P. Ingrao, *Le cose impossibili: un' autobiografia raccontata e discussa con Nicola Tranfaglia*, Rome, Editori Riuniti, 1990, pp. xxxi–xxxii, 199.

democracy.[22] Realising that they would be unable to defeat the proposal in the central committee, Occhetto's opponents opted to protract discussion of the change for as long as possible in the hope that a majority of the membership could be won to their side.

Despite the strength of Party feelings, Occhetto succeeded over time in persuading a clear majority of active members to back his design, first at the Nineteenth Congress in March 1990 and conclusively at the Twentieth and final PCI Congress in January 1991. The 65 per cent support his motion won in 1990 grew to 69 per cent over the next nine months. After many months of being known simply as 'the thing', the new party, dubbed the Democratic Party of the Left (PDS), was finally launched.

The Aftermath

The credibility of the new party, however, remained to be established. For Napolitano and the right-wing the party had to show that it had drawn the appropriate lessons from the collapase of Communist regimes by breaking unequivocally with important aspects of the PCI's history, moving beyond communism in general and overcoming totally any remaining rejection of social democracy.[23] Initially Occhetto appeared to share this agenda and some progress was unquestionably made. A serious effort was made to come to terms with the Stalinist phase of Communist history; party spokesmen rehabilitated or re-examined the role of such figures as Ignazio Silone and Angelo Tasca (both expelled for their opposition to Stalin at the end of the 1920s) and, in response to those who argued that the membership had been kept in ignorance of parts of the PCI's history, Spriano's works were made available in special cheap editions distributed through news kiosks with *L'Unità*. In the spring of 1990, after due soundings had been taken, a formal application for membership was lodged with the Socialist International. In terms of policy, it proved easier to absorb environmentalism and feminism than to devise specific proposals in other areas, but some useful ideas were set out on institutional reform, labour issues and the welfare state at a programmatic convention held in October 1990.

In other ways, however, the shift to reformism was forestalled. As democratic centralism dissolved, giving way to a complex map of tendencies and sensibilities that took on the appearance of formalised

22. All the motions are in *Documenti per il congresso straordinario del PCI*, vol. 3, Rome, *L'Unità*, 1990, pp. 50–3.

23. G. Napolitano, *Al di là del guado: la scelta riformista*, Rome, Lucarini, 1990, p. xv.

factions, Occhetto appeared to accord more importance to internal bargaining than to completing his programme of party change in a clear, unambiguous manner. There were a number of reasons for this. First, he was prepared to go to considerable lengths to avoid the breakaway of those on the Left who remained deeply attached to communism, which they argued could be recast on the basis of its non-Stalinist variants (Gramsci, Luxemburg etc.) Second, he recognised that if the bulk of the PCI membership was to be carried into the new party he could not ride roughshod over the feelings of the rank and file. Thus, while the leadership refused to compromise on the fundamental question of the new party's creation, it allowed the debate to proceed at length and it tilted towards the Left on some key issues. In a somewhat contradictory manner, anti-capitalist as well as pro-market views were granted citizenship in the PDS. In order to quash any impression that it would be sucked into the orbit of the Socialists, the term 'socialist' was not included in its name and Craxi's promotion of 'socialist unity' was rejected out of hand. The symbol of the new party, an oak tree (intended to recall the revolutionary symbol of the 'tree of liberty' as well as attract green sympathies), was designed in such a way as to include in miniature form the old hammer and sickle motif of the PCI. Finally, on the Gulf War an uncompromising pacifist stance was adopted.

In this way Occhetto was able to launch the PDS at the end of the PCI's twentieth and final Congress in January 1991 with the grudging support of most of the more prominent 'democratic Communists'. This was interpreted as a political success, but the long months of internal wrangling disillusioned many of the mainly intellectual 'externals' who had seen the 'constituent phase' as a unique opportunity to reunite the whole of the Italian Left on new bases. It also meant that the PDS was born with a rather tarnished image and a less than wholly clear identity. No longer Communist and not yet fully Social Democratic the new party could only properly be described as post-Communist. Moreover, despite the compromises, the party organisation did not survive the transition intact. After the initial upsurge of participation in party meetings following the announcement of November 1989, there was a falling away as political activity was displaced by acrimonious in-fighting and an estimated 300,000 members opted not to renew their subscriptions in the wake of the Nineteenth Congress. Moreover, a split occurred at the end of the final PCI Congress as Cossutta and other hard-liners announced the formation of 'Communist Refoundation', a transitional grouping committed to the creation of a new Communist Party that quickly attracted 150,000 pledges of support. This grouping drew in many who had refused to go along with the PCI's criticisms of the USSR in the 1970s and 1980s, but also younger activists who identified with Ingrao or the New Left party PDUP (which was reabsorbed by the PCI in 1983). Persuaded that the neo-Stalinist element would be minor, the only surviving component of the Italian New Left with parliamentary representation, Proletarian Democracy, also decided in the spring of 1991 to dissolve itself and join this new alignment of diehard Communists.

In the middle of 1991 Occhetto found himself in a fairly weak position. Paradoxically, it was the dramatic turn of events in the Soviet Union in August that allowed him to consolidate his leadership, push his internal opponents on to the defensive and reassert the PDS's extraneousness to communism. The short-lived coup was roundly condemned by both the Refoundation group and the PDS, but the subsequent downfall of the CPSU and of the Communist system of power in the USSR caused shock and anguish among many of those who continued to adhere to Communist principles. Occhetto and his collaborators, by contrast, could even welcome this historic event. They cited it as proof that they had been right to transform the PCI and they even opportunistically joined in the anti-communist commentary that abounded in the press. Communism, Occhetto said, had betrayed the interests of the workers and the fall of the Soviet system was proof that socialism could not survive without democracy. This point, he argued, had not been fully appreciated by the PCI under Togliatti not even under Berlinguer.

There was enormous relief in the PDS that the process of ideological and organisational renovation had been completed before the fall of Soviet communism. Yet many commentators noted that the political transition would only truly be over when the new party emerged as a credible alternative force of government: something which the PCI has never quite managed. Although the shadow of a historic defeat would probably fall, in the short term, more on the purists than on the PDS, the latter would unavoidably be affected; moreover it remains a fairly fragile force. Renovation has been achieved but only at great cost in terms of influence and cohesion. Moreover, the events of 1989-91 and the emergence of a neo-Communist rival on its left means that the electoral standing of the PDS is likely to fall well below that of the PCI.

As a necessary part of the process, the PDS faces the challenge of overcoming its diffidence towards the Socialists and setting about building unity on the Left. Even though Occhetto and Craxi issued a joint statement condemning the Soviet coup and demanding its reversal, the gulf separating their two parties persists. Swallowing their pride and accepting the possibility that their party could come to power but only as the junior partner in a left coalition remains the most difficult transition of all for Italy's ex-Communists.

–2–

Post-Communist Parties in Finland and Scandinavia: A Red-Green Road to the Twenty-first Century

David Arter

In May 1990, the Swedish Left-Party Communists (Vpk) became the first party in Western Europe to follow the example of its fraternal parties in the Eastern bloc and change its name. It became simply Leftist Party (*Vänsterpartiet*). At the September 1988 general election, the Left-Party Communists polled 5.8 per cent of the vote and gained twenty-one of the *Riksdag*'s 349 seats; three years later, the new Leftist Party won a reduced 4.5 per cent vote and sixteen parliamentary seats. In contrast to Sweden, communism in Finland had not presented itself as an explicit electoral option. Rather, the two wings of a long-divided movement contested elections as part of front organisations. A month before the renewal of the Swedish party, however, the two Finnish Communist parties and their umbrella bodies merged into a Leftist Alliance (*Vasemmistoliitto*) which, at the March 1991 general election, polled 10.1 per cent of the vote and won nineteen of the two hundred seats in the *Eduskunta*. These developments meant that the era of Communist representation in the Nordic parliaments was over. In the Finnish case, moreover, it denoted the demise of traditionally one of the largest Communist movements in Western Europe, claiming in its heyday in the 1950s nearly one-quarter of the votes.

Significantly, both the Finnish and Swedish Communist movements planned their change of name before the 1989 revolutions which swept away Communist control of the East European states. The majority in both cases, moreover, had for long charted a course of 'national Communism', which eschewed subservience to the Moscow line. Indicatively, whilst the (former) Soviet President, Mikhail Gorbachev, was strongly criticised for his intransigence towards the legitimate claims of the Baltic states to independence, there was equally vehement condemnation of the hard-line coup attempt against the Soviet President on 19 August 1991. Lars Werner, the Swedish Leftist Party leader, emphatically rejected the coup, expressed his unreserved support for Gorbachev (then under house arrest) and his democratisation programme and expressed concern for the plight of refugees from the disintegrating USSR. In Finland, the Leftist Alliance and the Greens were the only parties at the time to condemn the attempted coup.

Both former Communist parties have a history of real political influence: the Swedish Left-Communists exercised influence disproportionate to their size as the legislative ally of the ruling Social Democrats, whilst the Finnish Communists participated in government between 1966-83 more regularly than any other party of its kind in a pluralist democracy. Before focusing in more detail on the post-Communist parties in Finland and Sweden, a note on the present state of the Radical Left in the Nordic region in general is in order.

The State of the Nordic Radical Left

Across the Nordic region, minuscule Communist parties continue to exist, although they have long lacked a toehold in the national assemblies and relied on forming electoral alliances with other non-parliamentary groups on the Radical Left. They have also witnessed deep divisions over future strategy. Indeed, far from being impervious to the wider crisis of legitimacy facing communism in the wake of events in Eastern Europe, it may well not be long before the Danish and Norwegian Communists follow the example of the Dutch party and vote themselves out of existence.

Founded as a section of the Komintern in 1918, the Danish Communist Party (DKP) entered parliament for the first time in 1932. It was banned during the German Occupation, when several of its activists were imprisoned, but worked industriously in the Resistance movement and, accordingly, gained representation both in the Danish Council of Liberation (*Danmarks Frihedsråd*) and the Liberation Cabinet. In the first post-war election, DKP won eighteen parliamentary seats, and in 1977 it managed to win seven, but at the October 1979 election it lost its footing in the *Folketing* and has not regained it since. By 1990 DKP's membership had slumped to only ten thousand and the party was plunged into a financial crisis which threatened to close its organ *Land og Folk* (a paper it first published illegally in 1941 during the Occupation). Earlier the same year, an attempt by the Stalinist old guard to replace the party chairman, Ole Sohn, was repulsed – weakened by East European developments, the Stalinists managed only five of the thirty-five seats on the central committee – and Sohn's line on cementing electoral alliances with other very small radical Socialist groups prevailed.[1] However, at the last general election in December 1990, the DKP continued its slide.

In much the same way as in Denmark, the Norwegian Communist Party (NKP) and the Marxist-Leninist Red Electoral Alliance fought the 1989 general election as part of a new umbrella organisation, 'Solidarity and the Environment' (*Fylkeslistene for Miljø og Solidaritet*). This managed only 0.8 per cent of votes, however, and it seems that at least half its potential support ultimately opted for the Left-Socialists, who polled 10.1 per cent.[2] Like its Danish sister party, NKP gained its best result, 11.9 per cent of the vote, in 1945, elected its last *Storting* delegate in 1957 and has declined to such an extent that by 1990 it had only 950 members. At its party congress at the end of March that year, NKP split into two groups. The majority, under Kåre Andre Nilson, resolved to co-operate with a number of extra-parliamentary red-green groups; a minority, however, preferred more direct co-operation with the Left-Socialists. Significantly, in 1989, the Left-Socialist delegates were returned for precisely those constituencies which in 1945 had elected Communist members of the *Storting*.

The striking feature about communism in Sweden in the period from the shift to unicameralism in 1970 was its electoral stability. The Left-Party Communists narrowly, but consistently, crossed the 4 per cent national threshold necessary to qualify for parliamentary seats, even if its performance was indebted in no small measure to tactical votes from Social Democratic supporters concerned to ensure that Vpk continued to play the role of faithful legislative ally to the ruling party. In 1982, when a six-year interlude of 'bourgeois' government was ended by the return of a minority Social Democratic cabinet, the size of this so-called 'comrade vote' was estimated at nearly 2 per cent. In 1988, when the Social Democrats won a third consecutive term, it was probably closer to 1 per cent. Vpk never participated in government, but its leaders were able to wheel and deal with minority Social Democratic cabinets. This was the style of an older cohort of leaders who joined the party in the 1940s and 1950s – the likes of Lars Werner, C.H. Hermansson and Lars Ove Hagberg. They were increasingly opposed not by the survivors of the split in 1967 or the purge in 1977 (which led to the formation of a Communist Workers' Party), but by a younger generation which was critical of the pragmatism of the Vpk chairman, Lars Werner, and demanded more principle in the party. For these 'young conservatives', at least, communism was not to be

---

1. 'Udrensning hos kommunisterne', Nordisk Kontakt, February 1990, pp. 24–6.

2. 'Sosialistisk Venstreparti valgkampens store vinner', *Nordisk Kontakt*, December 1989, pp. 61–4.

sacrificed on the altar of opportunism and considerations of short-term electoral expediency.

Finnish communism was at its electoral peak in the 1950s during the long period in opposition (1948–66). In 1958 it equalled the Social Democratic vote of 23.2 per cent and when the left-wing won a parliamentary majority in 1966, the ensuing Popular Front coalition included the Communist front Finnish People's Democratic League. The issue of government involvement split the Communists, and the rift in their ranks deepened in the wake of the Warsaw Pact invasion of Czechoslovakia in August 1968. By the mid-1970s, the Finnish Communist Party had achieved the rather unusual status of being at once a member of the government (the majority favoured participation) and a party in opposition. The hard-line Stalinists refused to 'collaborate' and ultimately, in 1984, were expelled from the Party. The internecine warring of the two Communist factions contributed to a period of electoral decline. In 1975 the Communist vote was down to 19 per cent and by 1987 the combined share of the two Communist parties was only 13.1 per cent.

Despite their contrasting electoral and governmental profiles, there were several common denominators in the modernisation of the Finnish and Swedish Communist movements. As in the case of the Italian PCI and Spanish PCE, plans to reform and refurbish the Communist movements in both states predated the autumn revolutions of 1989 and the concomitant collapse of communism across much of Eastern Europe.[3] Pressure for renewal built up in the Finnish movement as early as November 1987, whilst in Sweden a concern to reappraise the party's whole position dated back to spring 1989, and is reflected in Vpk's congress slogan, 'Modernise, Liberate and Reform'.

Moves to reorientate the Radical Left were taken against the backdrop of a history of enervating internal division. In both Finland and Sweden, the Communist movements were also predominantly class-based movements of blue-collar workers which sought, somewhat belatedly, to transform themselves into modern catchall parties appealing to the growing body of educated middle-class voters. True, the Swedish Vpk began to recruit a greater proportion of the tertiary white-collar population in the central and southern towns under C.H. Hermansson's moderate and pragmatic leadership between 1964 and 1975, and by 1976 it was estimated that 12 per cent of senior civil servants under the age of thirty supported the party. Indeed, by February 1989, a quarterly report showed that Vpk's strongest support no longer derived from members of the central trade union federations,

3. Martin J. Bull, 'A new Era for the Non-Rulers Too: West European Communist parties, Perestroika and the Revolution in Eastern Europe' *Politics* vol. II, no. 1, 1991, p. 21.

Landsorganisabonen i Sverige (LO) and Tjänstemännens Central Organisational TCO), but from among highly-educated academics.[4] But the Finnish Communists were far slower both to see the need and also to act to extend the social base of its support.

In transforming themselves as radical leftist groups, the Communist parties in Finland and Sweden sought to distance themselves from the governing Social Democrats and to capitalise on disaffection with the latter's performance. Except for a six-year interlude of 'bourgeois' coalitions between 1976 and 1982 and the Conservative-led coalition, formed under Carl Bildt, following the September 1991 general election, the Social Democrats have dominated government in Sweden since the adoption of a single-chamber assembly in 1970, albeit without enjoying majority backing in the *Riksdag*. In Finland, the Social Democrats were the largest single party between 1966 and the March 1991 general election and became the fulcrum of coalition-building. In many respects, indeed, the momentum for the modernisation of the Communist movements of Finland and Sweden derived as much from dissatisfaction with the right-wing policies of the Social Democrats in government as the impact of Gorbachev's reforms in the Soviet Union, although the latter clearly lent immediacy to the need to seek a new identity and legitimacy. It was the accentuated market orientation of social democracy and its apparent lurch to the right which the redesignated Communist parties hoped in no small measure to profit from.

Finally, in both Finland and Sweden, the Communists had lost much of the radical initiative to expanding environmental movements during the 1980s. The Finnish Greens first gained parliamentary representation in 1983 and the Swedish Greens followed suit five years later, both parties making a strong appeal to the (otherwise relatively passive) cohort of first-time and young voters. Importantly, in contemplating revision, the two Communist parties found ready role models in the form of the Socialist People's Party in Denmark and the Left-Socialists in Norway. The success of these parties suggested that a judicious admixture of 'red' and 'green' policies could be electorally appealing, and that a brand of 'eco-socialism' might well offer reformed communism a route to the twenty-first century.

The Socialist People's Party (*Socialistisk Folkeparti*) was, in fact, a product of revisionist communism. It was formed in 1958 when the Danish Communist Party expelled its former chairman, Aksel Larsen, together with other 'Titoist revisionists', for refusing to follow the Moscow line. These reformist figures had then willy-nilly to seek to

4. David Arter, 'The Swedish Leftist Party: "Eco-Communism" or Communist Echo?' *Parliamentary Affairs*, vol. 44, no. 1, 1991, pp. 69–78.

adapt radical marxist socialism to the conditions of a welfare capitalist state in which there was growing affluence and economic security. The new party initially targetted blue-collar Socialists disillusioned with both the Communists and Social Democrats. The exiled Communists in SF originally believed they were creating a party which differed from the DKP only in not having the burden of 'defending Soviet reality as the Socialist utopia'.[5] After 1968, however, the character of SF changed and it began to attract a younger generation of educated, middle-class radicals and to develop a distinctive New Leftist mix of red-green ideas. SF nonetheless remained a relatively small party between 1968 and 1981, polling 5–6 per cent of the vote, but in 1981 it surged forward to 11.3 per cent and in May 1988 to 13.1 per cent of the vote, before falling back to 8.4 per cent at the last general election in December 1990.

The Norwegian Socialist People's Party (an anti-NATO Labour splinter group formed in 1961) joined the Norwegian Communists, left-wing Labour dissidents and other anti-EC elements in a Socialist Electoral Alliance which won a remarkable 11.2 per cent at the 1973 general election. These radical leftist elements subsequently merged forces as the Socialist Left Party (*Socialistisk Venstreparti*), or Left-Socialists. At the last general election in September 1989, SV advanced from a modest 4.6 per cent to 10.1 per cent of the vote and trebled its *Storting* representation – largely, it seems, at the expense of the governing Labour Party, whose 34.3 per cent was its worst result since 1930. Opinion polls in 1991 made the Left-Socialists Norway's third largest party. Under its leader, Erik Solheim, the party has promoted more of a green than a red image and it was significant that in a survey in autumn 1990, 31 per cent of respondents saw SV as the most credible environmental party. By presenting itself as the 'caring party', SV has also directed itself towards the public-sector workers who have comprised the mainstay of its support in recent years. Solheim's style has become increasingly populist, and the socialism in SV's title is of a diffuse, pragmatic and essentially humanistic character.

For the modernising Communist movements in Finland and Sweden, the example afforded by well-established radical leftist parties of a non-Communist genre elsewhere in the Nordic region was crucial on at least two counts. First, it illustrated the potential appeal of red-green policies to a younger generation of voters. In 1977, for example, 49 per cent of Danish SF voters were under thirty, whereas in 1989 every second voter for the Norwegian SV was aged between twenty-six

---

5. John Logue, *Socialism and Abundance: Radical Socialism in the Danish Welfare State*, Minneapolis, University of Minnesota 1982, pp. 4, 56, 79, 89–90.

and thirty-nine. SV, however, fared less favourably than its rivals among voters in their forties, suggesting that the party had lost its hold on the generation of 1968. A second important lesson was the ability of the Danish SF and Norwegian SV successfully to compete with the Social Democratic/Labour parties in a highly volatile 'voter market'. This was particularly true in Norway, where at the 1989 general election 40 per cent of voters opted for a party other than the one they had backed four years earlier. Not since 1973, when traditional voting patterns were shattered by the EC question, had electoral stability been as low as 1989. Equally, the relative decline in SF's support among young persons and their tactical shift to the Social Democrats – presumably in an attempt to end an eight-year period of Conservative-led rule in Denmark – accounted for much of the Danish SF's 4.3 per cent loss at the polls in December 1990, and served as a reminder that parties can never assume the support of even their core constituencies.[6]

The Origins of the Finnish Leftist Alliance

Since the Finnish Communist Party was in its prime one of the largest in Europe, and participated in coalitions more frequently than any other West European fraternal party, it seems appropriate to concentrate at this stage on the factors underlying its decision to choose a non-Communist route forward. What were the origins of the new Leftist Alliance and on what basis does it seek to appeal to voters? In truth, electoral necessity was in large part the mother of a proposal on 11 March 1989 to merge the Finnish Communist Party (SKP) and its umbrella organisation, the Finnish People's Democratic League (SKDL) and found a new party, the Leftist Alliance. So much was acknowledged by Reijo Käkelä, the SKDL chairman, who admitted at a League Council meeting that SKDL had lost over half its traditional share of the labour movement.[7] At the 1987 general election, SKDL – comprising in addition to the Communist Party (majority-wing), the Democratic League of Finnish Women (SNDL), the Democratic Youth League (SDNL) and the Socialist Students' Union (SSYL) – polled only 9.4 per cent of the vote – and this represented the worst election result since its creation in 1944. From a position as the best-supported

---

6. 'Hor socialdemokratisk valgsejr', Nordisk Kontakt, issue 18 1990, pp. 21–4; 'Rorgængeren sagde farvel efter 17 år', *Nordisk Kontakt*, April 1991, pp. 22–3.

7. SKDL:n (puheenjohtaja) speech by Reijo Käkelä, at the SKDL: Executive meeting (liittoneuvosto), 11 March 1989, *Helsinki*.

group in 1958, SKDL had slipped to fourth place behind the Social Democrats, Conservatives and Centre by 1987.

Although on the eve of the Twenty-second Party Congress in February 1990, the Communist Party chairman, Jarmo Wahlström, noted that the historic events in the Soviet Union and elsewhere had reinforced the need to modernise the Finnish Radical Left, he insisted that the idea of a Leftist Alliance (LA) had not originated in the events in Eastern Europe. The initiative for reform clearly predated the autumn revolutions of 1989. If there was an exogenous causal factor, it was probably more the strong aversion felt towards the predominance of the New Right in Western Europe than a response to the crisis of socialism in Eastern Europe. Certainly the distinctive Conservative-Social Democratic cabinet under Harri Hoikeri, formed after the 1987 general election, led leading Communists to conclude that the Finnish Social Democrats had become mere pawns of the New Right and were demonstrably assisting in the realisation of Thatcherite goals. According to the so-called 'April Manifesto' of the nascent Leftist Alliance (which was approved by its provisional executive committee on 7 April 1990), the new party would open its doors to all those wishing to play a constructive role in its development, irrespective of their ideological conviction. However, the new party was a joint venture involving the Finnish Communist Party and Finnish People's Democratic League and, in its original conception, the LA did not envisage the incorporation of the hard-line Stalinists who had been expelled from the party in 1984. They, in turn, had proceeded to found their own party, the Finnish Communist Party-Unity (SKP-y), which through its front organisation, the Democratic Alternative (DEVA), had polled 4 per cent of the vote at the 1987 general election.

A history of deep internal factionalisation, therefore, had thrown up the curious spectacle of two competing Finnish Communist Parties, the reformist majority which was instrumental in the Leftist Alliance project and an orthodox minority which wanted nothing to do with it. As late as autumn 1989, the hard-liners – often known as 'Taistolaiset' after the Christian name of their long-standing leader Taisto Sinisalo – remained totally opposed to the Leftist Alliance. By the turn of the new year, however, they had performed an abrupt *volte-face* and joined the new party. The inauguration of the LA thus signified the demise of communism as a meaningful electoral option in Finland and the effective reunification of the Communist movement, albeit under non-Communist colours.

The hard-liners were undoubtedly caught on the horns of an electoral dilemma. Opinion polls early in 1990 indicated that DEVA had the support of only 1.9 per cent of voters and to have gone into the

1991 election on its own lists would almost certainly have meant the Finnish Communist Party-Unity losing its slender toehold in parliament. Equally, the hard-liners in SKP-y could scarcely fail to ignore the fact that as the sole remaining Communist party, and the one most closely associated with Moscow,[8] it would struggle to maintain voter credibility given the incipient collapse of the Muscovite empire in Eastern Europe and, in particular, the fall of hard-line Stalinism in Romania. The fissures appearing in the fabric of Communist systems may thus be said to have contributed to making reluctant partners out of the hard-liners and they pooled their resources with a reformist majority in the Communist movement which had taken the road to renewal ahead of the autumn revolutions of 1989.

The inaugural conference of the Leftist Alliance was staged over the weekend of 28–29 April 1990. On the final afternoon of the weekend's proceedings, extraordinary congresses of SKDL and SNDL voted to wind up their respective organisations. In practice SKP also ceased to exist. Perhaps the biggest question mark surrounding the renewal of the radical Left concerned the future of the Finnish Communist Party-Unity. SKP-y had adopted a generally recalcitrant attitude to joining the Leftist Alliance and its chair, Esko-Juhani Tennilä, initially favoured preserving the minority party, although he ultimately recognised that the Leftist Alliance offered both an electoral lifeline and a career safeguard. Elements among the hard-liners remained irreconcilable, however, and the small minority of 'Taistolaiset' who refused to collaborate in the Leftist Alliance subsequently formed a new party, the Communist Workers' Party (KTP).

KTP claimed (rightly) during the 1991 general election campaign that this was the first time in Finnish history that Communists had expressly stood as Communists, rather than as part of a front organisation. Uniquely among the parties, the Communist Workers' Party came out strongly against Finnish involvement in the negotiations that were underway on the creation of a European Economic Area (encompassing the EC and EFTA states) and opposed to the whole process of European integration. On a platform of 'Peace and Socialism', KTP ran candidates in all fourteen mainland constituencies in 1991, but gained a mere 0.27 per cent of the national vote. Its best result was just under 0.5 per cent in Uusimaa constituency in the hinterland of the capital city, Helsinki.

For the architects of the Leftist Alliance, the Finnish Communist Party (majority wing) and the Finnish People's Democratic League, the new party had three main objectives. First and foremost, it was

8. Taisto Sinisalo, *Vastaus on vasemmistopolitiikka*, Kursiivi, Helsinki, 1980, p. 161.

conceived as a vehicle for stemming the ebb tide in the electoral fortunes of the Radical Left. Käkelä, the SKDL chair, spoke of the desire to double the movement's strength by the turn of the century – this meant seeking to capture about one-fifth of the active electorate – and, in effect, returning to the support level SKDL had enjoyed before the advent of internal strife in 1966.

At its peak in the 1950s and 1960s, the Finnish Communist Party was *par excellence* a party of the blue-collar work-force. Just over one-third of the working class voted for SKDL and this represented more than two-thirds of the party's overall support. SKDL, in short, was primarily a party which recruited from the industrial workers of the south and west and the farm-forest workers in the peripheral north and east – the so-called 'backwoods Communists'. A period of accelerated development in the late 1960s, however, propelled Finland towards a post-industrial economy and enabled proponents of the Leftist Alliance to argue with much force that the pace of socio-economic change had served appreciably to erode the class base of the Radical Left.[9] They could also insist that the protracted conflict between revisionists and hard-liners within its ranks had prevented the Communist Party from making a determined enough effort to win the expanded service sector of salaried employees spawned by de-industrialisation. The belief that the Radical Left could indeed broaden the economic base of its electorate to become a catch-all party – as well as attain a vital generational renewal of its support base by attracting a influx of younger voters – was given a fillip by Kalevi Kivistö's performance as the SKDL presidential candidate in 1988. Kivistö and his support group, 'Action 88', succeeded in projecting a softer image which attracted a modicum of support from outside the Radical Left's traditional catchment.

A second goal of advocates of the Leftist Alliance was a corollary of the first, namely that increased popular support would enhance the political standing of the Radical Left and facilitate its participation in government. Between the formation of a broad left-centre Popular Front coalition in 1966 and SKDL's resignation from the cabinet early in 1983, the Communist Party was a regular governing party, although the issue of coalition involvement, which President Urho Kekkonen actively encouraged, was an important factor dividing the 'Eurocommunist' majority wing from the hard-line minority. A final objective in creating the LA was the realisation of a single, cohesive party machine which would replace the duplication of separate SKP

9. David Arter, 'Finland: a Typical Post-Industrial State?' in Engman and Kirby (eds.), *Finland: People, Nation, State*, London, Hurst, 1990, pp. 227–43.

and SKDL organisations, both possessing traditional (and costly) pyramid structures and suffering from declining membership and morale. Among Leftist Alliance supporters, there was an undoubted sense that it was high time to renounce the hoary notion of a vanguard party based on professional revolutionaries and to supplant it with a model of an open, fluid and democratic organisation in which decisions derived from the rank-and-file and which would be member-centred rather than elitist in character.

When the hard-line minority belatedly entered the mainstream of modernisation, it plainly did not concur with all the principal objectives of the Leftist Alliance. The unwritten trade-off had seen the majority-wing Communists and People's Democrats achieving the appearance of unity on the Radical Left in return for the hard-liners gaining an extended lease of parliamentary life. It was, in short, a marriage of convenience which did not *ipso facto* betoken a lasting, still less harmonious, relationship. In large part, the prospects of domestic accord revolved around the answer to two leading questions. One, would traditional hard-line voters back a Leftist Alliance which had as a main objective the type of collaboration with the bourgeois state, i.e. participation in government, which had been anathema to the minority wing of the Communist movement? Two, would the expelled districts that had formed the mainstay of SKP-y merge fully into the LA or, alternatively, seek to retain an identity as part of a vanguard movement?

The 'Ideological Crisis' of the Leftist Alliance

According to Elisabeth Nordgren, writing in the theoretical journal, *Kommunisti*, the most attractive feature of the incipient Leftist Alliance was not that it offered ready answers, but that it posed relevant questions.[10] The Leftist Alliance, with its apparently piecemeal pronouncements, she inferred, represented a healthy antidote to the doctrinal politics of old-style communism. Nonetheless, as a new party formation, the Leftist Alliance was clearly obliged to engage in a process of systematic ideological renewal in order to sustain its position in the political market-place. Ideally, there appeared to be three prerequisites for the successful adaptation of Radical Leftist thinking to the 1990s and beyond. First, there was the need, especially pressing in view of events in Eastern Europe, to advance an explicit

10. Elisabeth Nordgren, 'Vasemmistoliito?' *Kommunisti*, February 1990, pp. 12–14.

critique of command economy systems to complement the classical Radical Leftist thinking to the 1990s and beyond. First, there was the need, especially pressing in view of events in Eastern Europe, to advance an explicit critique of command economy systems to complement the classical Radical Leftist indictment of capitalism. A recognition that state socialism was in retreat did not, of course, necessarily imply the rejection of socialism as a value system. A distinction could legitimately be drawn between a Marxist party, which viewed socialism as a goal to be aimed at, and one 'inspired by Marxism and its labour movement heritage', which was committed to the diffusion of Socialist values throughout society. Perhaps the most important point, though, was that the Leftist Alliance's socialism should appear to be pragmatic, in the sense of offering a practical code of conduct, rather than being dogmatic and intolerant.

Second, it was important, if possible, to formulate an alternative critique of capitalism to that devised by Marx: one which clearly acknowledged both the extent and the structural implications of the socio-economic change occurring in the late twentieth century. Both capitalism and the working class had evolved significantly and the working class movement had perforce to respond to the changed realities. If this clearly involved jettisoning the more deterministic elements of 'scientific socialism', it did not, of course, require an acceptance of the inevitable inequalities and injustices of the capitalist system. On the contrary, it underlined the need for a programme of innovative social reform, not least to counter the advance of New Right thinking.

Third, there was the need to generate a body of New Leftist thought which, while retaining a deep commitment to a root-and-branch reform of the social structures perpetuating inequality, nonetheless constituted a distinctive synthesis of progressive tendencies culled from outside the Marxist tradition. A recognition of its heterogeneous ideological foundations (and the collective debt it owed *inter alia* to humanism, environmentalism and feminism) was ultimately, perhaps, less important to the Leftist Alliance than that the hybrid should be electorally saleable. Put simply, the product should differentiate the new party from other left-wing groups – the Social Democrats and Greens – and be capable of attracting both old and new voters.

The Leftist Alliance's launch was accompanied by the so-called 'April Manifesto', which contained an outline statement of its principles, along with a detailed party programme entitled 'Sustainable Development – A Just Society'. The central thread in both documents was the quest for a mutually satisfactory relationship between the economy and the environment, and the pivotal analytical tool used in the search for such an accommodation was the concept of 'sustainable development'. This gained prominence following the report 'Our Common Future', published by World (Brundtland) Commission on Environment and Development in 1987. By 'sustainable development' the Brundtland Commission denoted economic activity which would serve the needs of existing citizens without endangering the possibilities of future generations satisfying their needs. Obviously, 'sustainable development' presupposes the attainment of a compromise between the dominant Western lifestyle, based on conspicuous consumption, and the underlying dictates of the ecosystem. Interestingly, however, the Leftist Alliance deploys 'sustainable development' as a multifaceted concept which informs the whole party programme. In short, it is given an application outside the economic arena and the need to plan the economy on an environmentally sound foundation.

Importantly, the ecological perspective which is the primary imperative of 'sustainable development' permits the Leftist Alliance both to broaden the premises of the time-honoured Radical left critique of capitalism, whilst also allowing for a novel condemnation of state socialism. There is, to be sure, the traditional concern for the casualties of capitalism – the homeless, unemployed and low-paid – and emphasis is given to the way the capitalist system marginalises groups and produces alienation. But with its commitment to unlimited growth and ever-increasing consumption, the market economy is held to be incompatible with sustainable development. Capitalism, in brief, impoverishes and subjugates citizens, destroys the natural environment and eschews responsibility for future generations. Significantly, the state Socialist economy is held culpable on similar charges: it has devastated the environment, debarred people from running their own lives and denied citizens any meaningful participation in setting societal goals. Predicated on a rejection of both capitalist and command economy models and the cardinal importance of achieving sustainable development, the Leftist Alliance's programme in April 1990 espoused the type of 'eco-socialism' which is mirrored in its key slogan, 'Red Politics for a Green and Just Future'. Socialist it indubitably was (albeit of the non-Marxist variety), in counterposing the traditional left-wing values of liberty, equality and solidarity with the inequality, injustice and individualism of the unbridled market. Eco-Socialist it was too, in the way an attempt was made to combine 'red' values with a 'green' concern for global problems such as international peace, Third World poverty and, of course, environmental pollution.

The principal postulates of the Leftist Alliance were: a defence of nature and the environment of future generations against the spoliation and destruction of resources; a defence of the poor against oppression and indifference; a defence of work against the power of capital; a defence of women against discrimination; a defence of citizens against market forces and centralised control; a defence of peace and international harmony against war and images of hatred; and a defence of human values against life-alienating structures. Ultimately, the Leftist Alliance programme asserted, the onus must be on human growth (the growth of people) rather than economic growth (the growth in production).[11] This was not to argue that a sustainable economy was incompatible with economic growth, provided that growth did not threaten future resources and the environment. But a 'casino economy', with its attendant speculation and profiteering, clearly violated the concept.

The Leftist Alliance's programme appeared to contain relatively few hard, vote-winning promises of the type likely to attract the wider electoral constituency the new party was seeking. Really the only 'handout' was a 'citizen's wage' (how it was to be funded was not made clear), which would be a statutory allowance guaranteed to all citizens, irrespective of whether they were employed or not. The benefits of instituting such a provision would, it was claimed, be extremely wide-ranging. Thus the 'citizen's wage' would enhance study opportunities; enable young persons to become independent of their parents; increase the economic independence of women; allow workers to decline 'poorly paid, exhausting and morally questionable work'; and revitalise rural areas by permitting people to live and work there. As the 1991 general election approached, there were naturally more tangible offerings: promises to increase house construction, standardise taxation on work-related and capital-based income, raise the level of study support, unemployment benefit and pensions, and abolish the wage differentials between men and women.

The Leftist Alliance programme also contained several 'restrictive measures' likely to have a potential appeal to the (mostly educated) groups on the 'green left'. For example, Finland's energy consumption was to be frozen at the 1990 level by the year 2000 and the 1990 level reduced by at least 10 per cent by 2010; there was to be no fifth nuclear power station and nuclear power was gradually to be phased out; a comprehensive environmental protection act was clearly to prohibit water, soil and air pollution; and there was to be a ban on the construction of new motorways. But the new party faced strong competition for the environmental vote from the Greens and, indeed, the Centre, which also claimed to embrace the concept of 'sustainable development'.[12]

---

11. Internal publication series No 1.: Vasemmistoliiton ohjelma, *Kestävä kehitys – Oikeudenmukainer Yhteiskunta* Vasemmistoliiton julkaisuja 1.

12. Paavo Väyrynen, *Yheinen tehtävämme*, Porvoo-Helsinki-Juva, WSO 1989, pp. 81–5.

The Leftist Alliance in the Electoral Market-Place

In the build-up to the 1991 general election, there were three main questions relating to the Leftist Alliance's performance. First, would the new party achieve its target of 10 per cent of the vote and preserve the twenty parliamentary seats which the two Communist parties and their umbrella organisations had won between them at the polls four years earlier?[13] Second, could the Leftist Alliance succeed in presenting itself as a unified force after nearly a quarter of a century of bickering in the Communist movement? Clouds had already appeared on the horizon of internal solidarity. Reijo Käkelä, SKDL's last chair and a leading architect of the LA, had defected to the Social Democrats and although no longer a registered party, the Finnish Communist Party-Unity continued to exist within the Leftist Alliance. Third, could the Leftist Alliance profit from the onset of an economic recession which, after years of sustained growth, queered the pitch of Hoikeri's Conservative–Social Democratic coalition in the months before the election? Predictably, the Leftist Alliance inveighed against a government which, in the mould of Margaret Thatcher, had increased disparities in income and wealth, and it coupled a vigorous concern to promote the cause of the low-paid and underprivileged social groups with a package of environmental measures designed to conserve energy and protect valuable natural resources like the Finnish forests.

External events in the early part of the campaign served to dispel doubts regarding the independence from the Kremlin of a party which had incorporated the vast majority of pro-Moscow hard-liners. The bloodbath in the Lithuanian capital, Vilnius, on 14 January 1991, stirred young Finns to demonstrate against Gorbachev and led the Leftist Alliance to condemn the violence and support the aspiration of the Baltic states to achieve independence by peaceful means. So strongly did the LA chairman Andersson feel on the Baltic question that individual members of the Leftist Alliance's parliamentary group were asked formally to declare themselves – all came out against the violence – and the party chair subsequently conceded that any equivocation would have been in violation of the party line.

Ironically, Andersson's strongly supportive stance on the independence of the Baltic states prompted a reprimand from President Kivistö. This took the form of a letter which the Leftist Alliance leader

---

13. Shortly after its formation, the Leftist Alliance's aim was to win 26–7 parliamentary seats. Puheenjohtaja Claes Andersson, Polittinen tilannekatsaus Vl :n liittovaltuuston Kokouksessa Kuopion Rauhalahdessa 2–3 June 1990. *Vasemmisto Liikkeellä* Vasemmistoliiton julkaisuja 2, p. 13.

received whilst attending the thirty-sixth annual session of the Nordic Council (a consultative body of regional parliamentarians) in Copenhagen in February 1990. For the first time ever, the Nordic Council had invited the presidents of the Baltic states to attend and Kivistö, whose official line was that the Baltic question was an 'internal Soviet matter', plainly felt that it was timely to counsel Andersson to proceed prudently. This was not perhaps without good reason since, during its session, the Nordic Council received a memorandum (which it simply noted and filed) from the Soviet Foreign Ministry, warning it against co-operation with 'separatists and those forces working to destroy the Soviet Union'. According to Andersson, however, Kivistö's note was 'perhaps unnecessarily dramatic, recalling the style of former president Urho Kekkonen', and he played down his differences with the Finnish head of state on the issue, claiming they were more nuance than substance.[14] In any event, the episode was widely reported in the media and gave welcome publicity to the fact that although (in the words of its programme) 'prepared to engage in co-operation with the CPSU', the Leftist Alliance was no servile apologist for the Kremlin. By contrast, ten years earlier, the hard-line leader, Taisto Sinisalo, had expressed great incomprehension of, and regret over, the anti-Soviet pronouncements of several West European Communist parties.

Ultimately, the Leftist Alliance failed by only one to retain the twenty seats the two Communist parties had won in 1987. The distribution of its seats between former hard-liners (four) and majority-wingers (fifteen) remained essentially unchanged. The overall loss of only a single parliamentary seat (and one actually gained in Helsinki) persuaded *Kansan Uutiset* to describe the result as a 'Defensive Victory'.[15] The fact remains nonetheless that the Leftist Alliance failed to attract a significant proportion of former Communist voters and managed to appeal to relatively few new supporters. Its 274,000 votes (10.1 per cent of the active electorate) was 118,000 or 30 per cent down on the combined SKDL/DEVA total in 1987, and it lost ground in all fourteen mainland constituencies. The Leftist Alliance was strongest in the geographic and economic periphery of northern Finland ('backwoods' Communist terrain), polled relatively well in several areas in the densely-populated south and south-west (the heartland of 'industrial communism'), but fared generally very poorly in the centre and east of the country. Overall, its electoral topography can be summarised as an erosion in support across the entire national

---

14. Interview with Claes Andersson, 13 March 1991.
15. 'Torjuntavoitto', *Kansan Uutiset*, 19 March 1991.

territory, but with the new party inheriting the 'peaks' and 'troughs' of its Communist predecessors.

When the Leftist Alliance vote in 1991 is compared with the SKDL/DEVA aggregate in 1987, it becomes evident that the new party's decline is roughly equivalent to DEVA's share of the poll in 1987. An exit poll directed by Sten Berglund showed that whereas 93 per cent of Leftist Alliance's support derived from previous SKDL/DEVA voters, only 64 per cent of those favouring the two last-mentioned groups in 1987 voted for the Leftist Alliance. Nearly one-fifth of the Radical Leftist electorate abstained (particularly in the northern regions), whilst 4.3 per cent shifted to the opposition-based Centre Party and 4.0 per cent to the Social Democrats.[16] The Leftist Alliance, in short, failed to mobilise its previous voters (and there is a strong *prima facie* case for suggesting that abstentionism was highest among former hard-liners) and largely failed to attract new voters on its red-green 'eco-Socialist' ticket. Despite a low turn-out of 72 per cent, the Greens, for their part, increased their support to 6.8 per cent – the largest environmental vote in the Nordic states – and the Centre Party emerged as the clear election winner, becoming the largest single party for the first time since changing its name from the Agrarian Party in 1965.

When the Centre Party leader, Esko Aho, was requested to form a government, it is clear that there was division in the Leftist Alliance's ranks regarding participation and that (as previously) the former hard-liners were opposed to it. In a survey of members, however, it emerged that a *majority* or respondents wanted the new party to enter government, albeit, if possible, with the Social Democrats and Greens. The Social Democrats (for whom the election result was their worst since the war) made it immediately clear that they would revert to an opposition role (for the first time in twenty-five years) and the Leftist Alliance ruled out serving in the same cabinet as the Conservatives. The withdrawal of the Leftist Alliance and, shortly afterwards, the Greens from the negotiations on a new coalition duly opened the way for the formation of a three-party (Centre, Conservative, Swedish People's Party) non-Socialist government under Aho's leadership.

The Leftist Alliance's International Links

The Leftist Alliance asserts that co-operation across state boundaries is an essential precondition for the resolution of such global issues as

16. 'Vasemmistoliitto sai vain vähän uusia ääniä', *Kansan Uutiset* 23 March 1991.

environmental pollution, the North-South divide and the search for peace and disarmament. In the latter context, the Leftist Alliance, in addition to emphasising the importance of the Conference on Security and Co-operation in Europe (CSCE), has argued the case for the Nordic Council breaking with its convention of not taking a stance on foreign and security policy questions in favour of an active propagation of a nuclear-free zone in Northern Europe.[17] So as to make a tangible contribution to the goal of continental disarmament, the party is committed to cut the size of the Finnish army as a prelude to its eventual abolition.

Unlike its Communist predecessors, the Leftist Alliance did not initially regard itself as having fraternal parties or forming part of a wider movement anchored in a common ideology. Its natural partners, it held, were those parties with a red-green philosophy, although it declared itself willing to establish links with left-wing groups in the European Community and Council of Europe and possibly, too, with the Socialist International. In fact, the Leftist Alliance has regarded its fraternal parties as comprising the group of non-Communist parties of the Radical Left that provided the initial role model: the Socialist People's Party in Denmark and Norwegian Left-Socialists, together with the Icelandic People's Alliance and the redisignated Leftist Party in Sweden. Importantly, the new party has actively supported leftist parties and popular movements in Estonia and the other Baltic states.

In November 1990 (two months before the unrest), the Leftist Alliance adopted a resolution urging Finland, when the circumstances permitted, to take the initiative in the creation of a permanent con-sultative organ, a Baltic Council, along the lines of the one which functioned in the 1930s. On 15 January 1991, the day after the deaths in Lithuania, moreover, the Leftist Alliance's parliamentary group addressed a note to President Gorbachev, condemning the violence and pressing him to recognise the independence of the Baltic states. In order to avoid further violence, the Soviet President was entreated to engage in negotiations with the newly-elected Baltic Supreme Soviets. Significantly, the Leftist Alliance's line on the Baltic question went considerably further than President Kivistö who, on geo-political grounds that reflected a tactical concern not to alienate Moscow, preferred to adopt a noncommital stance and to view developments as an internal Soviet matter.

In common with its kindred parties in Norway and Sweden, and the Greens across the Nordic region, the Leftist Alliance has adopted a critical stance on the issue currently foremost on the Finnish political

17. 'Vasemmistoliiton sata tapaa arvostaa ihmistä ja säästää luontoa' *Vasemmistoliiton julkaisuja*, No 6, p. 105.

agenda, namely European integration. The new party, of course, recognises the importance to Finland of Western markets and, accordingly, endorsed the nation's participation in the negotiations which in November 1991 led to agreement on the formation of a European Economic Area embracing the EFTA states and the EC. But it is totally opposed to Finland taking the Swedish road to an application for full European Community membership. At very least, it holds, there would have to be a public debate and a popular referendum before proceeding to take such a step. The Leftist Alliance's recalcitrance on the Community appears to reflect the feelings of the bulk of its supporters. In a survey published before the March 1991 general election, it emerged that whereas 51 per cent of Social Democrats and three-quarters of Conservative voters favoured Finland joining the EC, the Leftist Alliance was the only party in which a majority of supporters were opposed to membership.

The Future of the Scandinavian Post-Communist Parties

For both the new post-Communist parties in the region, the Finnish Leftist Alliance and the Swedish Leftist Party, the immediate period ahead will be a testing time. They will need to complete a more detailed party programme and maintain a radical identity in opposition, whilst flanked by the Social Democrats, themselves seeking to radicalise and refurbish their party's image, and, in the Finnish case, the Greens, who spurned the chance of government to pursue their own radical alternative. Co-operation among these opposition parties will not be easy. In contrast to the Social Democrats, who are moving progressively closer to supporting a Finnish application to join the European Community, the Leftist Alliance and Greens are adamantly opposed to membership. The same is true in Sweden, although the Greens lost their *Riksdag* toehold following the September 1991 general election. Significantly, Swedish public opinion appears relatively split on the EC question. A poll published just before the New Year 1992 showed 48 per cent in favour of membership, 24 per cent against and 27 per cent undecided. Many of those opposed were from northern Sweden and comprised predominantly public-sector workers who were supporters of the Leftist Alliance. Bildt, the Prime Minister, has promised a referendum on EC membership in conjunction with the next general election in 1994, and the Leftist Party can, perhaps, make capital out of the declining popular enthusiasm for full membership.

For both the new post-Communist parties there is also an urgent need to attract a younger generation of voters and, in the Finnish case, to mobilise former hard-liners and convince them that the party represents their best interests. Throughout the Nordic region, the electorate is less stable and there is a susceptibility to populist, anti-establishment parties – witness, for example, the extraordinary rise of New Democracy in Sweden which polled 6.7 per cent at its first election in 1991. The success of the Left-Socialists in Norway in 1989 has demonstrated that the Radical Left can profit from volatile young voters by playing a red-green card, although in both Finland and Sweden, recent election defeats have pointed up the scale of task ahead. Leadership is clearly an important electoral factor. Indeed, despite Andersson's creditable performance in the 1991 election campaign, it would not be surprising if a change at the helm of the Finnish party was imminent. In large part, the future of the Radical Left in both Finland and Sweden depends on securing a younger generation of leaders lacking a close association with the Communist past.

Tentative or makeshift as the exercise might have been, the reappraisal of communism, which was viewed with suspicion by the diehard elements, has witnessed the post-Communist parties of Finland and Scandinavia mapping out a red-green road to the twenty-first century. In the face of incipient pluralism in Eastern Europe and the ascendancy of the New Right in the West, communism was jettisoned and replaced by an 'eco-socialism' which sought to combine the ethical principles of socialism with the practical goal of 'sustainable development' and incorporated, too, an explicit critique of both capitalist and command economy systems. In Norway, it appears that the Left Socialists' recent success has resulted from vesting eco-socialism with a populist character and bringing out the green at the expense of the red in its appeal. In Finland and Sweden, however, competition for the green vote includes Green parties who have an established foothold in the legislature. In these circumstances, it may be more prudent for the Finnish and Swedish Radical Left to emphasise their Socialist credentials, especially at a time when social democracy appears to have lost its way and historically dominant left-wing parties are on the defensive. Parties who change their name/colours rarely reap rapid electoral dividends: it took the Finnish Centre over a quarter of a century to 'make good'. New images, styles, and appeals take time to evolve. Indeed, if the immediate future does not look particularly bright, judgements about the prospects of the new post-Communist parties in Finland and Sweden are best deferred. The neo-liberal tide must eventually turn.

–3–

French Communism's Final Struggle

David S. Bell

The French Communist Party (PCF), like other Western parties, was in
a long-term decline before the collapse of communism in the East and
the August 1991 coup against Gorbachev. At the Liberation the
Communist Party, which had participated in government and been
associated with the prestige of the Resistance and the victorious Soviet
ally, had polled a startling 28.6 per cent in the Assembly elections of
1946. From that time on there was a 'saw tooth' decline until the
1980s, when its collapse became precipitous: the party polled 15 per
cent in the presidential elections of 1981, 11 per cent in the European
elections of 1984, 9.8 per cent in the Assembly elections of 1986 and
6.7 per cent in the 1988 presidential elections. In the 1988 Assembly
elections it returned only twenty-seven deputies, too few to form a
parliamentary group.

Of course a Communist Party is no mere electoral machine, but the
dimensions of decline were apparent in other areas. The main party
front, the CGT unions, steadily lost members and voters (in social
security and labour elections) and lost ground relative to competing
labour federations (the Force Ouvrière and CFDT). Other party fronts,
such as the peace movement and the 'friendship societies', lost their
ability to appeal beyond the committed Communists, and party
membership also clearly declined (but by what figures it is difficult to
guess). The Communist press, once a substantial empire, was reduced
by 1992 to one national and three regional dailies. In short, the
Communists' once formidable ability to mobilise a constellation of
institutions around its political objectives was reduced to nothing as the
party became a marginal force in French politics. The 'fellow
travellers' and intellectual sympathisers who had once adorned the
party's campaigns were no longer present, and dissidence became a
regular feature of French Communist life, even reaching the
Secretariat.

Yet at the beginning of the Fifth Republic the French Communist
Party had dominated the Left: the SFIO Socialist party was weak and

divided but the Communists, massive, well organised, polling strongly, were unreformed and committed to the Leninist vision. In 1956 the party had started to seek an alliance with the SFIO and had entered a 'reformist' phase – the parliamentary road to power. The Fifth Republic, with its bipolarised politics – presidential competition with the revival of the Socialist Party around a credible presidential candidate (which a Communist could never be) – was an even more hostile environment for the Communist Party than the Fourth, for all its anti-communism, although the awesome resources of the party disguised this basic weakness for some time.

The Communist Party, following the line set in 1956 by the Kremlin, embarked on a suicidal course – the policy of left-wing unity around a joint manifesto (the 1972 'Common Programme'). The precondition of an alliance victory was that the Communists be the junior partner and very clearly subordinate to Socialist leadership. The alliance was unstable from its outset. The Communists reacted to the growth of the Socialist Party under François Mitterrand in the 1970s (then the only credible left-wing presidential candidate) by trying to compete with it 'modernising' and presenting a more attractive face to the electorate (the so-called 'Eurocommunism'). However, these attempts to renovate an old-fashioned Bolshevism were superficial and unconvincing.

The French party's inability to steer a constant course, veering between agreeing with the Socialists and attacking them as surrogate versions of the Right (and even varying wildly within the sectarian anti-Socialist line), must have contributed to its continuing decline.[1] It changed from alliance to sectarianism in 1977; participated half-heartedly in government in 1981–4; and became extreme sectarian again in 1984 but continued to ally with the Socialists for electoral and local government purposes. By the same token its vacillations about whether it was the 'eldest daughter of the Church', faithful to Moscow, or prepared, like the Italians, to be critical were also baffling.

The roots of French Communist crisis are therefore to be found in its untenable position in domestic politics, in the competition with the renovated Socialist Party. Neither the modernised 'Eurocommunism" nor the hard-line sectarian stance which the party adopted after 1977, when it decided to scrap the alliance with the PS, had been paying propositions and it is, in retrospect, hard to see how the party could have been saved. However, it made things worse for itself by returning to an aggressive pro-Sovietism, and ending the alliance with the Socialists.

In the 1930s, when French Communism had benefited from the Popular Front alliance with the Socialists, the Soviet Union had not

1. *Le Monde*, 4 September 1991.

been an 'anti model' (quite the contrary), nor had it been after the Second World War, but it was by the 1970s. It was one element in the disenchantment with the PCF and it went against the tide which was strongly anti-Soviet in France after the publication of the *Gulag Archipelgo* (the 'Solzhenitsyn effect') in 1973 and the invasion of Afghanistan in 1979.

The early Komintern had wrought better than it knew: the French Communist Party was thoroughly Leninist. In fact, the French Communist Party has been for half of its existence a sectarian party, and its 'reformist' phases have been short (1934–9, 1942–7, 1956–77). The French Communist Party was not one of those parties which pushed at the outer edges of Leninism in the search for a 'third way' in between social democracy and capitalism. It accepted the Leninist model and promoted the Soviet system as 'Socialist', really existing socialism (as distinct from the 'unreal' socialism of the Social Democrats). All of which makes the 'Eurocommunist' interlude something of a puzzle, and it must therefore be re-examined.

The French party evidently saw itself, with its 'mass organisations', fêtes and active memberships as a 'counter society', a part of a Popular Democracy detached in a capitalist country – as an outrider of the 'Socialist camp' – and it was an enthusiastic participant in world Communist institutions. Only in the mid–1970s did the PCF find itself out of step with the centre, but this was on the most sensitive issue and explains the paradox of how an ultra-orthodox party came to be at odds with the Kremlin. The Soviets had two major objectives and one minor interest in Western Europe at the beginning of the Cold War. These were, firstly, to divide the NATO alliance; secondly, to push the Americans back out of Western Europe; and thirdly, to gain some legitimation from the West for the regimes in the 'Socialist camp'. They were, with one exception, and despite an eleventh-hour diplomatic offensive in the 1980s, unsuccessful in these aims. The West remained united and the American forces were not pushed out despite the Communists' encouragement of anti-Americanism – *tous azimuts*. Even in countries with big parties – like Italy – and where the party was quasi-insurrectional – like Portugal – Moscow had little success.

There was, however, one exception: France. For Soviet diplomatic purposes the most advantageously disruptive state in Western Europe was Gaullist (and then right wing) France, which encouraged anti-Americanism, withdrew from NATO and sought a 'special relationship' with totalitarian regimes of the East. A left wing government – even, or especially, one including Communists – would not deliver these diplomatic benefits. The entry of the Italian

Communists into government would have delivered a gain for the USSR (or the Portuguese, Spanish, or Finnish parties) but the French party in government would not. In fact, Mitterrand's Socialists, after 1981, brought France to its closest co-operation with NATO in twenty years.

Hence the alliance of the Left imposed constraints on the French Communist Party: it needed to be modernised to compete and it had to redefine its links with Moscow. Thus there was, although it was not immediately evident, a conflict between Moscow's strategy and the French party's attempt to come to power as part of a left-wing coalition. Mitterrand, supported by the party, had run a muted but emphatically Atlanticist presidential campaign in 1965, and any coalition of the Left was bound to be influenced by the pro-NATO Socialist Party. For the purposes of this alliance, Waldeck Rochet had effectively dropped the party's opposition to French membership of NATO in December 1962. In 1965 this did not matter bacause Mitterrand could not defeat de Gaulle. All the same, the tension was there and PCF support for Soviet foreign policy and the totalitarian systems prevented the party from improving its appeal.

The dispute between the CPSU and the French party sprang up in the mid-1970s, when the French party were widely regarded as being on the verge of government. The immediate cause of the polemic had been the clear preference of the Soviet Union for Giscard, whom the Soviet Ambassador visited in between rounds of the 1974 presidential elections. *L'Humanité* protested but the dispute did not stop there; Brezhnev continued to make his preference for Giscard clear – a Soviet foreign policy imperative. The PCF's International Department insisted on 'the condemnation of the theses which states that peaceful coexistence means a political and social status quo . . . . By the same token the interferences intended to prevent peoples like our own and others in capitalist Europe from freely choosing their destiny are also condemned.'[2]

By the time of the East Berlin 'European' Parties' Congress in 1976 called to legitimate the USSR's international objectives, the French party was one of the dissenters amongst the twenty-eight delegations. On the prospect of further meetings Georges Marchais had declared,

On this issue we must say that it appears to us that this type of conference no longer corresponds to the needs of the time. Since the elaboration of a strategy common to all our parties is henceforth excluded, it appears to us opportune to look for new forms of collective encounters, more vital, more supple, more efficacious, facilitating a deeper discussion, frank and direct,

2. *France nouvelle*, 12 June 1976.

on the great problems of the moment and not always concluding with the adoption of a document.[3]

Although Marchais did not see the need *always* to have a common declaration, he did allow for the possibility of conferences on specific issues. The French concept of the mutual obligation of Communist Parties was the heart of the problem: the French replied to unspecified accusations that they wanted to create a 'national' or regional socialism in the following terms: 'Proletarian internationalism does not in any way mean uniformity. It implies mutual solidarity.'[4] The French wanted the Soviets to take into account the interests of 'fraternal' parties when framing policy. This was highly unrealistic.

Marchais was particularly keen to emphasise that *détente* did not imply a cessation of the 'struggle against capitalism' in Western Europe. Jean Kanapa, then head of French Communist international relations and credited with the responsibility for the PCF's new boldness, had argued that the most important action was to 'roll back imperialism' and that, as 'peace objectives' had been attained, priority should be given to the struggle for 'social progress and the defeat of the monopolies' in France.

The CPSU sent three angry letters to the French party in 1976–7 – perhaps the lowest point in relations.[5] *L'Humanté* wrote:

> For the concept according to which the Communist Parties were 'detachments' of a world movement . . . was substituted the idea of the independence and equality of the various Communist Parties; the idea that the international Communist movement is not, and cannot be a centralised organisation; the conviction that no party or group of parties is in a position to define an exemplary line or strategy which would be valid for others. In solidarity, because they are fraternal Communists, it is together that the parties consitute the world's Communist movement .

Marchais said that the break in relations with the USSR came for one reason alone: 'because it [the CPSU] did not accept the editing of a joint communiqué laying out the divergencies which I have just recalled'.[6] This small change, a right to disagree, was disguised by the breakup of the French alliance of the Left, which enabled close relations between the PCF and the CPSU once again.

By the end of 1976 the PCF had begun to use the term 'Eurocommunism' freely. Although Eurocommunism was not a

3. *L'Humanité*, 10 April 1976.
4. *France nouvelle*, 29 March 1976.
5. *Cahiers du communisme*, October 1991.
6. *Le Monde*, 21 August 1988.

coherent movement it did serve to dramatise the attempt by the three parties to break out of their ghettoes. Eurocommunism also involved a modernisation, a repackaging, of the party's appeal and an attempt to compete with the Socialists for the radical reformist vote. Amongst the more serious incidents was the (disingenuous) reaction to the report on the goulag in Riga: 'the Political Bureau of the PCF declares that, if the reality corresponds to the images which have been diffused, and they are not made the object of a denial by the Soviet authorities, it [the French party] . . . will express its profound surprise and most categorical reproval'.[7]

Yet it was too little and too late. What was never in question, for the French Communist Party, nor for the other Eurocommunists, was that the Soviet Union was *Socialist* and therefore a superior form of society. Incidents and 'errors' were condemned – sometimes quite obliquely. The bases of the system – central planning, the one-party state – expressed as the 'laws of Socialist development' , were never questioned (even though the party claimed not to take the USSR as a 'model'), nor was the 'progressive' role of the USSR in world politics: just because there were spots on the sun it did not mean that there was no sun. Marchais declared:

> It is wrong to make out that socialism does not exist on the grounds that it takes forms which are not consistent with our way of looking at things. Moreover, the balance sheet of the Socialist countries, their daily activity, confirm their original character, their superiority over capitalism in tackling the great problems facing society, above all if one takes into account their starting points and the conditions they met. We believe that the balance sheet is globally positive.[8]

The Eurocommunist Parenthesis Closed

The return to good relations with the CPSU took place at some time in late 1978. The end of *détente* also marked the return of the French party to revolutionary sectarianism. The legislative elections of 1978 had been a setback for the Left, which had been expected to win, but the Communist Party polled a creditable 5,870,402 (20.6 per cent, or eighty-six seats), and was to that extent satisfied. Yet the drift back to uncritical pro-Soviet positions gathered pace: a significant event had

7. *L'Humanité*, 14 December 1975.
8. *L'Humanité*, 11 December 1978.

been the pulping (at considerable expense) of the *Viver* election brochure which showed Pierre Juquin shaking hands with the Soviet dissident Leonid Plyushch. By 26 July 1979 *L'Humanité* was making copious use of the phrase 'globally positive' (consecrated at the Twenty-third Congress in 1979) to describe the Eastern bloc regimes. The same day there was an announcement of CPSU meetings with the French party, and from 19 to 24 November Zagladin was in Paris to meet Maxime Gremetz, the head of the French Communist International Department. The infamous 'globally positive' formula caused such a rumpus that it was abandoned, although the party continued to publish glowing accounts of Socialist systems. In other words, the French had decided to choose their 'camp' and it was the 'Socialist camp' as distinct from the 'imperialist camp' led by America, which had, they said, 'gone onto the offensive'.

The test for the new orthodoxy came with the Soviet invasion of Afghanistan in 1979. Marchais had decided to go to Moscow to meet Brezhnev at the beginning of 1980 despite the invasion and produced his justification of Soviet action on live TV from Moscow. The French party was one of the select group which approved of the invasion and it repeated, without qualification, the Soviet justifications that the Red Army had entered Afghanistan at the government's behest to put down a feudalistic rebellion financed by 'imperialists' from abroad. In this it was at one with the Austrian party, which had also condemned the invasion of Czechoslovakia but which hailed the invasion of Afghanistan an 'internationalist act'; the Cypriot party, which praised Soviet 'generous internationalist aid'; the West German party; the Greek party; the Portuguese, Luxembourg, Danish and Norwegian parties. However, the Political Bureau tried shortly afterwards to limit the damage by drowning the approval in a general statement in which there was no mention of 'Socialist solidarity' or 'proletarian internationalism'. Yet even the docile front *Mouvement de la Paix* expressed its quite reasonable disquiet and the CGT also had difficulties in imposing an approval of the invasion.

The invasion of Afghanistan went alongside another international issue of the 1980s, and in this too the French party followed – the opposition to the 'Euromissiles'. According to Juquin, Marchais asked the Soviet leader on the Euromissile issue 'quels mots d'ordre précis doit-il avancer?'[9] The French party (along with the Italians and other Eurocommunists) flung themselves into the 'peace movement' with varying degrees of success.

9. P. Juquin, *Autocritiques*, Paris, Grasset, p. 217.

In recognition of this new settlement with Moscow, a conference on 'peace and disarmament' was held 26–28 April 1980; although the French and Polish parties were the ostensible hosts, the conference was generally thought to have been the work of the CPSU. The timing, procedure (the abandonment of any attempt at consensus decision-making in the world movement) and the content of the conference broke the unwritten rules established since the mid-1960s and showed the importance the Soviets attached to the campaign. The result was that this attempt to fix the world Communist line on disarmament was attended by a mere twenty parties – only five out of fourteen nonruling parties plus Italian and Spanish 'observers'. However, a 'peace offensive' was launched in France, where the 'peace movement' had been big in the 1950s and where the French party was presumed to have strength, but it was a fiasco: it had no echo and fatally failed to rally non-Communists. All the same, Marchais' role in the 'peace offensive' was later recognised; he was one of the few Western Communist leaders to meet Andropov and the only one to be met twice – a significant warmth of relations.

But the party had fared badly at the elections of 1981, partly as a result of its philo-Sovietism, but mainly because of its extreme hostility to the Socialist Party (even advising its inner faithful of the need for a 'revolutionary vote for the Right' on the second ballot) and from its own lack of modernisation. Its presidential cadidate Marchais polled only 15 per cent and was outdistanced by Mitterrand (with 29 per cent); it emerged as junior partner in the subsequent Assembly in which the Socialists had an absolute majority (the part took 16.2 per cent of the vote in the Assembly elections and won only forty-four seats).

The Party's comprehensive defeat at the polls led to a rapid change in line to seek a place in the Socialist government. An agreement was signed between the Socialist and Communist Parties in June 1981 which permitted four PCF ministers to enter the government (none had any responsibility for foreign or defence matters). The agreement enabled the party to stick to its positions on Afghanistan, on the intermediate-range nuclear forces (INF) talks in Geneva and on Poland, but the party had to mute its anti-Westernism to a small extent. Moscow's 1980s 'peace offensive' led to a further conflict between the party's support for the USSR's foreign policy and the foreign policy of the 1981–4 governments of which it was then a part, and the party responded by criticising the government's positions indirectly (usually reporting Eastern bloc comments in *L'Humanité*). The Communist Ministers supported the government in its apporval of 'Euromissiles' but the party remained very critical and the position was summed up by Roland Leroy (Publications Director of the party press), who said that the PCF was in government but not of government.[10] This was typical of the party's previous strategies in government (1944–7): tried to run 'independent' campaigns, often using the seemingly independent CGT, to exploit discontents, but ministers remained loyal.

The events in Poland, which were an embarrassment to other Communist Parties (the suppression of Solidarity flung the Italian party into a vigorous exchange of denunciations with the CPSU) and to the PCF ministers, but further fixed the French party in Moscow's orbit. While some Communist Parties supported the Polish strikers, the French party played down Solidarity and then hailed the state of emergency as a 'triumph' for the Polish Communist government. When General Jaruzelski's state of seige led to protests from other unions and parties in France, the Communist Party boycotted both the demonstrations and a token strike because, as the party put it, 'they hampered the search for a peaceful outcome', and they blamed the 'excesses' of Solidarity for the Polish crisis. The French Communist Party was well re-established in Moscow's orbit by the time Brezhnev died, and the brief Chernenko/Andropov interregnum before Gorbachev was established in power made no difference to its role.[11]

The French Communists and Gorbachev

Gorbachev came to power in March 1985 and could hardly fail to make an impact after the gerontocracy of Brezhnev, Chernenko and Andropov. But to general surprise, Gorbachev quickly overtook the supposed master of the media, President Reagan, in public relations (and in popularity in Western European countries), and put the Americans onto the diplomatic defensive. This was initially welcomed by the French Communist Party, which hoped to draw strength from a reinvigorated Communist leadership, and a Soviet 'socialism' once again on the march. In the first phase of Gorbachev's policies, the Soviet leader applied traditional remedies to salvage a system in which he apparently believed, and this caused no problems for the PCF. As late as 1988 Marchais said, 'Gorbachev has said: "what we need is not less socialism but more socialism"; I also totally support his point of view.'

In 1986 the French party supported the Soviet inclusion of the French nuclear weapons in the Geneva arms talks in defiance of the

10. *L'Humanité*, 8 July 1981
11. H. Timmermann, *The Decline of the World Communist Movement* , Boulder, Colorado, Westview, 1987.

Socialist government's stance and of his own party's 1977 positions (which reaffirmed the need for a French nuclear deterrent). The party followed this up with a series of 'peace' initiatives to support Gorbachev's 'peace offensive' and his appeal for a nuclear-free world by the year 2000 (the party joined anti-nuclear demonstrations or tried to run their own) and by attacking the notion of a 'European' defence. The French party echoed Moscow's condemnation of Reagan for the failure of the Reykjavik summit meeting and the continuation of the Strategic Defence Initiative. The Americans and their 'NATO tool' were accused of 'hegemonic' and 'imperialist' aims in Europe and the Middle East and remained the principal target of French Communist propaganda.

The French party tried to use their relationship with the new Soviets to the maximum. Marchais was later to declare that he was the French politician who was closest to Gorbachev, he took opportunities to visit Gorbachev in April/May 1987 and attended the seventieth anniversary of the Revolution. The French party also tried to profit from the dynamic created by the Gorbachev reforms, but the conservatism of its posture (that is its closeness to the Brezhnev regime) was such that it found itself frequently and loudly having to deny that it opposed reform in the USSR and devoted energy to the praise of *perestroika*. Like other parties it claimed to be the 'onlie begetter' of *glasnost* and *perestroika*, stating, for example, that it was the Soviets who had taken up French positions and not the contrary. The party started by promoting the idea of a 'revolution in the revolution' taking place in the East and that, because the Eastern bloc was moving, the PCF had been correct to deny that they were 'stalemate societies'.[12] The Twenty-sixth PCF Congress in 1987 was vibrant in praise of Gorbachev, although one speaker declared that it had been prepared by Brezhnev, and it was attended by Kremlin hard-liner Egor Ligachev. But things began to go sour when Gorbachev became more radical and it was realised that the reforms implied the destruction of 'socialism' and the ending of traditional Soviet diplomatic objectives (Gorbachev eventually stopped trying to divide the Western allies). Gorbachev looked favourably on Eureka (which the PCF disparaged); and ended the USSR's scorn for the process of European integration.[13]

At this juncture, some time in 1987, there was a parting of ways and not just with the French. The PCF soon made itself part of a 'Third and a half' international which included the hard-line regimes of Eastern Europe (East Germany, in particular), Cuba, North Korea and the Portuguese

12. Georges Marchais, *Cahiers du communisme*, 29/30 September 1986.
13. G. Wettig, *Changes in Soviet Policy Towards the West*, Pinter, London, 1991, p. 101.

Party. Speaking at the Portuguese Party Congress, Marchais stated that *perestroika* was not an 'obligatory example' for other countries and (Juquin revealed) in December 1988 the French party Political Bureau warned the CPSU against Gorbachev's 'adventurist' drift.[14]

The French party's hopes of a rise in popularity resulting from the association with Gorbachev were not realised. The party's isolationist stance and its unpopular policies more than compensated for any 'Gorbachev' effect and at the 1986 elections its vote fell further to 2,873,234 (9.8 per cent). The party's negative domestic policy was pursued during 1986–8 and had a predictable impact on the party's performance at the presidential elections of 1988: the vote fell to 2,055,995 (6.76 per cent). At the subsequent legislatives the party polled 11.3 per cent but the historically low turn-out meant that this could not be taken as a sign of revival. The sequence of disasters at the polls, which meant that the Party had become irrelevant to the political game in France, was remarked on by the Soviets and Gorbachev took the PCF for a negligible quantity. On 5 April, shortly after the first round of the presidential elections of 1988, *L'Humanité* editorialist Claude Cabanes attacked Alex Bovine (*Izvestia* correspondent in Paris) who had asserted that the poor vote for the PCF's candidate was caused by 'ideological stagnation'.[15] On 4 March *Literaturnaya Gazeta* was scolded by the PCF for forgetting the class struggle for its analysis of the Munich agreements (i.e. Stalin was right) and Yeltsin and his supporters were labelled 'rightists'.[16]

The Soviet search for an understanding with the Second International Socialists was counter to French Communist domestic strategy. A feature of the Twenty-seventh CPSU Congress in 1986 had been the unprecedented numbers of Social Democrat delegations. The strategy was a continuation of the early 1980s – to mobilise broad fronts around Communist objectives – but pursued with more vigour.[17] The French party, which had been running an intensified anti-Socialist campaign since leaving government in 1984 (and consecrated the *nouveau rassemblement populaire majoritaire* – the old Leninist sectarian 'unity at the base'), once again found itself going against the grain.

In the mid-1980s, which were the years of French party decay, the Italian Communists started a polemic with the PCF, asserting that the decline was a result of narrow sectarianism (though the Italian party had not fared any better), and by the same token relations with the

---

14. *Libération*, 3 December 1988.
15. *L'Humanité*, 4 May 1988.
16. *L'Humanité*, 4 March 1988.
17. G. Iglesias PCE leader; see the conclusion to this book.

more hard-line parties were strengthened. In July 1986 Pierre La Roche riposted, asserting that the Italian party was no longer a revolutionary party but a mere reformist party.[18] The visit of the Italian party leader to France in 1989 did not include Marchais in its itinerary, and in the European Parliament the Italians sat in the 'United European Left' group with the Spanish, Greek and Danish sympathisers and Communists apart from the 'Communist' group of the French, Portuguese, Irish and Greek hard-liners.

The position for the leadership was made more difficult in that dissidents in the French party used the reforms in the USSR, the new international alignment and Gorbachev's 'charm offensive' to the Socialists in their attacks. (They may have thought that by playing the Gorbachev card they could displace Marchais.) Fiterman was the centre of this unco-ordinated group and in 1990 took the opportunity to table a statement drawing 'lessons' from the collapse of communism in Eastern Europe. The CPSU showed no inclination to interfere in the French party, although two meetings between Gorbachev and Marchais in 1989 were described as 'chilly'.

The complete change in emphasis away from Brezhnev's hard-line had made the French party *persona non-grata* and the Italian party *persona grata*: in Moscow the Italians became welcome and the French unwelcome. This U-turn was symbolised by the meeting in January 1986 of A. Natta (then PCI Secretary General) with Gorbachev, Ligachev, the CPSU's Ponomarev and Zagladine. In June of the same year Napolitano (the PCI's International Affairs head) visited CPSU International heads Dobryinie and Zaglandine in September 1986 a return visit to the Italian party's Féte was made by Zagladine, and the newly-elected Italian Communist leader Achille Ochetto met Gorbachev and Ligachev whilst on vacation in the USSR. Although an effort was made by the Soviets for the seventieth anniversary of the Revolution in 1987, Gorbachev met only five secretary generals: the Austrian, West German, Italian, Japanese and Uruguayan (and some Socialist leaders).

Hence the implications of the CPSU's strategy went distinctly counter to French Communist domestic strategy. While the USSR looked for an understanding with non-Communist forces on the Left, Social Democrats in particular (symbolised by the revamping of the World Communist journal the *World Marxist Review* and its opening to non-Communists in 1988), the French party refused to ally with the Socialists. The Italian Communists were exemplary in this strategy – as their criticisms of the 'Socialist' systems extended, they also hoped for formal relations with Western Socialists.

18. Pierre La Roche, *Cahiers du communisme*, July 1986.

The French party had been increasingly at odds with developments in the Eastern bloc. *L'Humanité* turned on the new powers in Poland, accusing Solidarity of forming a new elite[19] and pointed out that the workers were now being led in strikes by the (formerly official) Communist (OPZZ) unions.[20] Hence the French party was less like the Italian in its receptivity to Gorbachev's policies and more like the Portuguese who, under Cunhal, tried to maintain a revolutionary purity. As late as 20 October 1989, *L'Humanité* was warning that the Eastern regimes were being threatened by an 'orchestrated operation' by the Second Internaional against 'socialism.' Marchais reiterated this at the beginning of 1990, saying Eastern Europeans 'are mistaken when they want social democracy'.[21]

The French Communist Party was no more prepared than any other organisation for the collapse of socialism in Eastern Europe. However, it distinguished itself by trying to ignore or minimise the importance of what happened. The party daily *L'Humanité* avoided headlines about the revolutions until the beginning of November 1989, and the party put off a discussion of the events until December. Georges Marchais was asserting at the annual Fête de L'Humanité in September 1989 that there had been a crisis in Soviet society, but that Socialism was giving proof of its superiority by overcoming it; and he never despaired, he said, of socialism's ability to overcome its faults. At the same time the problems of 'socialism' arose from inherited 'backwardness' of the sort that no capitalist society had had to face.

Events outpaced even this explanation of the party's positions and Gremetz, even in 1990, defended the party view that the Eastern regimes were 'globally positive'. The party's foreign affairs spokesman again declared that the crisis was not a crisis of Socialism, and claimed that the fault lay with the leaderships of the GDR and Czechoslovakia, which had refused to implement *perestroika* and whose obscurantism had led to a break between party and people. The party was harking back to its Twenty-seventh Congress view that the Communists in the East had been insufficiently Leninist – they had not rallied the masses to party objectives. Although Gremetz claimed that the party's analysis of socialism had been confirmed in the events of 1989 – and it could therefore be proud – it had no knowledge of certain facts such as the lack of discussion in the Politburos.[22] Two dissidents (Rigout and Damette) reposted that the argument from ignorance was, at that point,

19. *L'Humanité*, 5 February 1990.
20. *L'Humanité*, 29 January 1990 and 20 January 1990.
21. Ibid.
22. *Le Monde*, 17 December 1989

disgraceful[23] but other sometime critics were satisfied with the party's response. None of this 'analysis' prevented warnings about the capitalist course or nostalgic looks back to the Socialist past. Marchais explained events in the USSR to the Central Committee: 'It is at the summit in the name of *perestroika* that these forces [capitalist] are fighting the party.'[24] Thus the pace and depth of reform in the heartland of communism itself left the French party very isolated and the leadership attacked within its own party.

By late 1990 the break-up of the world movement was well under way. The biggest nonruling party, the Indian (twenty-nine million votes, 400,000 members and fifty-two seats), was very critical of the CPSU. The Twenty-eighth congress of the CPSU in July 1990 showed the contemporary state of relations between parties: there were no fraternal delegates and no speeches from foreign delegations. The condition of the front organisations was also dire. Most of them, deprived of the support of the parties and governments, found themselves without a home and with the problem of finding finance to replace the Eastern bloc subsidies. *World Marxist Review*, the last co-ordinating body of the world movement, folded in June 1990, but although that left the bilateral relations between the local parties and Moscow intact, they also (as the criticism of Moscow from the Indian party shows) were coming under increasing strain.

Even in the dying days of the International Communist Movement the French party tried to retain some semblance of internationalism. In the absence of a co-ordinating centre the party promoted its own bilateral contacts and campaigns of 'solidarity'. The most famous of these was the equipping of a petrol tanker for the beleaguered Cuban regime, but there were many others, including exchanges and round tables for regional Communist parties. The party retained its contacts with the former Communist Parties of Eastern Europe (and former state unions). The French party had supported the new Soviet tactic in 1989 to emphasise 'common values'. This started at the Warsaw meeting of the WFTU with a campaign against 'attacks on union rights', for which purpose the International Centre for Trade Union Rights was created. The party also assisted in the setting up of international unions supposedly independent of the WFTU – the International Miners' Organisation was sited in Bobigny in the Paris suburbs. The main aim of these was to make overtures to 'Third World' workers, and the French delegates found themselves in the company of the Chinese, Cubans and Indians in a hard-line opposition to Gorbachev inside the

23. *Libération*, 19 December 1989.
24. *L'Humanité*, 13 October 1989.

WFTU. Krasucki, the CGT leader, did not want union action restricted to strike demands and wanted a world-wide struggle to continue against 'imperialism'. This split was consecrated at the last meeting of the WFTU in Moscow in November 1990.

The Gulf crisis provided a further challenge to the party's loyalty. Moscow having supported the Allied operation in the Gulf, the party was at odds – implicitly – with Gorbachev. The Communists tried to exploit the antiwar and anti-American themes which had served it so well in the past, and hoped to gain from the disagreements in the Left. The main vehicle for this was the committee opposed to the Gulf War (*'Appel des 75'*), another index of Communist decline being the unreliable nature of this movement, which included Trotskyists (of various persuasions), ecologists and anarchists – an association which would have been unthinkable for Communists ten years previously. On the Gulf War issue the French party was at odds with its own voters (who supported the government and the allies) and in the same camp as the National Front: it did not gain support as a result of this antiwar stance.[25]

The French party found itself, vis-à-vis the CPSU, in the 'conservative' camp without ever overtly rejecting Gorbachev's reforms. The party mailed its colours to the mast with outspoken condemnations of Yeltsin and 'so-called democrats' were vivid in what was a clear preference for the plan over the market.[26] The French party was critical of Gorbachev for opening the Pandora's box of Eastern European liberation and for not stopping German reunification – though how this could have been done without recourse to armed force was not made clear.

The PCF's reaction to the coup in August 1991 has to be seen in this light. The party leadership's first reponse was not to fly to the defence of the Soviet leader but to say that, whilst the manner in which Gorbachev was evicted was unacceptable, conditions in the USSR under Gorbachev were strikingly bad and the country had slipped behind the capitalist world (by implication this slippage was Gorbachev's failure and the cause of the coup). The party's initial reaction was one of benevolent neutrality towards the putschists, although a dispute broke out in the Political Bureau when it was asked to endorse this attitude, and the declaration was made more forceful. This was the last straw for a number of critical Communists (especially the party's economic department aound Herzog), and Fiterman and others accused the leadership of endorsing the coup. The next day the

25. *Le Monde*, 20 February 1991.
26. *L'Humanité*, 30 March 1991.

d its revenge in *L'Humanité*, it published disobliging
Gorbachev along with the full coup 'pronunciamento'.
not given any support.) The CGT followed exactly in the
e party, though it too suffered from internal dissidence as
the coup had failed the party turned on the putschists and
on the CPSU.

Whilst the Soviet Union was intact, the party had been able to argue
that the collapse of the Eastern bloc did not detract from the
achievements of socialism in the heartland of the Revolution. Fifty-
seven per cent of delegates to the party's Twenty-seventh Congress
were happy to aver that the Soviet Union remained 'Socialist'[27]:
socialism in one country was possible. But after August 1991 that
conviction became impossible. In 1992 very little was left of the model
to which the party had been devoted and the movement it had hoped to
help to hold together was shattered. As the Red flag was run down over
the Kremlin the French party proclaimed that this made no difference
to its ideals. The party was not able to ignore the collapse of the East,
but it did dismiss it.

Conclusion

The August coup came at the end of what was a long and probably
terminal crisis for the French Communist Party. The decision by the
French Communist leadership to sabotage the alliance with the
Socialists at the cost of a victory for the Left in the 1978 elections
caused a wave to dissidence which inaugurated a period of open
internal criticism and the party's intellectual capital was dissipated.
With each subsequent election setback the dissidence got worse, and
the dissenters reached further into the apparatus until, in 1989, they
reached the secretariat. In that year Charles Fiterman, former
Communist Minister and a man wholly in the stamp of the party
professional, declared his hostility to the Marchais line. It was a
measure of the party's devastation that no action was taken to
discipline this 'factional' and increasingly structured movement of self-
styled 'refounders'. Meanwhile the departures continued from a
debilitated party.

On the one hand the French party's future will be determined by
domestic rather than international factors, but here the omens are not
good. The party is locked into declining social sectors and irrelevant

27. *Le Monde*, 3 January 1991.

ideological issues, and is no longer even an efficient party of protest. The genie, the Socialist Party, is out of the bottle, and unless it can be returned there is no 'space' for a second 'reformist' party of the Left. On the other hand the changes in French culture and the collapse of the Soviet regime have also meant the end to the 'revolutionary' lyricism which passed for a project on the French Left: there is no longer a widespread belief in the revolutionary transformation of society as a shortcut.[28]

The weak and divided French party had ceased to be an element of fear or repulsion in French politics in the 1980s, but its clear preference for the old-fashioned Bolshevism of the Brezhnev style poses a further problem. Whilst the party was small and preoccupied with internal quarrels the PCF was neglected, but it was an acceptable alliance partner with the Socialists (in local and regional government). However, after August 1991 it was no longer possible to overlook its devotion to Leninist totalitarianism; groups in both the Socialist Party itself and the conservative Right condemned the 'hypocrisy' of such alliances. In particular the Communist Party has strengthened the arm of those on the orthodox Right who wish to conclude alliances with the National Front. The Right can argue that if it is proper for the Socialists to make agreements with a totalitarian Communist Party, then why not make deals with Le Pen's National Front? The French party may be in its final state of decomposition, but its capacity for damage is not yet ended.

28. François Furet, *Libération*, 28 August 1991.

– 4 –

The Portuguese Communist Party: Loyalty to the 'Communist Ideal'

Maria Teresa Patricio and Alan Stoleroff

The Portuguese Communist Party (PCP) energetically resisted the trend to Communist breakup associated with the post-1989 collapse of 'really existing socialism' until the autumn of 1991. The leadership unapologetically maintained its dedication to orthodox Leninism, and despite pressures to change the party as a whole held to a fundamental consensus regarding its role in Portuguese society. Although *perestroika* inspired a number of attempts by Communist intellectuals to 'renovate' the party, the PCP leadership was able to ward them off without provoking a major internal organisational crisis, and the core of the party's support remained intact, although the party's electoral results suffered a continuous gradual decline after 1979.

However, in the autumn of 1991 the PCP faced two very important challenges. The first was the position it would have to take about the attempted coup in the Soviet Union. This was a test of its credibility as a 'democratic' actor and of its adjustment to the emerging post-Cold War order. The second, the legislative elections of October 1991, was a test of the support for the PCP's line following a period of Portuguese political stability, economic growth and European integration as well as a test of the influence of the collapse of communism and the international Communist movement on the PCP's electorate. The first challenge left the PCP divided; the second showed it to be significantly weakened.

In this chapter we will first ask how and why the PCP was able to resist the successive crises of communism and maintain a substantial stability during the breakdown of 'really existing socialism' as well as what happened in 1991 to bring about a crisis in the PCP. We will analyse the sources of the relative stability that the PCP experienced in this period and contrast this relative stability with the party crisis following the August coup and the 1991 legislative elections. It is difficult, however, to evaluate the most recent trends within the

Portuguese Communist Party without the background of fundamental political continuity manifested in its programme from the final phases of the dictatorship to the present. We will therefore illustrate the continuity in the PCP's political orientation, examining the evolution of the party programme in the context of Portuguese society. We will then attempt an analysis of the social-cultural and political-institutional sources of the PCP's support.

The PCP and Dictatorship

The PCP was founded in 1921. Within five to seven years of its foundation, and coinciding with its 'bolshevisation', the party had moved underground to evade the military regime and the dictatorship. In 1933 the authoritarian-corporatist regime of Antonio Salazar, known as the 'New State', was launched, and with it began a period of severe repression, during which the PCP had to remain clandestine. Following an abortive insurrection against the New State's incorporation of the trade unions, led by anarchists in January 1934, and the subsequent repression, the working-class movement was left leaderless. After suffering great damage, the PCP underwent a fundamental reorganisation in the early 1940s and on the basis of this organisational stablisation, the party tried to grow, to lead struggles, and to forge alliances. During the 'strike wave' of the early 1940s the PCP, the only effectively organised opposition force, was able to achieve the leadership of the Portuguese working class, a position it would maintain throughout the struggle against fascsim. The 1950s, however, were once again a period of retraction for the PCP: arrests of a significant part of the experienced leadership broke the party's organisation.

In 1961, with the reappearance of Alvaro Cunhal in the leadership (following a dramatic escape from prison), the PCP repudiated its policies of the 1950s as 'right opportunist' and adopted the line which it held to thereafter. At the Sixth Congress of the PCP, held in September 1965, the last in clandestininity, the party characterised the contemporary stage of the revolution as 'democratic and national'. The democratic character of the revolution envisaged by the PCP programme was the ending of the dictatorship, the restoration of political liberty, an end to the power of the monopolies and the latifundia and the implementation of a series of reforms which would benefit the majority of the Portuguese population. The 'national character' of the revolution involved ending the 'imperialist domination' of Portugal and also Portugal's colonial domination over other peoples, promoting the development of national resources, guaranteeing sovereignty, territorial integrity and the true independence of the country. The goals set by the party programme were the destruction of the Fascist state and the establishment of a democratic regime.[1]

Several factors from the 1960s on were used to justify Cuhnal's characterisation of this period as a 'permanent crisis' of the regime: the deterioration of the economic situation, the colonial war and the Portuguese regime's increasing internal and international isolation.[2] In the 1960s Portuguese society had entered a new phase. Economic growth moved away from the previous pattern of state industrialisation. New, large-scale industries emerged, with them new working-class communities were formed and serious opposition to the corporatist official state trade unions grew. In parallel with this economic and social change, the corporatist regime also evolved, but not towards democracy. In 1968 Marcelo Caetano took over from Salazar and the 'New State' was transformed into the 'Social State', but although the change in government produced an initial political thaw, this 'spring time' was temporary. This evolution of the state, however, initiated a phase of constant crisis, intensified by the colonial wars, during which the working class and democratic movements emerged as the main opposition to the regime. The PCP played an important role in the struggles of this period, and these movements were to provide the PCP with new recruits and long-lasting support.

The PCP and the April Revolution

On 25 April 1974 a military coup overthrew the regime, but the PCP was only indirectly involved; its activity had contributed to the crisis and it had influenced the real architects of the coup, the insurgent army captains. However, once the coup took place, the PCP was in the privileged position of playing a prominent, and at times determining, role in the revolution. After 11 March 1975, when nationalisation and agrarian reforms were undertaken in response to an apparent counter-revolutionary threat, the situation in Portugal bordered on a revolutionary crisis. During this time the PCP was in close alliance with the Armed Forces Movement (MFA) and came very close to taking power through Vasco Gonçalves' Fifth Provisional Government. However, after the events of 25 November 1975, when moderate military forces intervened to end left-wing influence in the armed forces, the PCP was definitively excluded from government. From then

1. Alvaro Cunhal, *A Revoluçâo Potuguesa*, Lisbon, Ediçôes Avante!, 1976, p. 21.
2. *Ibid.*, p. 32.

on, in spite of the very long period of governmental instability, there was a steady consolidation of parliamentary democracy.

Although consistently excluded from government, the PCP nevertheless managed to establish a distinctive role for itself in the Portuguese political system. In his speech to the Eighth Congress of the PCP on 11 November 1976, General-Secretary Alvaro Cunhal presented his view of the transformation brought about by the revolution: the nationalised sector of 245 enterprises, the intervention of the state in 261 enterprises, the 200 semi-state enterprises and the 787 co-operatives, as well as the Agrarian Reform. According to Cunhal, this 'revolutionary' transformation produced a diversified economy consisting of a non-capitalist economic sector, a capitalist economic sector, an economic sector of petty commodity production an economic sector with a tendency to State capitalism. He insisted that the 'Portuguese economy as a whole is situated in an intermediate and transitory state between a capitalist economy and a Socialist economy . . . with a determinant non-capitalist element.'[3] From this Cunhal drew the conclusion that the only progressive and therefore economically feasible policy was one that sought to develop the Socialist character of the Portuguese economy. Such a policy had to be based upon the dynamic impulse of the nationalised sector.[4] Hence any policy based upon a weakening of the public sector was considered counter-revolutionary and reactionary by the PCP and therefore anti-democratic. The PCP's reference to 'democratic' forces was based on its evaluation of those forces' policies towards the public sector and not on the evaluation of how they behaved with regard to abstract rules of parliamentary democracy and 'bourgeois' civil liberties.

For the PCP pro-capitalist political forces in the post-revolutionary period were by nature not democratic.[5] It is for this reason that the PCP's analysis does not link capitalism and political democracy. PCP theory equates 'capitalist' or liberal economic policy with 'counter-revolution', and explicitly assimilates this 'counter-revolution' with 'dictatorship'. Cunhal stated: 'The real alternative at the moment is between democracy [and democracy means taking the conquests of the revolution as definitive and irreversible and moving towards socialism]

3. Alvaro Cunhal, *'Discorso no VIII Congress do PCP'*, in A. *Cunhal Em Defesa das Conquistas da revolução, Discursos Politicos*, vol. 10, Lisbon, Ediçôes Avanti!, 1978, p. 23.

4. *PCP A Via de Desenvolvimento Para Vencer a Crise*, Lisbon, Ediçôes Avante!, 1985.

5. See Alvaro Cunhal's 'Speech in Marinha Grande' 2 October 1982, in A. Cunhal, *La Luta Popular e a Derrota da 'AD' 1981–1982*, Lisbon, E diçôes Avante!, 1985.

or capitalist recovery, which means, in the short term, the liquidation of the democratic regime and the installation of a new dictatorship.'[6]

The PCP's analysis of events since 1976 has been founded first on 'capitalist recovery' and secondly on 'counter-revolution'. These two concepts leave extraordinarily little room for manoeuvre. On the one hand, the PCP mobilised its electoral and nonelectoral forces to counter 'non-democratic' governmental coalitions and to demand 'a new politics' (which would only have been new if it had corresponded to the PCP's policies), and on the other hand it called for an electoral alliance between the Socialist Party (PS) and the PCP. The other basic elements of the PCP strategy of mobilisation which complement this electoral objective, were trade-union leadership, local-municipal power and organisation-building.

The PCP's attitude to the constitution of the Portuguese Republic illustrates this narrow outlook. The original democratic Constitution, ratified in 1976, contained explicit references to Portugal's path to socialism and the establishment of a classless society. This Constitution, according to the PCP, consolidated the 'conquests of the revolution', and the most important clause for the PCP was the one which stipulated that the 'nationalised enterprises' could not be denationalised. For the PCP the Constitution became the guarantee that the revolution, begun and suspended in 1975, would establish the permanent framework for Portuguese development, but these clauses in the Constitution were a guarantee that one stage of the revolution had been achieved. The revolutionary PCP became the staunchest defender of the Constitution.

Yet two events had a particularly significant impact upon the PCP and its line. The first was the entry of Portugal into the EEC, which was seen as a new economic and political arena. The other important event was the election of a Social Democratic majority to the National Assembly in 1987 and its formation of a government which came to power on a programme of 'structural reforms' aimed at eliminating a number of what the PCP considered to be 'victories of the revolution'. The reforms included privatisation of public-sector enterprises, the end of the Agrarian Reform, and the repeal of labour legislation. This was the first time since the revolution that a single party had obtained a majority in Parliament and the government was able to pass its programme of 'structural reforms' without obstacle.

In particular the Constitution was revised during the 'Democratic Alliance' government in 1980, limiting the powers of the President and eliminating the supra-governmental Revolutionary Council. However,

6. Cunhal, *Em Defesa das Conquistas da Revolução*, vol. 10, p. 24.

revision left intact the 'Socialist' content of the Constitution; the PCP asserted that this change constituted a coup against the democratic regime. Even more important for the PCP, the constitutional revision in 1980, on the back of an agreement between the Social Democratic Party (PSD) and the PS (normally seen by the PCP as a 'democratic' force), annulled the prohibition of privatisation. The PCP's analysis of the 1980 constitutional revision is twofold. On the one hand, it 'did not imply a rupture with the political regime which retains deep marks of the April revolution . . ., but it opened a new stage in Portuguese political life in which the Right has seen its efforts rewarded both with the political legitimation of previous institutional action and the acceleration of measures demanded by big capital and the latifundia'. The PCP maintains that its objective of 'advanced democracy' can still be attained within the framework of this revised Constitution. On the other hand, the revision of the Constitution opened a new phase in the process of the reconstitution and restoration of monopoly capitalism and latifundist property.[7]

For over twenty years the PCP had based its strategy on the objectives of national democratic revolution and the transformation of this revolution into a transition to socialism. It had been decided in 1988, at the Twelfth Congress, that this programme was out of date. The party adopted a new programme, made changes to its statutes and elected a 'renewed' Central Committee.[8] The Congress recognised the party's failure to meet the objectives it had set itself at the Tenth Congress of 1983 (to which it continually referred back). It considered the fundamental victories of 25 April to be intact but acknowledged that twelve years of 'counter-revolution' (as the PCP refers to the consolidation of liberal democracy) had their impact. The PCP also stated that it was not possible to relaunch a process of Socialist transformation which it had thought to be merely suspended. The party's new objective was summed up as the goal of achieving an 'advanced democracy'; democracy was considered in political, economic, social and cultural terms. This objective meant: a regime of democratic political liberties; a democratic representative state, based on popular participation; economic development based upon a mixed economy; social policies guaranteeing the improvement of the people's living conditions; a democratic cultural policy which would be a factor in individual, social and national emancipation; national independence and sovereignty and a policy of peace, friendship, and co-operation

7. PCP Theses for the XIII Congress (Extraordinary)'*Avante!*', 8 March 1990.

8. PCP, *XII Congresso PCP: Com o PCP Por uma Democracia Avancada no limiar do Seculo XXI*, Lisbon Ediçôes Avante!, 1989.

with all peoples. The achievement of this state of 'advan(democracy', that is the deepening of democracy, was conceived or as the 'road to socialism'.

The PCP after the Collapse of 'Really Existing Socialism'

The history outlined above illustrates the stability of the PCP's basic posture, but after 1989 the leadership found itself working against very strong ideological and political pressures coming both from the crisis of the International Communist movement and internal Portuguese forces. The party consequently found itself struggling to maintain a 'Communist' continuity. Changes in the economy and in the working class and in Portugal's urban environment made it particularly difficult for the party leadership in the unions and cities, and labour-market volatility complicated their task. The growing hegemony of Portuguese liberalism, combined with the restructuring, meant that the PCP's traditional approach intensified the problems of political control. When responding to the 1989 crisis of communism, the party leadership reacted by clinging to old certainties and reinforcing both its historical identity and its links with its traditional support. The Portuguese party had further adapted its programme in 1988 (at the Twelfth congress), but this had been a further intensification of 'orthodox' theories and methods based on the notion of 'advanced democracy'.

A substantial part of the Thirteenth Extraordinary Congress in May 1990 was dedicated to analysing the Soviet Union's *perestroika*, its consequences and the events in Eastern Europe.[9] An Extraordinary Congress had been called because the party had recognised the importance of the events in the Eastern bloc and because of the organisational need to manage the effects of a growing critical opposition whose emergence in the party had been very much encouraged by Gorbachev's *perestroika*. At the Twelfth Congress of 1988, the interpretation of *perestroika* as a revolutionary process for the perfection of socialism in the Soviet Union was the predominant view in the party. At the 'Extraordinary' Congress of May 1990, the party found the causes of the crisis of the Socialist bloc in 'errors' and 'deviations' from Leninism. Such an analysis could have avoided breaking the party consensus except that when it came to its own functioning, the PCP sought a reaffirmation of orthodoxy rather than a liberalisation. In reaffirming its Leninist character, the party reasserted

9. The most explicit case for *perestroika* by a PCP member in public was Zita Seabra, *O Nome das Coisas*, Mem Martins, Europa-América, 1988.

the validity of democratic-centralism as a method of party functioning against its more critical internal elements.

Although the PCP made the events of 1989 the priority of the Thirteenth Congress, its analysis of the revolutions did not question the principles of Communist politics in the affected countries. Firstly, the PCP reaffirmed the orthodox Marxist-Leninist interpretation of the course of history, that is the fundamental place that the Soviet Revolution held within it. Secondly, it repeated that social advances had been made by Soviet socialism: industrialisation, mass literacy, education, health, social security, the elimination of unemployment and national cultural development.[10] In particular it interpreted *perestroika* as a measure to reinforce socialism. The PCP also distanced itself from the effects of these revolutions by stating that they did 'not invalidate the justice and validity of the Communist ideal'.[11] The Communist ideal was defined as

> the abolition of exploitation of man by man, of social injustices and all forms of political, social and national oppression, as the construction of a new society without antagonistic classes and based on humanitarian values, the primacy of individual and collective enterprise and creativity, the permanent and creative intervention of the masses in every aspect of the social, political, economic and cultural life of society, raising the material and spiritual well-being of the workers and the people in general, the realisation of equal rights between men and women and the integration of the young as a creative and dynamic social force in the life of the country.[12]

More important, however, were the party's fundamental characteristics, based on the Communist ideal, with 'its class nature as the vanguard of the working class and of all the workers, its Marxist-Leninist ideology, its structure and functioning through democratic centralism and its patriotic and internationalist policy'.[13]

Thus the 'errors' and 'mistakes' in Eastern Europe and in the Soviet Union (which the PCP leadership claims not to have known about) did not, for it, invalidate or contradict the justice and loftiness of the 'Communist ideal'. By contrast with the Eastern Bloc the Soviet Union, said the PCP, had recognised in time the contradictions between the organs of political power and the people, between the leadership of the party and the base of the party and between the party and the people, as well as the abuses of power and the inevitable and generalised corruption and tried to put right these

---

10. 'Thesis 1.5', in 'PCP Theses for the XIII Congress (Extraordinary)'.
11. Ibid.
12. 'Thesis 4.1.8', in Ibid.
13. Ibid.

mistakes.[14] Indeed, the 'Communist ideal' both stemmed the potential disillusionment of staunch activists and reasserted Marxist-Leninist orthodoxy against people within the party who had launched a threatening campaign for reform and renovation (and who the leadership considered to be 'social-democratic').[15]

The reaffirmation of the 'Communist ideal' as the PCP's main response to the new world situation was an inadequate response to the complexity and variety of problems posed by the evolution of external and internal events. For example, the PCP's foreign policy had been reduced to a radical anti-imperialism, aligning it with Gadaffi and the PLO, but isolating it from almost everywhere except Cuba, China and North Korea. The 'Communist ideal' has also proven to be inefficient as a control mechanism relative to the internal problems of Communist trade unionists – a crucial party resource. The experience of Communists in the leadership of the CGTP trade union confederation particularly throws into sharp relief the struggle between orthodoxy and pragmatism in the PCP, revealing as it does the emerging conflict of priorities between the party's leadership and the Communists' trade unionists. Events such as the negotiation of a national labour relations agreement within the tripartite (state, union and management) Permanent Council for Social Consensus have led to divisions between Communist trade unionists about concrete strategy and tactics.[16]

In 1990 a comprehensive economic and social agreement was reached, to which all parties present on the Permanent Council for Social Consensus had actively contributed. When the time came to sign the agreement, the CGTP leadership was divided. The PCP supported those who opposed the agreement and declared that the CGTP would not be party to an agreement 'to control class struggles'. The position was justified by union leaders and members of the PCP, because it would constitute a giving away of the 'rights of the workers' won in the revolution. These rights were considered non-negotiable, even in exchange for higher wages. In the face of growing unity between Socialists in the UGT unions and reform Communists in the CGTP, who were willing to sign the agreement, and the probability of labour agreement being successfully concluded with a government 'of the Right', the PCP reinforced its control of the orthodox activists in the unions and ensured the CGTP's rejection of the wage agreement. What

14. See, for example, the Chinese Communist Party's praise of Cunhal's 'resolute defence of socialism' in *Diário de Noticias*, 6 July 1991.

15. See M.T. Patricio, 'Orthodoxy and Dissent in the Portuguese Communist Party', *Journal of Communist Studies*, vol. 6, no. 3, September 1990, pp. 204–8.

16. A. Stoleroff, 'Reflexões sobre a evolução do sindicalismo e do movimento operário na era dos governos de Cavaco Silva', *Vertice*, no. 31, October 1990, pp. 45–56.

is important here is the perception by the PCP leadership, and a fraction of PCP union activists, that concessions on 'rights' would constitute a betrayal of the working class and jeopardise union gains. The PCP union pragmatists believed the linkage of the CGTP to the agreement to be a strategic resource because it ensured their institutional integration and active participation in future negotiations. Clearly, this faction was not willing to subordinate the autonomy of what it considered the CGTP's interests to the PCP's political strategy.

Even on issues that had no direct bearing on labour relations, such as the reaction to the attempted coup in the Soviet Union, Communist trade-union leaders were divided. Most significantly, the divisions on this issue coincided with the divisions on strictly labour issues. Given the realities of labour relations, the party's imposition of a hard line in the trade-union sphere may actually jeopardise the position of the very confederation it controls to the benefit of the UGT union confederation led by the Socialists.

Clearly, therefore, the reaffirmation of the 'Communist ideal' did not achieve what it was intended to even amongst the Party's traditional supporters. Moreover, the PCP Political Commissions's hasty support for the Soviet putschists in August 1991 and the Central Committee's radical opposition to the post-coup turn of events opened divisions within the party's conservative 'intellectual sector'. Indeed, Communist intellectuals, who had accepted the justification for the PCP's support of the invasion of Czechoslovakia and the tacit support for the Chinese party's repression in Tiananmen Square, finally reached the point of publicly displaying their reservations about the party. At the time of writing, only the party's core traditional support, in particular traditional socio-cultural communities, appears unquestioning. Nevertheless, their support should not be underrated.

The Sources of the Relative Stability of the PCP

As we have argued, no fundamental changes have been made in the party's orientation: the PCP's basic strategy for participating in Portuguese liberal democracy has undergone only very minor adjustment. The PCP has finessed some of its positions (on economic restructuring and Portugal's integration into the European Economic Community), but this has been consistent with its fundamental orientation. The party's conception of the world system is a good example of its consistency. The PCP's ideology has a distinctly nationalist component. It is in many ways similar to the Latin American Communist Parties in its objections to 'dependence', but it has also developed a defence of national sovereignty in the face of European integration. The PCP sees Portugal's relations with the more powerful industrial nations as subject to 'imperialist domination' and not as a partnership in the club. The PCP has not moved in its fundamental appreciation of the relations between 'capitalist' or 'imperialist' states and the 'oppressed peoples' and it has not changed its view of the Western military alliances. In short, if the Cold War between the US and the USSR has ended, for the PCP the basic adversarial relationships on a world scale have remained unchanged, except that, with the collapse of Soviet socialism and the Eastern bloc, imperialism has been fortified.

Although in parallel to the programmatic continuity that we have analysed the party has experienced a slow electoral and organisational decline, the PCP has not suffered from a lack of relevance in the political life of the country. The party obtained 17 per cent of the vote in the 1975 elections for the Constituent Assembly; its decline since then has been gradual, and it has kept its important pockets of support. The PCP's political programme and its objectives obviously continue to satisfy the perceived interests of significant portions of the population. The Portuguese Communist Party is the party within the Portuguese political system which most consistently speaks in terms of the interests of the working class, but this does not mean that it is the principal party of Portuguese workers. What little is known about the voting behaviour of workers in Portugal shows that it is the Socialist Party and not the Communist Party which obtains the majority of working-class votes. However, Communist Party representation of working-class interests involves a very tight link with the majority labour confederation, the CGTP. As long as the PCP maintains this link, it will keep its unique function within the Portuguese political system, and will retain more than a minimal base within the Portuguese working class.

By various other indicators, the party has also experienced setbacks. Claimed party membership declined very slightly from 200,753 at the Tenth Congress in 1983 to 199,275 (of which 25,000 were claimed to be new members) at the Twelfth Congress in 1988. We do not know the decline between the Twelfth Congress and the Thirteenth in 1990 because, while conceding that there had been a loss, the party reporter on organisation did not, and could not, quantify it. Membership problems must have been serious if the party leadership publicly acknowledged them.

Do these figures indicate a decline significant enough to label a crisis? With regard to enterprise cells, the report on organisation to the Twelfth Congress underlined the particular difficulties due to 'the increase in repression, increasing job insecurity, the rise in economic and social difficulties for the large part of the working masses'.[17] Given the importance that the PCP places on workplace cells, this situation is indeed serious. The party's financial situation is also not particularly bright. At both the Twelfth and Thirteenth Congresses it was reported that income had decreased and that expenses had increased. Measures have been sought to cut back spending. Yet, at the Twelfth Congress at least, the problems still seemed to be those of managing the organisational constraints resulting from 'the advance of the counter-revolution'. For example, it was reported that between 1983 and 1988 the number of party political full-time professionals decreased from 545 to 527, and the number of technical and administrative employees decreased from 273 to 250. But these appear to be symptoms of austerity rather than of organisational crisis.

It is possible to explain the PCP's capacity to resist ideological pressures resulting from the collapse of 'really existing socialism' in 1989 and the subsequent crisis of the International Communist movement through the way it has built up its support over the last three decades. It is important to take into account the ways in which the experience of revolutionary struggle against dictatorship has contributed to micro-sociological and even psychological sources of continuity within the PCP. Some authors attribute the PCP's peculiarities to a mentality, or intra-organisational psychology, derived from its prolonged experience of clandestinity.[18] The conditions of the struggle against dictatorship did reinforce the collective consciousness of Portuguese Communists (which is frequently dismissed as inward-looking and exclusive) as revolutionaries. It could be contended that this characteristic of the PCP derives from the transfer of the lessons of organisational maintenence learned under the conditions of repression of democracy. Indeed clandestinity is a source of the unanimity that produces acceptance of the discipline required for the democratic centralist operation of the party in the new context.

The PCP is not an organisation that has indulged in self-critical reflection. The fact that the PCP is structured around close-knit cultural communities facilitates this characteristic. Its leaders are generally not theoreticians but hard-nosed politicians trained in clandestine struggle and accustomed to reacting defensively to incursions from what is viewed as an extremely hostile environment. These are not people who will give up what they consider to be an historical war simply because

17. The number of cells in factories and businesses reportedly fell from 259 in 1983 to 175 in 1988.

18. J. P. Pereira, 'O PCP um partido do passando presente – Um interpertação', *Revista de Ciência Politica*, no. 5, Ist Semestre, 1987, pp. 5–29.

they have lost a series of battles, no matter how devastating their losses may be. As a result Portuguese communism has not been accompanied by the kind of continuous self-enquiry by prominent intellectuals on Communist experience that has given rise to 'crises of faith' in other European parties.

Nevertheless, it would be a misrepresentation to extrapolate from the apparent unanimity within the PCP to the conclusion that there has been no conflict over its political line. Episodes of political struggle within the party, such as the struggle between Cunhal's faction and the 'right opportunists' of the 1950s and the struggle between orthodox and Maoist currents in the 1960s (as well as the more recent struggles mentioned in this chapter) contradict this hypotheses. In our view the unanimity reigning in the PCP derives from three factors: the lack of communicative and critical capacity of a large portion of the traditional core support of the PCP, the very authoritarian democratic centralism practised in the party and the existence of a genuine agreement amongst the core of party activists. The first two factors derive from the persistence of the 'culture of clandestineness' within the party, although the incapacities of its supporters owe as much to the characteristics of the occupational and cultural communities in which the PCP is implanted. There is also the less rational emotive factor associated with the very recent experience (and the vitality of the memory) of the struggles for democracy and revolution under fascism and against 'counter-revolution'. The memory is still alive as well as the actors. Although it is subjective, this factor should not be underrated.

Another factor in the stability of the party is the generational division within the PCP. What could better symbolise the tenacity and continuity of the PCP in its evolution from a revolutionary party to a mass political organisation than the nearly fifty-year tenure of Alvaro Cunhal as General-Secretary of the party? Indeed, only in the late 1980s were some of the 1960s generation brought into the ranks of the leadership. Nevertheless, the fact that the PCP has cultivated a middle-generation corps of cadres, recruited after 1974 and notably loyal to the ideals and practice of the leadership, demonstrates the limitations of analyses centred upon these generational aspects. The intensity of the party's participation in the past, often heroic, struggle for democracy is important but not a sufficient explanation for either the stability or continuity of the party's orientation. Other Communist Parties were engaged in similar struggles, forging similar ties with society, and yet they have experienced both the radical decline and internal crises typical of Communism since the 1970s.

The PCP leadership was able, until the autumn of 1991, to neutralise internal political opposition and hold back the challenge from party reformers. The PCP leadership's management of internal opposition to its traditional orthodoxy has been based on the two interdependent tactics of integration and exclusion. At its Twelfth Congress in 1988 the party anticipated and dampened reformist efforts by incorporating notions of respect for political democracy into its programme while supporting *perestroika* as a movement advancing Soviet socialism. It also introduced subtle changes in its analysis of Portuguese society and brought a younger cohort of loyal activists into the leadership. It thereby placated the party's opposition while raising hopes that ideological renovation and modernisation were just around the corner. The leadership did not even need to resort to the extreme measure of expulsion as, with one notable exception, the most radical critics excluded themselves by resigning from the party following the failure of their unsuccessful attack on the leadership at the party's Thirteenth 'Extraordinary' Congress in 1990.

The comparative continuity of the Portuguese Communist Party derives in large measure from the endurance of its leadership's ability to reproduce an orthodox consensus within the party's decision-making bodies. However, this quality of the PCP's leadership as an explanation of the party's stability is limited in utility; the continuity of the leadership itself can only be explained as a result of the social-cultural and political-institutional factors which have provided it with support.

It would also be a mistake to see the PCP's recent electoral decline as exclusively being voters' reactions to the party's tie to the CPSU, since it may also be attributed to a variety of trends influencing the reorganisation of Portuguese electoral politics as a whole. Similarly, the opposition to the entrenched leadership was not stimulated uniquely by the positions taken on the international situation. Internal, evolutionary challenges to the stability of the party's traditional social and institutional bases of support have had and will probably continue to have an influence upon the party's fate equal in importance to the direct consequences of the ideological and political crisis associated with the break-up of 'really existing socialism'. Of course this assertion may involve splitting hairs, since evolution in politics is frequently manifested in a restricted series of events. For the PCP these included the leadership's lack of tact in dealing with the coup, the resulting coalescence of the party's critical tendencies and the discredit caused by the collapse of the Soviet regime: all these brought about a convergence of weaknesses within PCP support, intensifying the crisis in the party. There is a paradox here. The PCP now insists that it never wanted to import existing models of socialism to Portugal, in spite of its explicit commitment to Soviet leadership of the International Communist Movement since the 1940s. Its concept of socialism is, however, inextricably linked with notions derived from the history of the construction of the Soviet Socialist regime. This has resulted in its interpreting the collapse of the Eastern European regimes as a major setback for socialism, even a defeat, but rejecting a fundamental criticism of the concept of socialism as it was developed in the Soviet Revolution.

The PCP's distinctive support comes from the struggle for democracy and its immediate revolutionary legacy and from the persistence of social and demographic characteristics of Portugal's development. Of particular importance is the party's mass base, which is concentrated in regions or in occupational or cultural communities. The party obtains its major sources of institutional support from its role in the labour movement and municipal power and remains the predominant force in the major trade-union confederation, the CGTP-IN. The PCP and its electoral allies govern fifty municipalities. Its leadership of the CGTP-IN, which remains the country's major union confederation (although not as dominant as in the past) legitimises, according to the PCP, the party's claim to lead the Portuguese working class. The party's ability to preserve its institutional supports, trade-union leadership in particular, depends upon the ability of these institutions themselves to satisfy the demands of diverse constituencies. The political-institutional component of PCP support is therefore an impetus to pragmatism. We therefore further suggest that the problems provoked by external events in Eastern Europe and in the Soviet Union will influence the PCP to the extent that they correlate with new social and political problems generated by the tasks of trade union and local municipal leadership.

The PCP in Crisis

In August 1991 support if the PCP leadership for the attempted coup in the Soviet Union and its explicit opposition to post-coup developments confirmed the PCP leadership's resistance to the breaking up of the International Communist Movement and its willingness to risk the party's unity and electoral support in defence of Communist orthodoxy. The Political Commission declared that the coup was an attempt to limit the development of a counter-revolutionary process and resolve the Soviet crisis within the framework of socialism. This reaction caused an immediate revolt in the party by the 'loyal opposition'. As a result of this situation the PCP has been confronted with the most serious crisis since 1974, and its leadership has for once been placed in a decidedly defensive position. The reformist opposition, made up of prominent party members, challenged party discipline, organised and openly demanded that the leadership retract its initial support for the coup in the Soviet Union and submit their resignations. The group went so far as to organise a public meeting of protest by party members to the declaration of support for the coup. The revolt went beyond the usual group of reformers as a number of protests identified with prominent party members appeared in the press. Nevertheless, the Party's Central Committee went on to approve a document which reaffirmed the party's opposition to the measures taken in the Soviet Union following the coup's failure and the restoration of capitalism in the Soviet Union, criticising Yeltsin in particular and disparaging the demands of the party reformers. In the wake of the isolation that the PCP suffered in this situation, the approval of the Central Committee's document (with ony two votes against and four abstentions) was a clear sign of the unity of the party leadership.

If the coup provided the most serious outbreak of internal dissent the party had suffered, it also took place at a sensitive moment in the 1991 legislative election campaign. The PCP leadership went through the election campaign downplaying the influence of 'external events' upon the results of the elections. The core of the party's support still appeared intact, although the party's share of the vote had been gradually declining since 1979. The leadership did not express concern about the loyalty of this core and anticipated a stable 10 per cent vote in the legislative elections set for October 1991. In the first round of the presidential elections in January 1991, the previous test of electoral strength, the PCP candidate had obtained 13 per cent. The serious decline in the PCP vote on 6 October 1991 – from 12.2 per cent to 8.8 per cent of the national vote – is a good indication that PCP support was not as impervious to the effect of events in the Soviet Union as the leadership had hoped. In certain areas, such as Setubal and Beja in the Alentejo, the electoral results signalled a qualitative movement in what had previously been a slow and gradual decline.

Although the PCP made public statements immediately following the elections acknowledging its defeat and the need for serious reflection, this did not influence the basic stance of the PCP's leadership; it produced a reaction to internal and external challenges that is consistent with the most stalwart core of the party's hard-line leadership. The result has been a series of voluntary resignations of prominent and less prominent members, continuing internal instability and, finally, the resort to expulsion of the leading critics (for factionalism). The PCP leadership, in a demonstration of its lack of haste in drawing conclusions from the traumatic experience of the party since August 1991, convened the Fourteenth Congress for a suitably distant date.

Conclusion

We have argued that the PCP has felt pressure to change, from the need to adapt its revolutionary heritage to the conditions of institutionalised democracy and preserve its traditional social support, and from the isolation resulting from the extraordinary changes in the Socialist world and the collapse of the International Communist Movement. We have tried to demonstrate the degree of programmatic continuity and stability of the PCP and explain how the party has been able to resist the pressures upon it. While the leadership has unapologetically reasserted its orthodoxy, PCP activists have been profoundly moved by the events begun in 1989. Central Committee members, who otherwise continue to support the leadership, have done the previously unheard of by confiding to journalists that they need to 'reflect on events'. The increasing presence of reformist tendencies within the party's 'intellectual sector' is a symptom of critical reflection. Nevertheless, the opposition to orthodoxy within the PCP has been insufficient in its scope and content, and the leadership has been able to isolate or control it. Following each of the ideological skirmishes the most ideologically frustrated critics of the leadership have abandoned the party. The sporadic but significant resignations of intellectuals from the party over the last two years are indeed signs that members from this sector are increasingly giving up hope of being able to 'renovate' the PCP.

It is clear that the fate of the PCP as an organisation will depend as much upon what happens to its social and institutional bases of support as upon the ideological and political crisis resulting from the collapse of the Socialist bloc and the Communist Parties of those countries. If the PCP is relatively secure in, or can at least manage, its relationship with its traditional base of support within Portuguese society, it has little to lose from maintaining what it considers to be positions of principle.

–5–

The Greek Communist Party in the Post-Gorbachev Era

Ole L. Smith

It is something of a commonplace that the Greek Communist Party (KKE), together with perhaps the Portuguese Party, has been the most unquestioningly loyal ally of Moscow among the West European Communist Parties. However, this situation changed gradually after Gorbachev's coming to power: in the KKE there was considerable criticism of the Soviet government after 1989, and for the first time ever in the history of the KKE, party documents and party-sponsored publications started to openly question basic policies of the Soviet leadership. The repercussions of the crisis in the Soviet Union led in June–July 1991 to a split in the KKE along hard-core versus reformist lines. With the hard-core leadership in firm control, there is no doubt that the KKE will retain its orthodox Marxist-Leninist orientation.

Historical Perspective

The present situation of the Greek Communist Party cannot be properly understood without at least a cursory glance at Greek political history since World War II. From 1945 to 1949 the KKE fought a bloody civil war against the mainly British- and US-supported official government. The KKE was declared illegal in December 1947 and remained so until the downfall of the military dictatorship in the summer of 1974. When the Communists reappeared as a political force in Greece in 1974, the party had been indelibly marked by its long absence from Greek life, by its ties to the East European Socialist countries where the vanquished Communist partisans and their leaders in the Civil War had found refuge and by its inability throughout the years in exile to develop an independent political theory.

The feeble attempt in the years 1963–8 to adjust the KKE to a Greece and a world which had changed had led to a split between

Stalinist hard-liners and 'Eurocommunists'; the latter organised themselves in 1969–70 in the so-called Greek Communist Party of the Interior. In 1986–7 this party split again into two groups, the Greek Left and the Greek Communist Party of the Interior. The hard-liners kept the name KKE, and soon developed into the most powerful of the three Communist parties. In early 1989 the KKE and the Greek Left allied in a common front called *Synaspismos* (Coalition) (partly as a left-wing alternative to the Socialist PaSoK Party) for the parliamentary elections of 1989, but not without thoughts for a more permanent 'party-like' organisation. One of the great problems for the Greek Communists during the critical last two years was whether the *Synaspismos* should develop into a normal political party, or whether it should be kept as it was, as an 'umbrella organisation' of different parties, small splinter groups and individual political personalities. When the minority group in the KKE Central Committee in July 1991 decided to work for a further development of the *Synaspismos* the group was 'relieved of its duties', and in practice the members of the opposition in the leadership were expelled from their posts. They have now organised themselves within the *Synaspismos* as 'Movement for a New Left'.

Of particular importance when judging the impact of the Gorbachev revolution on the Greek Communists is the fact that the KKE leadership in exile in the Socialist bloc had further developed its strong ties with the Moscow establishment. After the Twentieth Congress of the CPSU, the leaders of the Socialist countries took the initiative in the destalinisation of the KKE (at the Sixth Plenum of the CC), removing in a summary fashion the then General Secretary of the KKE, Nikos Zakhariadis, who had been placed in the KKE in 1931 as the Komintern candidate, and replacing him with Kostas Koliyannis. All his life Zakhariadis, a member of the CPSU, remained unquestioningly loyal to Moscow. He was expelled from the KKE in 1957 and was sent to Siberia, where he was held under house arrest until his suicide in 1973. After the formal change in the KKE leadership in 1956, the Moscow authorities maintained control of the Greek party. In 1973 Moscow probably also made Harilaos Florakis leader in place of Kostas Koliyannis, because of the latter's inability to conform to the new imperatives facing the KKE, and because of his responsibility for the 1968 split between the Stalinists and the Eurocommunists. When Florakis finally stepped down from the post as Secretary General in 1990, there was no doubt that the Soviets were behind the choice of Grigoris Farakos. The irony is that Farakos' reputation of being 100 per cent loyal to Moscow proved wrong, for he emerged in the months after his election as a strong supporter of reform, and openly challenged the hard-liner Aleka Papariga, who was elected General Secretary at the Thirteenth Congress in February 1991. Farakos is widely regarded as the reformist leader and is the most important member of the old Civil War leadership generation to side with the younger reformist cadres. He was expelled with the other reformists from the Central Committee in July 1991.

Greek Communist Reactions

A tendency towards a sometimes highly critical attitude to President Gorbachev and his government could be seen even before the first public KKE pronouncements on the developments in Eastern Europe after the Romanian crisis.[1] The pre-Congress debate and the heated discussions at the Thirteenth Congress in 1991 clearly demonstrated that the problem of Gorbachev's reforms and more or less evident political goals were of central importance to the unity of the KKE. The two tendencies in the KKE, which have to a great extent been generated by differing appraisals of Eastern Europe developments, could not coexist in a party that was still dominated by Stalinist views of party discipline. It was obvious that unity would sooner or later be achieved either by a gradual opening-up of the party, or by a clean break.

For the Greek Communists, the old saying that loyalty and solidarity with the Soviet Union is the *sine qua non* for a true Communist was still valid, especially when the Soviet Union was the only Eastern Europe country where the Communists might be regarded as the governing party. However, there were evident signs that the KKE was aware that the CPSU had lost its dominating control for good. In the Greek party papers, Soviet affairs still occupied a large space, and interviews with Soviet personalities were frequently featured. However, apart from a short period before the Congress, the emphasis was now increasingly on official Soviet positions and policies rather than Socialist debate in the USSR. Even so, Greek Communist hard-liners protested against 'revisionist' views appearing in the party coverage of Soviet affairs.

I will now turn to the KKE attitude towards Gorbachev's reforms and the political developments in Eastern Europe as it developed during the last two years, culminating at the Thirteenth Congress in 1991, and more specifically, to demonstrate the central importance of

1. On the developments in the Socialist countries see the party documents *From the 12th to the 13th Congress*, Athens, Central Committee of the KKE, December 1990, 283–93 [in Greek].

these issues in the internal discussion in the KKE. The debate over developments in the Soviet Union and in the former Socialist camp should be seen as the main catalyst in the disintegration of the traditionally best-organised and most powerful left-wing party in Greece. On the other hand it must be emphasised that there was practically no discussion after the August events, because at that time the dissenters had already been thrown out from responsible positions and should be regarded as having been expelled from the KKE. As will be explained later, conditions for discussion in the party today are very bad. Irrespective of the new situation after the August events, what happens in the KKE will necessarily have great repercussions on the Greek political scene, and the final outcome of the continuous crisis in the Communist movement will contribute to a new definition of the whole of the Left in the country.

The Congress Discussions

The mood of the Congress debate was caught by Piraeus District Committee member Tasos Gargalakos: 'The developments in the Eastern Europe countries . . . contributed to breaking the silent apathy that characterised party functionaries and members. We began to talk loudly, more freely.'[2] The situation in the KKE did not seem, at least on the surface, to be so different from that in the other Western European Communist Parties. What made the KKE a somewhat different case was put very clearly by a number of delegates at the Thirteenth Congress: the KKE throughout its history has been a close copy of the Soviet party, the KKE has never doubted for a moment that the Eastern European countries had built 'real' socialism, Soviet bloc policies were supported without question and the party leaders, including Ceaucescu, hailed as great and truly revolutionary figures. The principles of Marxism-Leninism, proletarian internationalism, the dictatorship of the proletariat and democratic centralism have been sacrosanct in the KKE since the 'bolshevisation' of the party in the early thirties. The secretary of the Rethymno District Committee, Yannis Stathakis, put it this way: 'These [1989] developments are very much our own affair both for the reason that we uncritically supported the regimes in these countries and because we as a party identified ourselves with the governing parties there.'[3]

2. *Rizospastis*, 22 February 1991.
3. Ibid.; see also Giannis Maroukis ibid.

Gorbachev's *perestroika* had first hit the KKE in 1987, at the Twelfth Congress, where the leadership suggested the idea of a qualitative change in the party. This was widely interpreted as a reaction in favour of *glasnost* and *perestroika*, although it was obvious from the party documents and from *Rizospastis* that Gorbachev was regarded with some unofficial suspicion.[4] However, the qualitative change announced amid great jubilation and optimism at the Twelfth Congress remained largely on paper; there was no haste among the conservatives in the party apparatus to implement the democratic reforms, and virtually nothing happened. The Soviet government's various innovations in the following years were mostly favourably received in Greece, but then came the developments in the German Democratic Republic and Czechoslovakia, and the revolution in Romania. In January 1990 the Central Committee, under strong pressure from the rank-and-file and lower-lever party functionaries, finally issued a very mild statement on the changes taking place in Eastern Europe, but there was almost no discussion. Clearly, the party leadership was at a loss; they were not in doubt about the confusion among party members, but they must have felt that the best thing they could do was to wait and see, in the hope that the situation would somehow stabilize itself in a more beneficent way.[5]

The explosion came when the draft proposal for the Thirteenth Congress Theses was leaked in early summer 1990. On the committee, which had been appointed to work out a draft proposal for the Congress Theses, there were several well-known cadres from the reformist wing (one being the former minister in the ill-fated 1990 Tzannetakis government,Yannis Dragasakis[6]), and the work was supervised by Grigoris Farakos, the General Secretary of the party. When the draft proposal became known, an enlarged Central Committee meeting (much against the wishes of the top leaders in the Political Bureau) was called in June, in which district secretaries and other middle-level functionaries also took part, and where the proposal was discussed. Since this document was clearly an attempt to draw some preliminary conclusions from the political developments in Eastern Europe in order to revitalise the KKE, the discussion was very bitter and became the start of the open polarisation in the party between hard-liners and

4. For example Giorgos Psalidopoulos, *Rizospastis*, 23 February 1991, p. 12.

5. Central Committee member Flora Nikolidaki accused the leadership of having evaded the problems (*Rizospastis*, 22 February 1991, p. 22).

6. The Tzannetakis Government was a short-lived coalition between the *Synaspismos* and New Democracy, formed to carry through the purges after the Koskotas scandals, and thus mainly directed against PaSoK.

reformists. Sacred cows like proletarian internationalism, democratic centralism and dictatorship of the proletariat were almost sacrificed, and Marxism-Leninism was taken out of its Stalinist garb and rechristened the 'ideas of Marx, Engels and Lenin'. In this way the reformist wing of the KKE tried to save what it could: the reformists argued that the changes in Eastern Europe had made it impossible to uphold principles which were widely seen as the reason for the corruption of socialism in the former Eastern bloc.

The Political Bureau, however, refused to give in. The draft proposal was curtly dismissed (in spite of support from middle-level cadres), and a new set of Theses for the Thirteenth Congress was drafted and published in September, when it became the subject of an extensive discussion in the party press until the Congress in February 1991. Though far from strictly orthodox in its views, the revised (and now official) Theses kept traditional KKE language and ideology.

As far as can be judged from published facts, the KKE was divided. Among the rank and file, there was a small majority in favour of the new Theses, whereas among middle-level cadres the majority seems to have been against the revised document. Basically, there were among Greek Communists two views on *perestroika*: one negative view regarded the reforms as the factor that sparked off the collapse of the Socialist countries; the other, positive view, saw Gorbachev's policies as a serious attempt at democratic reforms, as the only possible way out of the crisis for the Soviet Union and as the precursor of a new Socialist development (not necessarily controlled by Gorbachev). At the Congress the first point of view was expressed by a representative of the KKE members living in Germany, Nikos Karageorgos, who claimed that *perestroika* was directly responsible for the débâcle of the Socialist countries.[7] On the second view, Panos Trigazis (now no longer a Communist), President of the KKE-dominated peace organisation EEDYE, was representative: 'I do not at all share the opinion of some comrades who denigrate the contribution of *perestroika*. I am categorically against an off-hand condemnation of *perestroika*.' Trigazis further warned against the tendency to see Gorbachev behind the downfall of the Eastern Europe regimes, and emphasised the great advances in international co-operation achieved on the basis of Gorbachev's policy.[8] Between these extremes there were of course several different shadings of opinion.

Both in the pre-Congress debate and at the Congress, developments in Eastern Europe and the attitude to President Gorbachev tended to

7. *Rizospastis*, 22 February 1991.
8. *Rizospastis*, 22 February 1991.

dominate the proceedings and to be the point at which the split became manifest. With very few exceptions the delegates began speeches with a statement about the meaning and the effect of the changes in the Socialist world. The supporters of a modernised party (influenced by the downfall of the Eastern Communist regimes) argued that the developments in the former Socialist countries were the source of the present split in the party and that they should be the object of a serious reappraisal irrespective of what stand individual delegates took on the basic issues. An Athenian delegate, Christos Tsakopoulos, put it this way:

> Let us accept that the present clash in the party has as its origin the different theoretical views about the developments in the so-called 'countries of real socialism'. The fact is that the basic theoretical dispute is whether these countries had built up socialism or not, and it turns on the differences in appraisal of other basic viewpoints on the causes of their crisis and the collapse. I think that all of us here agree that our party, parallel with the discussion in the international Communist movement, may continue our quest and our historical search through dialogue, and even through polemics between opinions. I also believe that even the comrades who encouraged the confrontation on the theme of ideological unity will agree that we cannot simply end such serious problems with a Congress vote. However, cries of the type 'Long live Stalin' or 'Gorbachev is a traitor' have no place in any kind of search or constructive discussion.[9]

According to the modernisers, however, the Eastern Europe developments showed the fundamentally erroneous nature of the Socialist experiment, in consequence of which the Greek Communists had to develop a quite different concept of socialism along with different tactics and strategies.[10] They argued that the carbon copy of Soviet experiences no longer had any validity. If the KKE was to regain lost territory, a radical change was necessary. For example, democracy, toleration of different views, independence of foreign models and a critical appraisal of heretical Leftist thinking were necessary. And first and foremost, the KKE had to dissociate itself from the crimes committed in the former Socialist countries. The demand for *glasnost* also made party history and its scrutiny a favourite topic of controversy. The reformers demanded that party archives be opened and made available for researchers, and claimed that the Political Bureau majority used the hermetically-closed party archives

9. *Rizospastis*, 21 February 1991; see also L. Vlisidis, *Komep*, 1991; Y. Stathakis, *Rizospastis*, 22 February 1991.

10. See Thessalonica delegate Giorgos Kokkinidis, *Rizospastis*, 22 February 1991: 'The socialism we advocated collapsed with the regimes that incarnated it.' See also Communist Youth delegate Anatoli Zarantiadou *Rizospastis*, 21 February 1991); 'Let us finally declare: No, this was not socialism; See further Tasos Kefalas, *KOMEP*, 1991.

against their opponents: in a remarkable contribution to the pre-Congress discussion, Vasilis Bartziotas even demanded that the Sixth Plenum in 1956 (where he himself and Zakhariadis were removed from party leadership) should be reassessed, along with the role of the Eastern Europe Communist Parties.

Among the orthodox there were several lines of defence. One group rejected out of hand any discussion of Gorbachev and Eastern Europe. They simply declined to talk about it. Several delegates downplayed the Eastern European problem, although it was on everyone's mind. If they had to mention the Socialist bloc at all they explained what had happened either as Gorbachev's treachery, or as the work of imperialist fifth-columnists; at most, they accepted that socialism had suffered a defeat.[11] This is typical. But they went no further and they never faced the fact that the débâcle had brought crimes and undemocratic institutions to light. Some explained that this would never have happened if the governments had kept strictly to Marxist-Leninist principles.[12] Few, apart from Florakis, went so far as to express optimism with regard to what was happening in Eastern Europe. A more supple attitude was shown by those orthodox Communists who were ready to admit errors and bad leadership without questioning the basic principles of the Socialist experiment. They apologised for their own acceptance of Eastern Europe communism by claiming that they did not know what was going on – an argument that has met with singularly little credence. Finally, not a few defended themselves and socialism by stating that they did not know enough, that the situation had to be studied in more detail and that developments had to be seen in a broader view and in a 'scientific' way.[13] Some also moved on to the attack by pointing out that the reformists were virtually denying that there had ever been socialism in these countries. By so doing, it was said, the reformists also rejected the vast progress made in Eastern Europe, the heroic struggle of the Soviet Union against fascism and the solidarity of the Socialist countries with national liberation movements.

At the Congress the basic discussion was polarised between those for or against party renewal to overcome the crisis. The majority of the

11. *Rizospastis*, 21 February 1991; Andreas Kalabogias (Central Committee member) spoke of an 'imperialist victory' supported by forces within the Communist Parties *Rizospastis*, (21 February 1991, p. 30). According to another member, Christos Logaras *Rizospastis*, (23 February 1991, p. 11), the international Socialist and progressive movement had suffered a serious defeat.

12. See, for example, Giorgos Dafoulis, *Rizospastis*, 22 February 1991.

13. Angeliki Michou, *Rizospastis*, 22 February 1991. More crudely the Corfu delegate Vasilis Armeniakos put it this way: 'We cannot answer the question of whether the creation of the People's Democracies in the 1950s took into consideration the local conditions in these countries or was based on the presence of the [Red] Army' *Rizospastis*, 22 February 1991.

delegates was in favour of what was a less than wholly orthodox Marxist-Leninist document, and the hard-liners, strongly supported by Florakis, were able to retain their hold on party machinery only through a small margin in the election of a new Central Committee. In spite of their statements to the contrary before the Congress, Florakis and the trade union General Secretary Mitsos Kostopoulos were prevailed upon to stand again for the Central Committee in order to lend their support to the conservative line. Of the 111 members elected to the new Central Committee, 60 belong to the conservative hard-liners and 51 to the reformist wing. The new General Secretary Aleka Papariga was elected at a dramatic session of the Central Committee, in which for perhaps the first time in the history of the KKE there were two candidates. Papariga had not even been elected delegate to the Congress by her own party organisation of Athens (where she had acted as Secretary). She participated in the Congress as an observer without right of vote, and was put up as a candidate by Florakis (she had even declared before the Congress that she would not be a candidate), whereas Farakos had proposed Yannis Dragasakis.

The Widening of the Gulf

This situation did not last for long; the KKE was obviously bound for a split. From March to July the Central Committee meetings were one unbroken series of violent controversies which almost paralysed the KKE. A few weeks after the Congress the editor-in-chief of the party newspaper *Rizospastis* was removed and then the party radio station was purged. In May the Central Committee majority sent out an open letter calling on the members of the KKE to put an end to the inner party struggle (implying that the rank and file should rally in support of the party leadership); at the same meeting a counter proposal (for further democratic discussion instead of an open break in the party) was introduced by the reformist spokesman Panayotis Lafazanis and supported by the minority. A number of party organisations rejected the letter (among them the three largest, the Athens, Thessalonica and Piraeus Town Councils) and voted for the minority proposal. At the next Central Committee meeting at the beginning of June, the majority again won a Pyrrhic victory on the issue of the *Synaspismos*. A resolution stated that party representatives throughout the organisational structure should be appointed by the parties themselves in the *Synaspismos* and not elected by individual members. This decision was also rejected by the big party organisations. At the same June meeting a minority report was tabled for the first time in party history, by Nikos Hountis of the Athens party organisation, and when the majority refused to put it to vote, the leading party economist Yannis Tolios walked out in protest. Also on this occasion the first public demands for measures against the minority were heard. It was by now almost certain that very soon the majority would have to re-establish 'law and order' by bureaucratic means, perhaps even by expelling members of the Central Committee. The process started at the Central Committee session on 23 June. A Party Congress was called to deal with the new situation and measures were taken to expel the opposition from the Central Committee. Finally, at the meeting of the Political Bureau on 9 July the split became a reality when about thirty leading cadres were relieved of their posts including five MPs. The official reason was that these cadres had taken part in the National Conference of the *Synaspismos* in spite of a majority decision in the Central Committee which ordered its members to stay away. The minority argued that by breaking up the *Synaspismos*, the Central Committee acted against the decisions taken at the Thirteenth Congress. Arguments and discussion had little effect at this stage; the party was split from top to bottom, and the published speeches from the Central Committee meetings in June show very clearly that there was nothing to talk about. During the next months the Central Committee majority tried to establish control of the party machinery by deposing the elected local councils.[14]

The split in the KKE can also be viewed from another angle. There can be no doubt, though it is often denied, that there is a generation gap in the party. There are very few among the reformists who belong to the older generation from the Resistance and the Civil War. The great majority of party veterans from that period – in so far as they have taken part in the discussion – seem to support the orthodox leadership, especially those older members who were in political exile in Eastern Europe. They tend to look upon the party very emotionally and, not unexpectedly, categorically reject any change in the profile of the 'heroic KKE'. An exception is Vasilis Bartziotas (Zakhariadis' close collaborator in exile in the 1950s), who declared himself a supporter of the reforms in the party.[15] There is also a marked tendency towards a split between intellectuals and workers. Some of the most vociferous

14. There are several obscure spots in the events at this critical point. For one thing I have not seen the decision from the 23 June meeting, but the speeches were published in *Rizospastis*, 28 June 1991. The formal decision was not taken until 9 July and published 11 July in *Rizospastis*. Just before the 23 June meeting Aleka Papariga was in Moscow for talks with the Soviet leaders. It is anybody's guess how Gorbachev told her to deal with the crisis.

15. *KOMEP*, Special Issue, 1990, pp. 57–61.

orthodox supporters are trade unionists, and it is no accident that the present General Secretary of the Labor Federation, Mitsos Kostopoulos, is leader of a strong anti-reformist group in the trade unions. On the other hand, among the reformists are such eminent trade unionists as Kostas Papachristodoulou (former President of the KKE trade union faction ESAK) and Panayotis Ploumis (President of the Athens Trade Union Center). The orthodox trade unionists at the Congress quite openly condemned intellectuals 'without class conscience'.

From the discussion about Marxist-Leninist principles and the Gorbachev reforms, the basic question dividing the two wings in the Greek Communist Movement now became the way out of the crisis in Greek politics and in the Greek Left. For the reformist wing the *Synaspismos* with its broad Leftist Popular Front programme offered the most promising answer to the new situation, and not a few of them openly stated before the split that the *Synaspismos* should replace the traditional Communist Party. The Stalinists, on the other hand, tried to keep control of developments in the *Synaspismos* by insisting upon the coalition's essential nature as a loose co-operation between independent political parties and movements. They also wanted to keep KKE representatives in the *Synaspismos* Executive Council on a very short lead, and emphasised the party leadership's right to withdraw or replace KKE representatives on the Council. The hard-liners did not want the Executive Council to be elected by a Congress, and they were strongly against any attempt to allow the *Synaspismos* to develop into an independent political organisation. They feared that their opponents would use the *Synaspismos* as a platform against the KKE leadership and carry on the inner-party conflicts supported by the *Synaspismos*. As mentioned above, the KKE split became a reality when KKE cadres insisted on taking part in the *Synaspismos* National Conference on 27 June. Since the National Conference the KKE has formally broken off relations with the *Synaspismos* and has now established itself as an independent party in Parliament and outside. The excluded KKE MPs now belong to the Parliament delegation of the *Synaspismos*.[16] Nonetheless, the KKE, after the split was a reality, stated that one of its main objectives was co-operation with the Leftist forces to establish an alternative to the Conservative government.

The coup against Gorbachev in August 1991 was met with a careful statement to the effect that the KKE would wait and see whether the events would lead to a stabilisation of the situation in the Soviet Union,

---

16. Among the MPs for the *Synaspismos* are former leading KKE members such as Farakos, Maria Damanaki and Mimis Androulakis.

which was regarded as highly critical and dangerous for the Socialist state. The party leadership seems to have believed that a removal of Gorbachev would put an end to what the KKE for some months had regarded as a re-emergence of capitalism in the Soviet Union. As a result of this attitude the credibility and public image of the KKE reached an unprecedented nadir. The KKE exposed itself by its blind subordination to anyone in power in the Kremlin and by its silent acceptance of the tanks in the streets of Moscow. Very soon, however, the leadership came out with a revised statement, and the official line now is that there was a coup that failed because of lack of popular support. The events following the coup and its sorry demise have been met with deep anxiety in the KKE. The dissolution of the CPSU and later of the Soviet Union itself seem to have rolled back the Greek Communist Party. The KKE is now entrenched in orthodox Marxism-Leninism and there is no attempt to analyse the situation in other than old-fashioned black-and-white terms. The recently published 'Theses for the Fourteenth Congress' regard the development in the Soviet Union solely as a question of bad leadership.[17] The collapse of the Socialist regimes does not mean the collapse of Communist theory and ideology. In 1991 outright neo-Stalinist views surfaced, and in the very lame discussion before the Fourteenth Congress rank and file views that the KKE should make a clear stand against anti-Stalinism have been aired.

The KKE seems as an organisation to have survived the split: the majority of party members probably have stayed. There is no doubt, however, that on the cadre level the losses have been great. It is very difficult to get precise information; after July 1991 party media became very reticent about the size and the effects of the split. The relative openness that characterised the party and its media before and after the Thirteenth Congress was effectively stopped. Probably about 40 per cent of party cadres either left or were immobilised. In some sectors the losses must have been still greater. The split took toll notably among intellectuals and there is hardly any doubt that the exodus among the intelligentsia will stifle initiative and discussion in the party. The KKE as far as both membership and political outlook are concerned, has been set back almost thirty years. Not surprisingly, the older members stayed; on the other hand, the Communist Youth Organisation (KNE) was barely alive and bore no similarity to the mass organisation with tens of thousands of members it was just a few years ago. Although the KKE recently succeeded in getting a party TV channel in the air, its mass media have been hit very hard. The daily newspaper *Rizospastis*

17. *Rizospastis*, 6 October 1991.

which was strongly oppositional even after the Thirteenth Congress must have changed over 50 per cent of its personnel and there is a very visible political censorship operating in the paper, with the result that it has lost its credibility and inventiveness not to mention a noticeable decline in quality.

The party is unlikely to regain its momentum and influence within the immediate future; for a number of years it will be supported at all costs by the older generation, but it is very much an open question what will happen when the Civil War generation is no more.

Conclusion

For those historians of Modern Greece who have looked into what happened in the KKE after the Twentieth Congress of the CPSU, all this seems *déjà vu*. History repeats itself: in 1956 and in 1968 international factors were behind the splits. This time, however, there is a difference. The KKE has lost its international orientation; the lifeline has been cut. There is no longer a powerful CPSU, there is no Soviet Union any more. Flirtation with China, and movement for solidarity with Cuba cannot make up for the lack of a source of ideological orthodoxy.

If there ever was a moment of truth for the Greek Communists, it is now. The Gorbachev experiment and all that followed in the wake of *perestroika* have effectively demonstrated what was wrong with the Greek Communist Party: its dependence on foreign theory and models and, as a consequence, its inability to formulate a credible perspective for Greek socialism.

–6–

Requiem for the
Spanish Communist Party

José Amodia

A cemetery seems an appropriate place to start this chapter. In November 1989 Dolores Ibárruri, Pasionaria, matriarchal figure of Spanish communism, was buried in the unconsecrated area of the Almudena, Madrid's gigantic necropolis. Her body was laid to rest a few feet away from the mausoleum which contains the remains of Pablo Iglesias, *el abuelo* (the grandfather) of Spanish socialism, founder of the PSOE (Spanish Socialist Workers' Party), who died in 1925. The proximity in death of the two greatest leaders of the Spanish Left becomes poignantly symbolic now that the world-wide crisis in the Communist movement is forcing parties of this ilk if not towards extinction, at least back to the Socialist fold they had abandoned in the past.

The Spanish Communist Party (PCE)[1] was born in the period 1919–21 as the result of a split in the Socialist ranks over the question of the Communist International, and after more than seventy years of hard struggle, meagre success, and almost permanent conflict with its left-wing brethren in the PSOE, now finds itself confronting the most painful of dilemmas – whichever path it takes it seems condemned to losing its own identity. The 1991 developments in the now defunct Soviet Union and their repercussions throughout the Communist movement only helped to accelerate a process which was already well advanced inside the PCE. Since Franco's demise in November 1975, the history of the PCE has been a chronicle of frustrated hopes, electoral failures, internal conflict, splits, purges and desertions: in short, sixteen years of crisis and decline.

After nearly four decades in exile and clandestineness, the legalisation of the PCE in the spring of 1977 awakened the hopes and

---

1. On the history of the PCE, see G. Hermet, Les Communistes en Espagne, Paris, A. Colin, 1971; V. Alba, *El Partido Comunista de España*, Barcelona, Planeta, 1979; or, for the party's official version, D. Ibárruri et al., *Historia del Partido Comunista de España*, Warsaw, 1960.

expectations of party leaders and membership alike. Many thought then that the PCE was likely to become the main standard-bearer for the Left in the nascent party system, with an electoral pull similar to that if its Communist counterparts in other countries of Southern Europe. Reality was to prove very different. And although this is not the place to analyse in detail the reasons for that failure,[2] it seems nevertheless appropriate to outline its main causes and some of its consequences, so as to make clear that when Gorbachev set in motion the process of change in the USSR, which would eventually uncover the profound sickness of Soviet communism, the PCE was already terminally ill.

Among the many factors that contributed to the PCE's initial lack of success and to its progressive decline, the following stand out. The long years of clandestine existence, which had turned the PCE into the symbol of the struggle against Franco's regime, had also served to ossify party structures, creating a rigid and authoritarian hierarchy totally unsuited to the demands of life in an open and democratic context. In sharp contrast with the experience of its main rival, the PSOE, the PCE returned to Spain and to democracy with leaders – Santiago Carrillo, Pasionaria, Ignacio Gallego, etc. – whose biographies were linked in the mind of many Spaniards with memories of the Civil War, thus reinforcing the fear of communism instilled in them by Francoist propaganda. At the same time, the attempts on the part of the leadership, in particular the PCE's General Secretary Santiago Carrillo, to impose a hierarchical and centralised party structure led to bitter confrontations with the younger members, who were hoping for a greater degree of decentralisation, and who were also expecting their leaders to listen and become more responsive to the aspirations and demands springing from the grass roots. Furthermore, these leaders, given their advanced age and their total lack of democratic experience, were unable to provide the party with the kind of face required in a modern electoral contest, based as it is on vigorous personalities and attractive media images.

Eurocommunism, which initially had been seen as a way of achieving autonomy from Moscow and as a public acceptance of the principles of political pluralism, soon became a major source of dissension within the PCE. For some, Eurocommunism amounted to an act of treachery against Communist orthodoxy, whereas others saw it as the first step towards a sincere and profound democratisation of the

2. On the PCE during the transition see, among others, E. Mujal-León, *Communism and Political Change in Spain*, Indiana University Press, 1983 or J. C. González Hernández, 'El PCE en el proceso de la transición', in J. F. Tezanos et al. (eds.), *La transición democrática española*, Madrid, Sistema, 1980, pp. 543–85.

PCE.[3] In practice the PCE's Eurocommunism never carried with it an unequivocal denunciation of past abuses under Communist regimes, nor of the latter's continued curtailment of freedom and disregard for human rights. In other words, Spanish Communists never went as far as totally severing the umbilical cord connecting them to mother Russia, nor did Eurocommunism ever allow the post-Franco winds of democratic change to reach the inner sanctum of party power. Instead of illuminating a new horizon for the party, the Eurocommunist torch was to ignite a large fire of ideological vagaries in which the last hopes of renewal would be burnt out.

The combination of the above factors, plus some others of lesser relevance, had fatal consequence for the PCE. The results in the first democratic elections, held in June 1977, were deeply disappointing. The PCE gained only 9.4 per cent of the vote, well below the level of its counterparts in other Southern European countries, and far away from the 29.12 per cent support obtained by their main left-wing rivals, the PSOE. But worse was to follow. Five years later, in October 1982, at the last general election the PCE entered as an independent party, its share of the vote dropped to just 4.13 per cent, and its number of parliamentary seats was reduced to four from the twenty they had gained in 1977. Party membership has followed a similar line of descent, though in this area it is more difficult to obtain reliable figures and impossible to verify official party claims. At the time of the Ninth Congress, held in April 1978, the party boasted a membership of 240,000, a figure which, though undoubtedly inflated,[4] made the PCE the largest organisation in the country. Five years on, at the time of the Eleventh Congress, in December 1983, the number of members had been more than halved, down to 85,000.[5] The dramatic losses in electoral support and party affiliation were accompanied by a long series of ideological swings and confused programmatic declarations, which in the end alienated on the one hand the more progressive sectors of the middle classes, who had seen in the PCE a suitable channel to contribute to the democratic transformation of Spain, and on the other many of those who still wanted the party to concern itself with working-class issues and to concentrate exclusively on the fight against capitalism.

3. A great deal was published on this subject during the late seventies ad early eighties. See, for instance, S. Carrillo, *Eurocomunismo y Estado*, Barcelona, Grijalbo, 1977; M. Azcárate, *Crisis del eurocomunismo*, Barcelona, Argos-Vergara, 1982; D. S. Bell, 'The Spanish Communist Party in the Transition', in D. S. Bell (ed.), Democratic *Politics in Spain*, London, F. Pinter, 1983, pp. 63–77.

4. A more objective assessment puts the figure around 175,000: J. Botella, 'Spanish Communism in Crisis', in M. Waller and M. Fennema (eds.), *Communist Parties in Western Europe*, Oxford, B. Blackwell, 1988, p. 80.

5. El País, 3 January 1985.

The antagonism and acrimonious confrontations which followed were to have disastrous consequences. Many members – some well-known figures among them – left the PCE, to join in many instances the ranks of the PSOE; a number of expulsions brought back memories of ruthless purges in the not very distant past; there were profound disagreements between the Madrid headquarters and Communist leaders in various regions, particularly those from Catalonia, the Basque Country and Asturias; some splinter groups of diverse Communist identity detached themselves from the main body of the party; and, as a final *coup de grâce*, a crisis at the highest level concluded with the self-exclusion (expulsion according to some) of Santiago Carrillo, PCE's General Secretary for more than twenty years.[6]

In 1985 Gregorio Morán, a former PCE member, published a long study of the party's history from the end of the Spanish Civil War to the present. His opening lines provide a suitable summary: 'When I started this history of the PCE I thought I would be testing the blood pressure of a seriously ill person. Now I realise it is something different, it is a postmortem examination'.[7] Although Gregorio Morán's words may read as over-dramatic hyperbole, they are certainly indicative of the depths of decay and disintegration the PCE had reached by the mid-eighties.

In Search of a Remedy

In years to come, when historians, with a wider perspective, try to assess the PCE's role during the post-Franco period, the figure of Gerardo Iglesias, Party Secretary from 1982 to 1988, is likely to be seen in a much more favourable light than it is today. Although his personal achievements were few and his popularity was never very high, he gave the party a much more open and receptive style of leadership than his predecessor, he struggled hard to bridge the deep divisions which had split the Spanish Communists into various factions, he unselfishly resigned his post when it became obvious that both the membership and the party apparatus wanted a new leader and, above all, he had the foresight to realise in the mid-eighties that traditional communism was reaching the end of its historical cycle and that the only way forward for the Left would be the creation of a new

6. On these various crises see P. Vega and P. Erroteta, *Los Herejes del PCE*, Barcelona, Planeta, 1982, and S. Vilar, *Por qué se ha destruido el PCE*, Barcelona, Plaza & Janés, 1985.

7. G. Morán, *Miseria y grandeza del Partido Comunista de España*, Barcelone, Planeta, 1985, p. 13.

coalition which would encompass other progressive forces side by side with the PCE. From this desire to find a new definition – wider, more open, and more flexible – of what the Left stood for, *Izquierda Unida* (United Left), IU, was born in the spring of 1986.

By 1986 Gorbachev had been in power for more than a year and *perestroika* was beginning to gather momentum in the Soviet Union. Its shock waves were being felt by all Communist Parties throughout the world, the PCE included, but it would be inaccurate to see the birth of IU as a direct result of it. It may have had some influence; the Soviet Union was still a point of reference for all Communist Parties. But relations between the CPSU and the PCE had been rather cool for a number of years and their contacts had been reduced to the occasional formal visit by PCE leaders to Moscow, or the presence of a Soviet delegation at the congresses of the Spanish party.

The rightward drift of the PSOE since its landslide victory in the general election of October 1982 had opened up an electoral gap to its left, providing space for a number of groups and factions of varied ideological hues, among them the PCE. Aware of their impotence to make inroads into the PSOE's hegemonic position individually, they opted for collaboration, pulling their electoral efforts together in a single coalition under the broad label of *Izquierda Unida*. What each member party was looking for in the new coalition is far from clear. There was probably a general desire to redefine the role and image of the Left. The smaller groups and parties in the coalition – and this applied to all of them save the PCE – were also hoping to find strength in the sum of their weaknesses. As for the PCE, as time would show, it was searching for a formula to arrest its rapid decline and it must have thought that IU would offer the much-needed remedy.

The creative impulse for IU was provided by the referendum held in March 1986 to ratify the question of Spain's membership of NATO. The PSOE, which had been against such membership in opposition, changed its mind once in government, and it used all the means at its disposal to encourage Spaniards to vote in favour of Spain staying in the alliance. On the other side, a wide spectrum of left-wing, progressive, and pacifist groups, among them the PCE, formed what they called a *Plataforma Cívica* in order to defend the international neutrality of Spain and advocate her withdrawal from NATO.[8] This proposal attracted considerable public support and, in the face of 'the government's contradictory, overwhelming and terrifying campaign,'[9]

8. On the question of Spain's membership of NATO see P. Preston and D. Smyth, *Spain, the EEC and NATO*, London, 1984; B. Pollack, *The Paradox of Spanish Foreign Policy*, London, F. Pinter 1987; F. Morán, *España en su sitio*, Barcelona, Plaza & Janés, 1990.

9. Thus described by the distinguished playwright Antonio Gala, president of the *Plataforma Cívica*, in 'Notas de un referéndum', *Anuario El País, 1987*, p. 65.

received more than seven million votes, which represented 39.85 per cent of the total cast. There was a considerable degree of success in this failure, and the main political forces involved in the *Plataforma Cívica* thought it might be turned into electoral capital. Five weeks after the referendum their leaders announced in Madrid the creation of a new coalition, under the name of *Izquierda Unida*, which would enter candidates in the general and Andalusian elections to be held in June 1986 and in the regional and municipal elections the following year.[10]

Yet from its inception IU was beset by problems of identity and organisation: how to blend its disparate components to offer the electorate a unified image; how to run and finance the coalition on a permanent basis; how to define the new left-wing ideology it was supposed to represent; and, above all, how to avoid the impression that it was little more than a disguise for the PCE. As we shall see later most of these problems remain unresolved.

Initially IU was nothing if not varied in its composition. As well as the PCE it included the *Federación Progresista* (Progressive Federation), led by the well-known economist and former PCE member, Ramón Tamames; the PASOC, *Partido de Acción Socialista* (Socialist Action Party), set up in 1983 by a number of PSOE dissidents; the pro-Soviet PCPE, *Partido Comunista de los Pueblos de España* (Communist Party of the Peoples of Spain), under the leadership of the veteran hard-liner Ignacio Gallego; three other minute parties – *Partido Carlista, Partido Humanista* and *Izquierda Republicana* – and a number of more or less prestigious figures who joined the coalition as independent members. This motley collection of political forces and individuals was variously and ironically described by its opponents as 'a gazpacho', 'a Russian salad' or 'a trade union of the resentful'.[11] With time its composition would alter. Some of the member parties – the *Federación Progresista* and the PCPE – would disappear; others – *Partido Calista* and *Partido Humanista* – realising the incongruity of their presence in a left-wing coalition, would abandon IU. What has remained constant to this day is the PCE's hegemonic position.

Electorally IU was not the success its founders had expected. The hurriedly patched-up coalition had to improvise a programme and to agree on the composition of its electoral lists in the two months which separated its foundation from the holding of a general election. Not surprisingly its offer to the electorate was extremely vague and incoherent, and, what made it worse for an organisation which held out

10. *El País*, 25 April 1986.

11. R. Gillespie, 'Izquierda Unida: The First Test', *Journal of Communist Studies*, vol. 2, no. 4, December 1986, p. 441.

the promise of a new Left, not sufficiently distinctive from that of the PSOE. The results showed an improvement in comparison with the PCE's performance in 1982, but they fell far short of the expectations raised by the NATO referendum. As an editorial in the Spanish daily *El País* indicated, 'nearly 6.9 million who said 'no' to NATO have denied their vote to IU'.[12] The root of the problem being, as the same editorial pointed out, that the PCE was trying to present a renovated and heterogeneous image through IU, whilst at the same time it was reverting to its old traditional ways to bring about unity in the divided Communist camp. In other words, the failure of IU was the PCE's failure. To emphasise the PCE's predominance in the new coalition, all seven IU's successful candidates were either PCE or ex-PCE members. The only real satisfaction for Gerardo Iglesias and his supporters must have been the failure of Santiago Carrillo and his curiously-named splinter group, *Unidad Comunista* (Communist Unity), to gain a single parliamentary seat.[13] IU fared better in the Andalusian election held at the same time as the general one, but here, as we shall indicate later, the charismatic figure of Julio Anguita at the head of its list of candidates had a considerable influence, particularly in the province of Córdoba, where the 'Red Caliph', as Anguita was called by his admirers, had been mayor of the provincial capital for several years.

Less than twelve months later, IU had to face its second test at three levels – local, regional and European elections were held simultaneously on 10 June 1987. This second test was to prove a second failure.[14] In the local elections IU gained some 370,000 more votes than in the previous general election, 'a sudden leap forward' in some journalistic estimation;[15] but a more meaningful comparison with the previous set of results at local level – those of May 1983 – showed a different picture: IU had fewer votes, fewer councillors, and controlled fewer municipal councils than the PCE on its own four years previously.[16] They almost lost control of 'the jewel in their electoral crown', the city of Córdoba, where their mayor found himself having to run the council with a minority government. Nor was there much sign of improvement in the regional elections. IU did not increase its

---

12. *El País*, 24 June 1986.

13. For an analysis of IU's performance in the 1986 elections see Gillespie. A broader view of the same election can be found in R. Robinson, 'From Change to Continuity: the 1986 Spanish Election', *West European Politics*, vol. 10, no. 1, January 1987, pp. 120–24.

14. See J. Amodia, 'Izquierda Unida: Second Test, Second Failure', *Journal of Communist Studies*, vol. 3, no. 4, December 1987, pp. 170–3.

15. *Cambio 16*, no. 812, 22 June 1987, p. 19.

16. On the 1983 local elections see J. Amodia, 'The Spanish Communist Party and Local Government: an Overall Assessment', in B. Szajkowski (ed.), *Marxist Local Governments in Western Europe and Japan*, London, F. Pinter, 1986, pp. 20–44.

overall number of deputies and found itself in the invidious position of having to lend its support to its Socialist rivals in order to stop the right-wing Popular Alliance gaining control of some regional governments. The picture was no better in the European elections, IU gaining only three of the sixty seats allocated to Spain in the Strasbourg parliament. It was becoming obvious that, in the short term at least, IU was not providing the remedies Spanish Communists were looking for. Their forthcoming party congress would have to confront this painful reality.

The PCE's Twelfth Congress

The party's congresses are rather irregular and infrequent. The Twelfth Congress held in Madrid between 19 and 21 February 1988, came more than four years after the previous one, which had met in December 1983. Spaced out so widely apart, their gatherings acquire particular significance. This was undoubtedly the case with the Twelfth Congress, which met at a time when the party's fortunes were almost at their nadir.

As explained earlier, *Izquierda Unida* coalition, of which so much had been expected, had not produced the hoped-for electoral improvements at any level. Under this new guise the PCE was not making substantial inroads into the Socialist hegemony, and Communists were still relegated to a secondary role in a party system dominated by two major forces, the PSOE and the conservative Popular Alliance – later renamed Popular Party. The Communist family was still divided into various factions unable or unwilling to patch up their differences. PCE's membership continued to fall.[17] while the financial situation reached crisis proportions, with debts of more than 1 billion pesetas – 1.6 billion if IU's electoral debts were included in the estimate.[18] It is hardly surprising that in such dramatic circumstances Gerardo Iglesias' leadership was called into question. In fact, the interest of the Congress delegates gathered in Madrid was almost completely absorbed by the leadership crisis.

Before discussing matters further, it might be worth restating that all the above issues and the concerns uppermost in delegates' minds appeared to have little to do with changes gathering pace in the Soviet Union. At most they were a distant echo. Some seventy foreign

17. By December 1987 it had been reduced to 62,342 members, according to official party figures published in *El País*, 19 February 1988.

18. *El País*, 20 February 1988.

delegations attended the Congress, among them three CPSU representatives,[19] but they were the silent guests at a Spanish ceremony. Suffice it to say that in the eighty-page summary of Congress speeches, debates and documents the Soviet Union is mentioned just three times and only tangentially.[20]

Leadership contests make good headlines. Reading the Spanish press of the time one is struck by the great attention paid to the question of who would be the new party leader. Gerardo Iglesias, aware of his loss of support, was willing to relinquish the post. In spite of his well-intentioned plans and proposals, his tangible achievements had been few; the party had made little progress in the previous six years under him. Moreover, he had not proved to be an effective electoral campaigner, nor a convincing parliamentarian. His replacement was inevitable, though finding a substitute was to prove far from easy, at least to begin with. Contrary to the norm in such cases, none of the more obvious candidates showed much willingness to take over from Gerardo Iglesias. The task of reviving the party was too daunting. Even Julio Anguita, the most widely-supported choice, was categorically stating, only hours before he was elected, his refusal to become General Secretary,[21] changing his mind only when he was able to extract from Congress a number of concessions and a central committee to his liking.

Anguita's election came as no surprise and was undoubtedly well received throughout the party. He had acquired considerable prestige as mayor of the beautiful Andalusian city of Córdoba – the first and only Communist mayor of a provincial capital – and had for some time been seen as man destined for higher things inside the party.[22] More recently he had headed IU's list in the Andalusian elections, markedly increasing its share of the vote. His reputation on taking on the mantle of party leader was that of a successful politician, a man with a charismatic image and a somewhat didactic and populist style.[23] Julio Anguita, who had always objected to any messianic view of his achievements, suddenly found himself cast in the role of party saviour, and in the end he accepted the challenge with gusto.

19. As reported in *El País*, 21 February 1988.

20. Partido Comunista de España, *El socialismo, una Búsqueda permanente*, Madrid, PCE, 1990, pp. 5–80.

21. The names most often mentioned as candidates, apart from J. Anguita's, were Francisco Frutos, a hard-liner in charge of socio-economic affairs in the PCE, and Nicolás Sartorius, Deputy General Secretary, ideologically on the more liberal wing of the party.

22. On his period as mayor of Córdoba see J. Anguita, *Textos y discursos (1979–1982)*, Córdoba, 1983.

23. A detailed and undoubtedly favourable study of Julio Anguita can be seen in J. L. Casas, *El último califa*, Madrid, Ediciónes Temas de Hoy, 1990.

Leadership apart, the Congress had to deal with two other important issues: a definition of policy aims upon which to base their programme for the forthcoming election, and the increasingly difficult question of the PCE's attitude to and relations with IU. The programme approved by the Congress was wide ranging but short in clearly-defined policies; many of them were couched in the political rhetoric of a party that knows it will not be confronted with the responsibility of having to implement such policies. Emptied of rhetoric there is little that can be called Marxist in the programme. There is no utopian 'Communist paradise' in the horizon, nor maximalist proposals of any kind. The mixed economy is accepted, albeit with a certain reluctance and with the emphasis very much on socio-economic planning and on the leading role of public capital. The most radical proposal in this area is the possible nationalisation of private banks. A similar attitude is taken towards the EC. The PCE proclaims its commitment to Europe, to the point of accepting greater political integration, but stressing too the need for a European social dimension and the reduction of regional imbalances within the Community.

The most radical part of the programme is the one dealing with institutional changes in Spain. The PCE is in favour of a federal state, which would comprise the right to self-determination and, in the long run, constitutional reform to take account of such changes. It favours too a political solution for the nationalist question in the Basque Country, including, if conditions permit, negotiations with the terrorist group ETA. The programme suggests electoral reforms to make the proportional system more representative. It advocates the introduction of public juries as part of a major overhaul of the judicial system, and also the demilitarisation of the Civil Guard. In the field of international politics the USA continues to be the PCE's *bête noire*. Peremptory demands are made for the cancellation of the bilateral agreements with the Americans, for the dismantling of their bases and the removal of all nuclear weapons from Spanish soil, and for the immediate withdrawal of Spain from NATO's military structure. References are made to various points of high international tension – Nicaragua, the Middle East, South Africa, etc. – but, surprising though it may seem, no mention is made of the changes in the Soviet Union and its satellite countries.

To conclude this summary,[24] the programme also includes a number of ecological, feminist and pacifist proposals, very much in line with the concerns and aims of the groups the PCE was hoping to draw into the IU coalition. In fact, IU was the third major topic discussed by the

24. This summary of the programme approved by the Twelfth Congress has been extracted from *El socialismo, una búsqueda permanente*, pp. 14-43.

delegates. Not, strictly speaking, IU as it them was, but the search for something similar though better: a great left-wing alliance, a new *Izquierda transformadora* (literally, a transforming Left) – the expression was repeatedly used during the Congress – which would converge round the values and goals contained in the programme summarised above. Until then IU had not brought about the expected upturn in the party's fortunes. It had been rashly conceived, many delegates thought, hence all the initial mistakes and disappointments. It had to be opened up to embrace a much wider concept of the Left. It might even have to include the PSOE, though it would obviously have to be 'a PSOE with different policies and a differently oriented leadership'.[25] What the Congress did not face up to was how to fit into this new model of *Izquierda transformadora* into its own party, a party which, though ideologically and financially in ruins, still considered itself 'the only revolutionary agent in Spanish society', a party which was loath to renounce its past as the following words make abundantly clear:

> we define ourselves as the vanguard of the working class and all progressive forces among the peoples of Spain, our objectives being the development of democracy, the Socialist transformation of Spanish society in order to arrive at Communism, and the struggle for peace and socialism in Spain and the world . . . The PCE is based on revolutionary Marxism and takes its inspiration from the Socialist revolution started with the October Revolution led by Lenin, and from all liberation and working-class movements.[26]

Julio Anguita: Saviour or Undertaker?

In 1991 Julio Anguita had been PCE leader for more than three and a half years. Looking back to the last party Congress, when he was elected General Secretary, it is not possible to ascertain whether, at that moment, the delegates saw in him a kind of witch doctor who would resuscitate the almost moribund party, or, with greater sense of realism, a skilful mortician whose task would be to inter the PCE's name and history in the fresher ground of IU in the hope that they might bear new fruit. Whatever the party Congress's intentions, Anguita saw himself in the former role from the moment of his appointment. His has been a deft balancing act. He has been quite happy to maintain and develop IU

25. Ibid., p. 44.
26. Ibid., p. 57.

as a programmatic and electoral vehicle, but, at the same time, his main efforts have concentrated on finding ways and means of guaranteeing the survival of the PCE. In his frequent appearances in the media, in his public lectures and political speeches, or when he addresses both the PCE's central committee and IU's federal assembly, his message is always the same: the PCE cannot and should not disappear.

Initially Anguita saw the salvation for the PCE in a return to more traditionally dogmatic positions, to the left of Gorbachev's *perestroika*. His interpretation of the Soviet leader's views underlines this point: 'I have read Gorbachev in depth, not just his best-seller book but his reports, and what I find in them is a return to pure Leninism, with democracy, debate and discussion. Pure Leninism and Marxism'.[27] And this was the direction in which Anguita tried to push the PCE in the initial stages of his leadership. His early radicalism was to include a Leninist view of the party, a revival of the Communist International, the use of extraparliamentary means such as political strikes, the total rejection of any form of collaboration with the ruling PSOE and even utopian pronouncements in favour of federal republicanism. Altogether Anguita was placing himself much closer to the unyielding positions of A. Cunhal in Portugal or G. Marchais in France, than to the more flexible and pragmatic attitude of A. Occhetto and the PCI.

The repercussions of Anguita's early extremism were surprisingly not all negative. It did frighten away some of the members who were hoping to see the party evolve towards some flexible form of democratic socialism, along the lines of the PCI; notably among them Enrique Curiel, former party Vice-Secretary, whose desertion in any case had been expected for some time. On the other hand, the PCE was able to exploit and, in the short term, benefit from the success of the general strike organised jointly by the Communist-controlled union *Comisiones Obreras* (Workers' Commissions) and the socialist *Unión General de Trabajadores* (General Union of Workers) on 14 December 1988.[28] It made possible too the return to the PCE of one of the groups which had left it in the aftermath of the Eurocommunist débâcle. It was Ignacio Gallego's *Partido Comunista de los Pueblos de España*. Gallego and his followers had abandoned the PCE in 1983 in order to defend what they considered to be the Marxist-Leninist inheritance of Spanish Communism, but in January 1989 were able to return, convinced that the party had regained its ideological purity.[29] So much

27. Interview in *El Independiente*, 26 March 1988.

28. For a broad discussion of this strike and its aftermath see S. Juliá (ed.), *La desavenencia Partidos sindicatos y huelga general*, Madrid, Aguilar, 1989.

29. The documents on the fusion of PCE and PCPE can be found in *El socialismo, una búsqueda permanente*, pp. 329–37.

so that a paper warned that unity had been gained at the cost of turning the PCE into a bolshevik-type party.[30] Communist harmony had thus been restored under Anguita's leadership, though at a price. The only group outside the PCE was the small faction surrounding Santiago Carrillo; but he was already drifting towards the PSOE, and totally unwilling to accept any compromise including IU.

Anguita's left-wing fervour and some of his over-the-top pronouncements during his first few months at the helm can be partly put down to his lack of experience on the wider stage of national politics. Such signs of immaturity provided ammunition for his political opponents, and even the more progressive press were soon advising him in admonitory terms to display greater calm and wisdom.[31] After all, pushing the PCE counter to the changes in the Soviet Union and in the Communist movement as a whole was hardly compatible with his avowed commitment to IU, a coalition comprising many political figures and groups of much more moderate views.

IU's First National Congress, held in Madrid in February 1989, chose Julio Anguita almost unanimously – there was just one vote against – as its leader and presidential candidate for the forthcoming elections. In his acceptance speech his enthusiasm ran away with him once again. He confessed with candour that he could already see himself as prime minister, and promised that IU would offer not just an alternative government, but an alternative state and an alternative society. There was no clear Marxist message because his audience was not exclusively Communist, but he rejected any form of agreement with the Socialist government on account of its right-wing values and policies. He even threatened the PSOE with another general strike if the government continued to drift towards the Right after the next general election.[32]

Time and experience have softened Anguita's discourse and style. He has not, however, renounced his Marxist convictions, nor, to this day, has he shown any inclination to consider the possible disappearance or transformation of the PCE. He prefers a double-fronted approach: PCE and IU side by side. And the results in the most recent general election have offered him some grounds to adhere to his position. Communist support or, more exactly, IU support – for the word 'Communist' was never mentioned in the coalition's manifesto –

30. *El Independiente*, 4–10 November 1988.

31. See for instance the ironic editorial entitled 'La inmadurez de Anguita' in *El Independiente*, 30 September 1988.

32. Extracted for J. Anguita's address to IU's First Federal Assembly, on 12 February 1989, reproduced in *El socialismo, una búsqueda permanente*, pp. 361–74. See also *El País*, 13 February 1989.

experienced a noticeable increase. IU's programme, though far from extremist, was the only left-wing one on offer to the electorate. As the slogan of its title indicated it was the only genuine alternative to all the other major parties.[33] There was some truth in this claim. The neo-liberal policies the Socialist government had been pursuing since 1982 had opened up an ideological space on its left which was to prove beneficial to IU. In the most recent parliamentary elections, October 1989, IU doubled its share of the vote and its number of deputies rose from seven to seventeen.[34]

However, with a wider electoral perspective the picture is different. If we consider all IU's results from its inception in the spring of 1986 to the present, we can see that the size of its support has fluctuated between 4.6 per cent and 9.1 per cent, well below the level reached by the PCE on its own in the late seventies. The high hopes that many had placed on IU as an original left-wing alternative and as a lifesaver for the PCE have not found a parallel enthusiasm among the electorate. Even Andalusia, a region with strong left-wing leanings and Julio Anguita's native land, has recently shown its disenchantment with IU. In the Andalusian elections of June 1986 IU, led by Anguita himself, obtained some surprisingly good results: 17.43 per cent of the vote and nineteen seats in the 109-strong parliament – one of the best ever Communist results in a Spanish election. Yet four years later, in June 1990, IU lost 42 per cent of the votes it had gained in 1986 and its representation in the Andalusian parliament was reduced to eleven seats.

Contrary to Anguita's claims IU has not helped to stop the decline of the PCE. Nor has it been able to acquire its own position, independent from that of the PCE, within the party system. The reasons for its limited success are many and varied. Some are rooted in the complexities of Spanish transitional politics, in particular, of course, the PCE's agitated life during the post-Franco years; others are linked to the crisis of international Communism and of the parties representing this ideology in the Western world. Amongst them all one stands out as the most relevant and influential: the lack of identity and definition of IU as a political project. As indicated earlier, its original impulse came from the PCE. The party leadership saw in the mass protests against Spain's membership of NATO in 1986 an excellent opportunity to lift the flagging spirits of the Left. What started as an electoral coalition at the time of the NATO referendum was later

33. The slogan used was *Somos la alternativa* (We are the alternative).

34. On the most recent general election in Spain see J. Amodia, 'Personalities and Slogans: the Spanish Election of October 1989', *West European Politics*, vol. 13, no. 2, April 1990, pp. 293–8.

upgraded to become a social and political movement[35] based, as Anguita tells us, on a flexible structure, on a collective elaboration of joint programmes, on shared responsibility and on a synthesis of the Socialist, Communist and other groups in it.[36] But this community of purpose and effort stops short of fusion into a single political organisation. Any move in this direction has been stubbornly resisted by the PCE leadership. In Anguita's own words: 'IU is plural and it must continue to be plural for the foreseeable future. If we were to dilute the PCE into IU, by transforming the latter into a political party, we would not have achieved anything; we would have to start all over again.'[37] Or, to quote another Communist voice, that of Antonio Pérez, member of the PCE's secretariat: 'for us IU is not a project devised by the PCE, but the organised political expression of a left-wing project in which the PCE takes part . . . The PCE is not then IU's executive body, only one of the groups fostering its development.'[38]

Such is the view from inside the PCE. From a distance the plurality, flexibility and autonomy attributed to IU are overshadowed by the dominating influence of the PCE. Its political opponents often refer to IU as the old Communist wolf under different attire. As things stand IU can only be seen as an extension of the PCE. PASOC and *Izquierda Republicana*, the only other parties in IU, are minuscule organisations, whose small membership hardly extends beyond the confines of Madrid.[39] The rest are independent members whose weight and influence are exclusively determined by the degree of personal prestige attaching to each individual.

The PCE has considerably more members that all the other groups in IU put together. Although in obvious decline the PCE is IU's mainstay. Its financial support, its regular publications and its nationwide structure make IU viable. Aware of this high degree of dependency IU has taken some compensatory measures – establishing a corporate presidency, downgrading the title of its leader to that of co-ordinator, and reducing to a maximum 25 per cent the representation of any group or party in IU's official bodies and committees. But in

35. It was IU's Second Federal Assembly, in November 1990, that decided to change the nature of the coalition.

36. J. Anguita, 'Izquierda Unida. La apuesta de los comunistas españoles', *Nuestra Bandera*, no. 145, 2nd Term, 1990, pp. 4–13. Text of a lecture at Deusto University (Bilbao) on 20 February 1990.

37. Ibid., p. 12.

38. A. Pérez, 'Reflexiones sobre Izquierda Unida', *Nuestra Bandera*, no. 146, 3rd Term, 1990, p. 23.

39. F. Jacobs, *Western European Political Parties*, London, Longman, 1989 gives an official membership for PASOC and Republican Left of 10,000 and 1,000/1,500 respectively, though I am inclined to think these figures inflated.

practice such steps can do little to reduce the PCE's predominance. To give but one example, the federal structure adopted by IU makes it inevitable that its electoral lists be dominated at all levels by PCE members, because the PCE is the only party inside the coalition able to offer candidates in sufficient numbers throughout the country. The face of IU is the face of Julio Anguita, its national co-ordinator. This is the way it is perceived and interpreted by the electorate. Herein lies the problem. Can IU take off as an independent political organisation as long as it remains dependent for its survival on the declining fortunes of the PCE?

The End Might Be Nigh

The demolition of the Berlin Wall, the collapse of the old Communist regimes of Eastern Europe, the change of name and identity of the Italian Communist Party and, above all, the 'August coup' in the Soviet Union have added tremors to the already shaky foundations of the PCE, though the official party line has been to pretend that all those momentous events have little to do with the state of Communism in Spain, because, they claim, the PCE had for years been moving ahead of the CPSU. Just a few days before the 19 August coup in the Soviet Union, Julio Anguita stated publicly: 'the PCE has nothing to learn from what is happening in the USSR; if anything, Gorbachev should learn from us'.[40]

Relations between the PCE and the CPSU had been less than cordial for some years, and Gorbachev has done little to improve them. When the Soviet leader paid an official visit to Spain in October 1990, he showed scant interest in either the PCE or IU. The real purpose of his trip to Madrid was to obtain financial aid from the Socialist government of Felipe González and some support from Spanish industrialists. Some newspapers in Madrid summed up the situation with the ironic words of an unnamed diplomat: 'Gorbachev is more interested in talking to Cuevas (Director of the Spanish Confederation of Business Organisations) than to Anguita.'[41] In the event, Gorbachev did have a brief meeting with Julio Anguita and cancelled his official engagement with Sr. Cuevas, but by then he had already obtained a $1,500m loan – the purpose of his mission had been accomplished. His meeting with Anguita was a mere formality. In his public pronouncements while in Spain he did not make any reference to the

40. Interview in *Tribuna*, 12 August 1991, p. 25.
41. *El País*, 26 October 1990.

PCE; in fact, the word 'communism' was never mentioned, Gorbachev preferring to declare himself, in line with his host Felipe González, a Socialist.[42]

The PCE's reaction towards the recent metamorphosis of the Italian Communist Party follows a similar pattern. The Italian changes are seen as erroneous and shortsighted. In his capacity as IU's national co-ordinator, Julio Anguita sent a telegram of congratulations to A. Occhetto when the latter was elected General Secretary of the newly-named PDS in Rimini in February 1991. The text of the telegram was reproduced on the pages of *Mundo Obrero*, PCE's official weekly,[43] but next to it *Mundo Obrero* inserted an article by Gregorio López Raimundo, former leader of the PSUC – the autonomous Catalan branch of the PCE – lamenting the decision taken by the Italian Communists. In his view all the PCI had achieved at its Rimini congress had been a change of name, claiming that 'in composition the new PDS is not significantly different from the old PCI'. This is no way to arrive at a new Left, he reasoned. What the Left needs is not a new party – 'parties are condemned to being propped up or replaced by other organisations more in keeping with the times' – but a political framework which, being wider and more flexible, will encompass a whole range of progressive groups and movements, the Communist parties included.[44] There is an obvious contradiction in opposing the creation or transformation of a party, on the basis that parties are outmoded, whilst at the same time obdurately opposing any suggestion to dissolve the PCE. Contradictions apart, the majority of the PCE leaders still see the Italian case as an example not to be followed. In an obvious reference to it Julio Anguita told the party's central committee in July 1991: 'there are certain features in the reality of other countries which offer resounding examples of how things should not be done'.[45]

However, during the last months of 1991, in the wake of the shattering news from the Soviet Union, even committed and lifelong Communists began to hesitate and ask questions about the party's future. Santiago Carrillo's reaction was perhaps predictable. His small party, *Partido del Trabajo de España* (Spanish Labour Party) had already made overtures to the PSOE in February 1991,[46] and finally joined it in October.[47] In his view 'the Communist movement as such

42. As reported in *El País*, 27 October 1990.

43. *Mundo Obrero*, no. 619, 6-12 March 1991, p. 8.

44. G. López Raimundo, 'La meta de Occhetto', *Mundo Obrero*, no. 619, 6–12 March 1991, pp. 7-8.

45. In Andalusian daily *Córdoba*, 29 July 1991.

46. Initially they joined the PSOE as a 'current of opinion', *El País*, 16 February 1991.

47. Report in *El País*, 27 October 1991.

has completed its historical cycle and it makes no sense trying to prolong it';[48] hence his sarcastic verdict: 'the Spanish Communist Party is a corpse and the only thing that remains to be decided is whether to bury it or to embalm it'.[49] Voices from inside the party are having a greater impact. In August, Antonio Gutiérrez, General Secretary of the Workers' Commissions and member of the PCE's Central Committee, expressed the view that all Communists bear some responsibility for supporting and defending in the past Marxist dictatorships in the Soviet Union and satellite countries, and he went on to demand the dissolution of the PCE in order to allow IU room to grow and develop.[50] At about the same time Nicolás Sartorius, IU's official parliamentary spokesman and one of the leading figures in the PCE, declared in the Spanish press his determination to leave the party if, after its next congress, it does not allow IU to become a fully-fledged political party.[51] Even the usually reticent Gerardo Iglesias felt the need to break a long period of silence to express similar demands, to stop, as he put it, 'the PCE swallowing up IU'.[52]

These were not, however, the predominant opinions in the party's Central Committee; not then, anyhow. At an emotional meeting at the beginning of October the majority of its members were adamantly in favour of maintaining the PCE alive, though they did accept, as a compromise with the minority, the need to reinforce IU by giving it full powers. But they stopped short of converting into a fully independent political party, because this would have eventually meant the disappearance of the PCE.[53] The decision taken by the Central Committee was in line with the desires of the rank and file in the party too. Earlier the membership had been consulted on a number of issues, and the results of the poll showed a considerable support for the continuation of the party, side by side with a strengthened IU.[54] This view, curiously enough, appeared to be shared by a sizeable number of Spaniards. In a poll conducted for *El País* newspaper at the beginning of October 1991, 44 per cent of those questioned expressed the view that the PCE should continue to exist, as against 35 per cent in favour of its dissolution, the rest being 'don't knows'.[55]

48. S. Carrillo, '¿Qué hacer?', *Cambio 16*, no. 1034, 16 September 1991, p. 119.
49. *Guardian*, 30 August 1991.
50. Opinions expressed during the course of a lecture at a summer course in El Escorial, reported in *A B C*, 31 August 1991.
51. Interview in *El País*, 30 August 1991.
52. In Oviedo's daily *La Voz de Asturias*, 6 September 1991.
53. Report on central committee's meeting in *El País*, 6 October 1991.
54. Results of poll summarised in *Mundo Obrero*, no. 633, 19–25 June 1991, pp. 14–16.
55. Full analysis of poll in *El País*, 6 October 1991.

Against this background of wishful resolutions taken by its leaders and of nostalgic hopes expressed by its dwindling membership, the PCE appears to be fighting a losing battle. Throughout this chapter we have argued that the party has for some years been showing all the symptoms of a terminal disease. The most recent reports on its deteriorating state do not augur any better. Financial problems have forced it to move its Madrid headquarters to a much more modest building away from the city centre; its glossy weekly magazine, *Mundo Obrero*, with a fast dwindling readership, was in September 1991 downgraded to a monthly newspaper; membership sank to its lowest level since the party was legalised in 1977: 55,000 members is the latest figure officially acknowledged.[56] The signs are all ominous. The delegates who will be attending the next party congress need not be superstitious to read into its number – it will be the PCE's thirteenth congress – the presage of an imminent end for Spanish Communism.

56. Figure obtained by the author from the party's headquarters in Madrid at the end of October 1991.

Endgame: The Communist Party of Great Britain

John Callaghan

The Communist Party of Great Britain (CPGB) has been shrinking in membership since 1964, when it could claim 34,281 activists, but its real crisis of identity can be traced to the revival of radical leftism for which the year 1968 has become emblematic. The Gorbachev phenomenon and the collapse of the Eastern bloc merely sealed its fate.

In Britain, as elsewhere, the certitudes of Marxism-Leninism were progressively corroded from within. The flowering of Marxist thought in the universities and the concurrent upsurge of radicalism among students, feminists and a variety of other activists resulted in priorities which could not be contained within the traditional categories of Marxism-Leninism. Of course faith in Soviet socialism had been in decline for many years prior to this ferment on the Left and received another blow, in 1968, with the Russian invasion of Czechoslovakia – which the CPGB duly denounced. But it was the growth in number and variety of left-wing constituencies which appeared in the late 1960s, combined with a rapid increase in the range of critical, often contradictory Marxisms, which pushed the party membership apart and fuelled the growth of factionalism.

By the mid-1970s the divisions within the party had become conspicuous. Party intellectuals were publicly questioning the organisation's habitual support for militant trade unionism by pointing to the lack of any correspondence between wage struggles and a developing Socialist political consciousness and arguing that the party's accustomed oppositional stance was correspondingly deficient in strategic terms (and, in the context, inflationary).[1] The twentieth anniversary of Khruschev's secret speech denouncing Stalin was celebrated with a debate on 'problems of socialist democracy' in the pages of the party's theoretical journal, *Marxism Today*, but only

---

1. D. Purdy, 'British Capitalism Since the War', *Marxism Today*, October 1976.

succeeded in demonstrating the depth of disagreement on this crucial issue within the membership.[2] After a year of controversy on Stalinism the Party turned to the question of modernising its programme; and so the period of acrimonious introspection was extended up to the thirty-fifth congress of November 1977. Along the way the leadership of the Surrey District of the party engineered a split and announced the creation of the New Communist Party (NCP), claiming sixty-five branches, but in fact taking just 2 per cent of the 25,300 membership. The departure of the pro-Moscow NCP in July 1977 did not mean, thus, that the opponents of revisionism within the CPGB had been seriously weakened numerically – though there can be no doubt that they had lost the intellectual initiative.

In 1978 on the eve of the first Thatcher government the division of party opinion on these issues was given focus when a party intellectual, Hobsbawm, pointed to a long-term decline in the Labour vote since its high point in 1951, to the growth in sectionalism within the working class and to the inability of trade unionism to spread much beyond its immediate post-war share of the British work-force. He argued that the upsurge in trade union militancy since the 1960s had been mostly confined to wage demands and a source of division rather than solidarity within the working class.[3] These arguments found favour with the wing of the party inspired by Gramsci, which was already inclined to stress a hegemonic project which, unlike economistic Marxism, recognised the importance of the cultural struggle.[4]

Until 1979 the Labour Left, with which the Communists had long sought a working relationship as a basic precondition for establishing the anti-monopoly alliance, was actually on the upgrade. Disappointment and disillusion with the Labour governments of 1964 – 70 and 1974–9, combined with the intellectual discrediting of the party's Centre-Right, produced a powerful movement for Socialist advance within the membership and the affiliated trade unions. This movement climaxed in the early 1980s with internal constitutional reforms – which apparently strengthened the mass organisations at the expense of the parliamentary party – and with the adoption of the most radical programme ever associated with Labour. But just as this programme was finally adopted by Labour the reform-minded wing of the CPGB was increasing its criticisms of the inflationary and statist implications of the programme's proposals for a major increase in public expenditure and nationalisation. Thus at the very time when the

---

2. *Discussion of Socialist Democracy*, CPGB, 1976).

3. E.J. Hobsbawm, 'The Forward March of Labour Halted', *Marxism Today*, September 1978.

4. S. Hall, 'The Great Moving Right Show', *Marxism Today*, January 1979.

Communist revisionists pointed to weaknesses in many aspects of the Left's case, most Socialists in Britain believed that it had never been stronger. Only after Labour was subjected to a crushing defeat in the general election of 1983 did the balance of opinion shift towards the rethinking inaugurated by the CPGB's theoretical journal *Marxism Today*. It then became commonplace to talk of a general realignment on the British Left, which placed the revisionist Communists alongside the new Labour leadership of Neil Kinnock while so-called 'fundamentalists' in both parties resisted the retreat from Socialist principles.

In summary we conclude that well before the advent of Gorbachev the CPGB – an organisation in seemingly irreversible decline – was very far removed from the disciplined, ideologically homogeneous organisation which had survived up to 1956. Indeed it was now plagued by an open factionalism conducted through the party's official publications as well as in a plethora of faction-sheets such as *Straight Left* and *The Leninist*, which proffered a variety of explanations of the party's current malaise. By 1982 ideological conflict within the organisation boiled over into a public row between the editors of the Party's daily newspaper, the *Morning Star*, and the revisionists in control of *Marxism Today*.[5] This rupture culminated in scores of expulsions and the eventual formation of the Communist Party of Britain (CPB) in 1987 and pointed to a broad-based disagreement along the fault-lines discussed above. The theoretical activists, led by Martin Jacques, the editor of *Marxism Today*, had succeeded (as far as the CPB opposition was concerned) in questioning and undermining just about every aspect of the Communist legacy by the mid eighties!

We have seen that the revisionist criticisms of 'real existing socialism' were initially elaborated in relation to the defects of Marxist-Leninist theory and its 'economistic' and authoritarian sins in particular. Their emphasis on the cultural and political fields of contestation evolved into a critique of the party's, as well as the Labour movement's, traditional policies – from statist conceptions of socialism to assumptions about class as a sufficient axis of social conflict and transformation. From 1977, when the *British Road to Socialism* was modernised around the strategy of creating a broad democratic – instead of an anti-monopoly – alliance, these theoretical developments led to a rediscovery of democracy and political pluralism and a corresponding critique of the authoritarian elements in the Leninist

5. See J. Callaghan, 'The Long Drift of the CPGB', *Journal of Communist Studies*, vol. 1, no. 3/4, September–December 1985, pp. 171–4; and J. Callaghan, 'Further Splits in the Marxist Left in Britain', *Journal of Communist Studies*, vol. 4, no. 1, March 1988, pp. 101–4.

legacy.[6] Those in the party who resisted were eventually forced out to form the Communist Party of Britain (claiming 1,500 members in April 1988). A much smaller group around *The Leninist* added to the confusion by announcing that it was the 'real' Communist Party of Great Britain although it traced the rot in the Communist movement back to the policies of 'Comrade Stalin'.

The real problem for all of these contending factions was the fact that in the ten years before the advent of Gorbachev the British party had lost its base in heavy industry largely as a consequence of the rapid decay of these sectors of the British economy. The fact that the lost cohorts were not replaced by new recruits from either the 'new social movements' or from more dynamic parts of the economy already suggested that the party was becoming an anachronism; Left-oriented militants were turning elsewhere. Thus, whereas the party had been able, as late as the mid-1970s, to provide a focus of opposition and a more or less coherent alternative line which organised a sizeable trade union Left at the annual Trade Union Congress, by the mid-1980s it had no influence at all at the TUC.

Monitoring the Progress of *Glasnost*

With the forced removal of their critics in the period between January 1985 and the end of 1986, the process of rethinking Socialist theory and Left politics begun by *Marxism Today* was accelerated inside the CPGB. The advent of Gorbachev undoubtedly helped this along, as did the fact that the party's shrinking forces – down to 11,000 members by 1987 – could claim only one success story: the rising circulation and intellectual influence of *Marxism Today*, which had reached monthly sales of 15,400 by October 1986.[7] But until Gorbachev even *Marxism Today* had had little to say about the Soviet Union.

It is true that the CPGB condemned the invasions of Czechoslovakia and Afghanistan, but there was no party position on the nature of the USSR beyond the accustomed acceptance of its Socialist credentials. The debate on Socialist democracy opened by John Gollan, the retiring General Secretary, in 1976 elicited every conceivable response from the membership – from those who traced the revolution's degeneration back to Lenin's time to those who wondered what all the fuss was

6. See, for example, A. Hunt (ed.), *Marxism Democracy*, London, Lawrence and Wishart, 1978.

7. *Report of the Executive Committee August 1983 – July 1987*, London, CPGB, 1987.

about.[8] Gollan himself suggested that the defeat of Nazi Germany proved that 'the basic Socialist foundations of the Soviet Union were unshaken despite the crimes in the period of Stalin's leadership'.[9] Even a leading revisionist, in a party pamphlet criticising the theory of state capitalism, was able to argue that 'there is a fundamental continuity between the achievements and conquests which issued from the October Revolution and the social role of the USSR's present leaders'.[10] But if the party failed collectively to systematically reassess the nature of the USSR, all the elements of such a critique were acknowledged separately by party members.

Thus on the eve of Gorbachev's elevation to the General Secretaryship, a leading member of the CPGB writing in *Marxism Today* observed that in spite of a decade of capitalist crisis 'the attractive power of the Socialist countries has diminished. Every socialist in Britain who is not completely isolated or blinkered knows this from his or her own experience'.[11] The detention of dissidents in psychiatric hospitals, the invasions of Czechoslovakia and Afghanistan, martial law in Poland – these had all taken their toll. And within the Socialist bloc 'growing signs of apathy, malaise and dissatisfaction' had given the lie to the alleged superiority of the command economies. It was thus possible to conclude that the sources of these problems 'are structural rather than conjunctural and arise from an authoritarian and bureaucratic form of socialism whose roots lie in the Stalin period'.[12] All attempts at reform had failed, according to Monty Johnstone, because they had left this bureaucratic authoritarianism untouched and the leadership of Chernenko offered nothing new.

Yet in Johnstone's analysis these authoritarian features of the political system had to go if economic reforms were to stand any chance of success. Economic rejuvenation was blocked by the combination of bureaucratic vested interests and the monopoly position of the CPSU.[13] Johnstone was pessimistic: 'What is certain', he argued, is that after Chernenko 'the greatest care will be taken by the Politburo to exclude anyone who might turn out to have the makings of a Khruschev, not to speak of a Dubček'. Gorbachev, on this reading, was therefore 'the best that realistically can be hoped for'. Economic

8. See *Discussion of Socialist Democracy*, London, CPGB, 1976.

9. J. Gollan, 'Socialist Democracy – Some Problems: the Twentieth Congress of the CPSU in Retrospect', *Marxism Today*, January 1976.

10. D. Purdy, *The Soviet Union: State Capitalist or Socialist?*, London, CPGB, 1976.

11. M. Johnstone, 'Back in the USSR: The Past Catches Up', *Marxism Today*, March 1985.

12. Ibid., p. 12.

13. Ibid., p. 17.

modernisation, 'no doubt with technocratic features', would then be on the agenda. According to Johnstone the reason why this was the best that analysis could suggest was because there were no forces capable of taking the initiative in carrying through a Dubček-style 'genuine socialist democratisation'.[14]

A month after this article was published Gorbachev was already in place as General Secretary of the CPSU and it was possigble for Johnstone to predict 'a period of important developments at home and abroad' including facing up to the USSR's 'structural problems', liberalisation of the media and movement on the arms race, Afghanistan and Soviet relations with China.[15] Nevertheless Johnstone and *Marxism Today* were attacked for their 'anti-Soviet' views by Alexey Pkozlov, a member of the CPSU who, distressed by Johnstone's analysis of the USSR's problems, confessed that he was not surprised by the appearance of this 'malicious falsification' considering 'your journal's generally unfriendly attitude to our Party and to Soviet society'.[16] *Marxism Today* itself had nothing to say on this issue until another year had elapsed.

Following the Twenty-Seventh Congress of the CPSU (February-March 1986), Monty Johnstone predicted that Gorbachev would go further down the road of reform than those who elected him ever imagined; he also perceived that the Soviet peace proposals were more serious and the steps towards a more open media more significant than fellow contributors to *Marxism Today* were prepared to concede.[17] Yet it was left to Labour's shadow Foreign Secretary, Denis Healey, to stress the doctrinal significance of Gorbachev's speech to the Twenty-Seventh Congress, which dropped the two-camp doctrine in favour of a vision of an integral world emerging from increasing national interdependence.[18] After the Reykjavik Summit, where the USSR proposed 50 per cent reductions in strategic nuclear weapons to be followed by total elimination of medium-range missiles in Europe, Healey again appeared in the pages of *Marxism Today* to declare that 'nothing will ever be the same again' and that both Soviet-American and US-European relations would be fundamentally' changed.[19] This estimate was typical of the euphoria surrounding Gorbachev's initiatives at this time, as was – at least on the Left – Healey's depiction of the Americans as the main obstacle to progress.

14. Ibid., p. 17.
15. M. Johnstone, 'Gorbachev Ushers in a New Period', *Marxism Today*, April 1985.
16. A. Pkozlov, 'Viewpoint', *Marxism Today*, May 1985.
17. M. Johnstone, W. Brus and D. Lane, 'Will Gorbachev Shake the World?', *Marxism Today*, April 1986.
18. Ibid.
19. D. Healey, 'Life After Reykjavik', *Marxism Today*, December 1986.

Throughout 1987 *glasnost* was the main focus of *Marxism Today's* Soviet analysis in accordance with the settled conviction that democratisation was the 'precondition for real economic changes'; the argument that real economic improvements might be the precondition for maintaining *glasnost* would come later. The absence of democracy in the factories and the continued monopoly position of the CPSU was noted disapprovingly by CPGB executive member Monty Johnstone, as was the failure to produce a more objective appraisal of the Stalin period and the lack of evidence that Green and feminist issues were coming to the fore.[20] But as non-Party academics such as Archie Brown and Fred Halliday pointed out, Gorbachev had exceeded expectations[21] and 'for the first time since Khruschev the eyes of the Western Left are turned eastwards with a genuine sense of excitement and anticipation: who would have guessed that in 1987 the best thing happening for the Left would be in Moscow?'[22]

This perception of Gorbachev as a new hope for socialism had probably more to do with the Soviet leader's championing of an agenda which the Western Left had made its own, but was largely impotent to do anything about, than with any optimistic reading of his ability to create a democratic socialism inside the USSR. Gorbachev's initiatives promised to undermine the rationale for the Cold War and the arms race; help along the 'Europeanisation of politics' which most of the Left in Britain and elsewhere now wanted;[23] and promote the realignment of the Left along the lines on which the Eurocommunists had been travelling for some time. Gorbachev's diplomacy buried the two-camp theory and finally – with the speech at the United Nations in December 1988 – subordinated class to universal human values. (Perhaps a vindication for those Western Communists converted to pluralism).

Thus after the British general election of 1987, in which the Labour Party was defeated for a third consecutive time, Hobsbawm's analysis of the voting figures – which showed clearly Labour's weaknesses within its natural working-class constituency – concluded that 'in practice "class politics" can no longer be realistically counterposed to "people's politics". In any case, an appeal which mobilises a minority of a class at the cost of pushing a majority elsewhere cannot realistically claim to be class politics.'[24] The CPGB was already converted to the need for electoral alliances between Labour and the

20. M. Johnstone, interview with F. Burlatsky, *Marxism Today*, February 1987.

21. A. Brown, 'The Gorbachev Offensive', *Marxism Today*, June 1987.

22. F. Halliday, 'The Gorbachev Era', *Marxism Today*, June 1987.

23. See E. Hobsbawm and P. Glotz, 'Ostpolitik Reborn', *Marxism Today*, August 1987.

24. E. Hobsbawm, 'Out of the Wilderness', *Marxism Today*, October 1987.

centre parties in order to remove the Conservatives; Hobsbawm simply emphasised that such an arrangement would succeed only around a modernising vision involving both planning and the market.

At about this time Gorbachev's *perestroika* was perceived to involve a much greater role for the market in the Soviet economy. There was no public dissent from this project emanating from the CPGB. On the contrary, the reintroduction of markets was now seen as inevitable for reasons I will explore later. But the focus of attention was still very much on *glasnost*. Monty Johnstone argued that 'a decisive turn to democratisation' had been inaugurated in the summer of 1986 when Gorbachev toured the USSR stressing the need for popular involvement in the reform process. But as late as November of that year Johnstone cautioned that any real progress was dependent on the development of a civil society independent of state and party control.[25] If Johnstone painted a bleak picture so did the history of *perestroika* without *glasnost*, as the unappealing record of economic reform in the Socialist bloc since the 1960s had demonstrated. The failure so far of *perestroika* was also undeniable, and within the pages of the CPGB's theoretical journal it was possible to liken the USSR to 'Upper Volta with rockets'.[26]

On two occasions between 1985 and 1989 articles in *Marxism Today* made fleeting reference to the need for the Soviet Union to overcome the Stalinist legacy by returning to Lenin; one of these references was made by a member of the CPGB – Monty Johnstone. But it was never part of *Marxism Today*'s publishing project under Martin Jacques' direction to encourage debate on the Communist tradition, or indeed to consider any history whatsoever. And there is every reason to suppose that in their zeal for 'rethinking', the CPGB's modernisers had destroyed at least as much as they had created – with their surviving attachment to the Communist tradition becoming purely sentimental. With the party losing members every year, the CPGB's decline was as out of control as the journey of intellectual discovery of *Marxism Today*, which had less and less to say on anything which could identify the journal as Marxist, let alone Leninist.

Facing Up to the Future

When the CPGB decided, in November 1987, to once again update its programme, the *Marxism Today* current was dominant. The

---

25. M. Johnstone, 'Glasnost and After', *Marxism Today*, November 1987.
26. M. Walker, 'What Is To Be Done?', *Marxism Today*, June 1988.

'preliminary' result of their labours was published in September 1988 under the title *Facing Up to the Future*.[27] The emphasis throughout is on the 'fundamental restructuring of the economy and social life' wrought by the breakdown of the 'Fordist era' and the advent since the 1970s of new organising principles in social, political and economic life under capitalism. While 'Fordism' is characterised in terms of centralised mass factory production and mass consumerism, the vanguard economic forces replacing it are held to reveal much greater flexibility, decentralisation and diversity. The old social blocs of the 'Fordist' era, which the document describes somewhat surprisingly as 'the symbolic armies of social conflict' of the past, are depicted as subject to a corresponding decay.

The upshot of all this was to deny the continuing validity of the Left's traditional assumptions. Class can no longer be understood as the product of a single polarity because increasing numbers of people occupy 'contradictory class locations' and a 'pure class identity' is in any case prevented by identities and inequalities structured around gender, ethnicity, region, religion and other rival social forces. Struggles around class issues can therefore no longer be regarded as primary; these erstwhile secondary factors are now 'alongside it, centre stage'. Thus the Left must create a new 'alliance of social forces, made up of diverse class and social interests', around a vision of democratic modernisation. A key component of this would have to be a new economic strategy which 'would aim at a continuing modernisation of the economy to make it more internationally competitive' – all this in the context of international economic integration and a necessarily European, rather than narrowly national, approach. A 'regulatory framework' is also preferred to outmoded 'statist notions of social ownership' on the grounds that it would politicise economic decision-making and allow for the market to play its role in the co-ordination of complex economic information and in responding to consumer interests.

Clearly the perceived failures of both the Labour Party in Britain and the command economies in the Socialist bloc have played a part in the evolution of the CPGB's thinking, as have the advance of ideas and political movements which worked to undermine confidence in a various aspects of Left ideology. One set of ideas that could simultaneously distance Socialists from the record of 'real existing socialism' and enable them to adapt to the new social movements while retaining the semblance of a radical outlook was that of democracy in its participative, decentralised and self-managing guises. This is what

27. 'Facing Up to the Future,' *Marxism Today*, September 1988.

the CPGB had embraced and so, to the extent that the Gorbachev reform programme was associated with this project, it could be perceived as a critical step in the 'remaking of socialism' rather than its destruction.[28]

Perestroika and Socialist Economics

For many decades supporters of the Soviet Union – and not just Communists – had regarded the economic system created by Stalin as a great historical leap forward. Socialists who abhorred the tyrannical political system and were fully aware of the concentration camps had convinced themselves that on this count the system was progressive. Well before the advent of Gorbachev, however, evidence of a deep economic malaise in the Socialist bloc had begun to undermine this conviction even within the CPGB. Indeed the splits in the CPGB which produced the New Communist Party and the Communist Party of Britain were in part connected with this issue; in these tiny fundamentalist groups faith in the command economies as somehow representing a higher stage in human social evolution continued to hold sway. Variants of market socialism – however qualified in some cases – had become hegemonic on the British Left (outside of the Trotskyist groups) by the 1980s. The dominant modernising current within the CPGB followed in the wake of these developments – all the more easily in view of the fact that Eastern European opponents of 'real existing socialism' began to see the market as the only alternative and largely abandoned attempts to address these problems within a framework of Marxist humanism, such as occurred in the 1960s. At the Central Committee meeting of the CPSU in January 1987, when Gorbachev seemed to embrace the argument that *perestroika* would fail unless economic restructuring entailed democratisation, a package of reforms was adopted which fell short of radical market reform but included measures designed to increase worker participation in decision-making and establish greater enterprise autonomy. But by the end of the following year the rising discontent resulting from the failure of Gorbachev's economic reforms was already acknowledged in the pages of *Marxism Today*.[29]

Communist commentators were of the opinion that the system of incentives and enterprise autonomy would fail unless a range of other

28. See J. Bloomfield (ed.), *The Soviet Revolution: Perestroika and the Remaking of Socialism*, London, Lawrence and Wishart, 1989.

29. M. Johnstone, 'Perils of Perestroika', *Marxism Today*, December 1988.

measures was taken to open the USSR to the world market, 'inject competitive pressure into the system' and enact a major reform of the price system involving the end of subsidies on food, housing and transport which were held to foster waste.[30] In short the market was required; there was no alternative. Gorbachev was thus championed as someone who recognised this imperative (and it now seems that he was in fact converted to a radical market solution in August 1990, only to back down the following October in the face of opposition led by the Prime Minister Nikolai Ryzhkov). Until this retreat became clear Gorbachev was thought to recognise 'the objective needs for economic decentralisation, for the use of market mechanisms to gauge consumer needs, for increased intiative by technically skilled labour and for much more active involvement by people in their enterprise and work'; it was these objective needs which were pressing for a 'more diverse, pluralistic system'.[31]

But if this meant that 'the USSR has the capacity to transform itself' and create 'a new socialism', there was very little idea of what this socialism would look like. All that was certain to CPGB commentators was that the old leftist debates – not only between Trotsky and Stalin but also between Lenin and Kautsky – were superseded and the split in the working-class movement since 1917 'becomes obsolete'.[32] The victory of social democracy in the ideological struggle waged since October 1917 was thus barely disguised in such formulations although the same Communist writers persisted in believing, as late as 1988–9, that progress in Eastern Europe was dependent on 'reform-minded Communists'.[33]

The Crash of 1989

It was left to non-party commentators such as Neal Ascherson, writing in *Marxism Today* in January 1989, to observe the contrary; that critics of the regimes in Eastern Europe were ceasing to be typically Communist or the offspring of Communist parents but increasingly from traditionalist, nationalist or even racist sources. A revival of peasant parties and aggressive nationalism could therefore be forecast – altogether 'a disquieting outlook'[34] In the Soviet Union itself the

30. J. Cooper, 'The Soviet Economy in Transition', in Bloomfield, *Soviet Revolution*.
31. Bloomfield, in ibid., p. 9.
32. Ibid., p. 15.
33. Ibid., p. 258.
34. N. Ascherson, 'Risings in the East', *Marxism Today*, January 1989.

nationalist violence in Nagorno Karabakh had signalled the end of 'the honeymoon period of *perestroika*' before the year began. The pace of change in Eastern Europe had also quickened as the Russians signalled their inclination to withdraw.

After the crushing of the student occupation of Tiananmen Square in Beijing in May 1989, the lead article in *Marxism Today* declared that the Communist Party-state had itself become an *ancien régime*; Leninism was dead, its totems and taboos were now purely formulaic.[35] By October Martin Jacques took almost the same view publicly by acknowledging that 'we are witnessing a terminal crisis of the Communist system as we have come to know it . . . it is the end of Leninism', not just Stalinism. Indeed Jacques argued that the uprisings in the East also represented a crisis for Western communism and 'inevitably a wider crisis of socialism'.[36] In spite of his comments concerning the end of communism, Jacques was still able to express the view that the prospects for the Western Left depended on the progress of reform in the relatively backward Soviet Union. This recognised the damage which all forms of socialism would suffer in the event of incessant bad news about the Soviet reforms. But Gorbachev had also evidently kept alive some residual faith in the reform-capacity of the Communist Parties and indeed was attributed with 'a Gramscian strategy for a progressive hegemony in international affairs' by one member of the CPGB Executive, who applauded the Soviet leader's 'progressive humanism' and ditching of 'the primitive model of class confrontation'.[37]

During 1989 the CPGB prepared for its forty-first congress with discussions around its *Manifesto for New Times* – a further attempt to identify the allegedly novel characteristics of modern capitalism and jettison those aspects of the Socialist legacy which the party now found redundant. This process effectively consigned the *British Road to Socialism* to oblivion; more to the point, it also rejected everything the party had hitherto stood for in its relationship with the Soviet Union. The Socialist bloc of former times was now found to consist of 'authoritarian' states 'riven with inefficiency, corruption, inequality, centralised control, repression, and environmental despoliation'.[38] Of its 'Marxist-Leninist' faith all that survived was a naïve conviction that Gorbachev could tackle this mess and redeem something for socialism. For the party leadership was equally adamant that *perestroika* was an

35. G. Stedman-Jones, 'Communism in Crisis', *Marxism Today*, July 1989, p. 9.

36. M. Jacques, *Marxism Today*, October 1989.

37. Bloomfield, 'From Proletarian Internationalism to Progressive Humanism', in Bloomfield *Soviet Revolution*.

38. *Manifesto for New Times*, London, CPGB, 1989.

attempt 'to confront this legacy and completely renovate Soviet society . . . with *perestroika*, the Soviet Communists are part of a worldwide process of radical renewal. The creative risks Gorbachev has taken with the meaning of socialism should be taken up by socialists in the West in search of renewal.'[39]

Approval for Gorbachev's 'creative risks with the meaning of socialism' (a phrase used more than once in the document) simply meant that the party had abandoned the old model and had nothing definite to put in its place. By the end of 1989 Martin Jacques announced that 'the historical distinction between Communism and social democracy is coming to an end' and while purporting to see little evidence that the crash in Eastern Europe was being celebrated in the West as a victory for capitalism, asserted that 'in one sense that is exactly what has happened'.[40] At its forty-first congress in November 1989, the party welcomed 'the process of reform and democratisation in the European Socialist countries' – but the word 'Socialist' must have seemed anomalous to many delegates. Actual events demonstrated that democracy – and even the market – was a more radical idea than socialism in Eastern Europe and the party's ideological development throughout the 1980s suggested that the CPGB believed the same was true in Britain. The party had abandoned Socialist blueprints and the idea that socialism could be considered as a superior alternative socio-economic system, while some of its leaders had explicitly depicted the future of socialism as existing within capitalism in the form of variants of social democracy.

The 'fundamentalist' Communist Party of Britain, on the other hand, initially took an altogether more confident stand on the achievements of the Soviet Union and the Eastern bloc. It had argued from its inception in 1987 that 'the function' of the CPGB was 'to promote reformism and class collaboration from within the labour movement itself'.[41] But it saw no evidence that Gorbachev represented similar tendencies. Thus when the CPB adopted its own version of the *British Road to Socialism* it fell back on the old formula which asserted that 'the world situation today . . . is at the most basic level characterised by the transition from capitalism to the higher system of socialism' – hence the 'deepening general crisis' of imperialism. In regard to *perestroika* the party programme expressed full support for the changes required to 'allow socialism to realise its full potential'.[42] The party leadership was in no doubt that 'whatever the problems in

39. Ibid.
40. *Newsweek*, 11 December 1989.
41. *Communist Campaign Review*, Winter 1987.
42. *British Road to Socialism*, London, CPB, 1987, p. 3, 9–10.

the Soviet Union today they are problems of growth and development'.[43] In 1987 Andrew Rothstein (a founder member of the CPGB and a casualty of its modernisation) even noted approvingly that since the advent of Gorbachev the CPGB's reports on the USSR marked 'an advance on the wholesale blackening . . . characteristic of the revisionist press three years ago'. If there was a difference between the two parties on the Soviet reforms it was, according to Rothstein, that the CPGB had succumbed to mere journalism and was no longer guided by Marxist-Leninist theory.[44]

This apparent improvement in the CPGB's appraisal of the Soviet leadership had allegedly come about because the one-sided expectations of the Eurocommunists had been disappointed' according to John Hoffman, '*glasnost* and *perestroika* renew, develop and extend Soviet democracy'; they represent 'an acceleration of the process of dissolving concentrated state power back into self-governing organs of society'.[45] For the CPB then, as these articles by its leading members demonstrated, there was no recognition of the systemic nature of the crisis in Eastern Europe, but rather a perception of growing strength and continuity with the pre-Gorbachev past.

The collapse of the Communist regimes in East Germany, Czechoslovakia and Romania was therefore contrary to all its Marxist-Leninist expectations. Like Ernest Mandel, the CPB at first denied that the upheaval in the German Democratic Republic had anything to do with a rejection of socialism and a desire for reunification. The purpose of the people was simply to give socialism more democracy.[46] But as it became clear that the uprising in the East involved more fundamental changes, the *Morning Star* adopted the tone of disinterested reportage. Thus it referred to 'the Christmas Day execution of the toppled despots Nicolae Ceasescu and his wife Elena' and observed that 'the demonstrators shouted "No More Communists"'; there was no hint that the CPB had supported this regime.[47] Similarly, the election of Vaclev Havel to the State Presidency in Czechoslovakia was reported with the comment that 'attempts by the now replaced authoritarian Communist Party leaders to silence him failed'.[48] Clearly the CPB's attempts to represent 'the complex changes' in the Communist states as evidence of the onward march of socialism had failed. By the summer of 1990 it

43. *Communist Campaign Review*, Winter 1987.
44. A. Rothstein, 'After Three Years', in ibid.
45. J. Hoffman, 'Revolutionary Renewal', *Communist Campaign Review*, Winter 1986.
46. *Morning Star*, 11 November 1989; *Socialist Outlook*, February 1990.
47. *Morning Star*, 27 December 1989.
48. *Morning Star*, 30 December 1989.

was forced to acknowledge that not only had the people 'repudiated "actually existing socialism" and its ruling Communist parties' – so too had 'the majority of communists'. Reactions within the CPB were reportedly 'mixed' though shock was 'universal'.[49]

The Democratic Left

The one thousand-strong CPB had indeed been seriously misled and had lost most of its *raison d'être* by 1990. But the position of the CPGB was little better. Down to seven thousand members by the same year, for all its 'facing up to the future', the party had also entertained thoughts that the future of Socialism hung on the success or failure of the Gorbachev reforms. There was no disguising the fact, however, that the USSR was now faced with chaos and disintegration. While Gorbachev had acquired dictatorial powers he had also begun to lose any popular mandate to continue. *Perestroika* had failed, but the old command system had been sufficiently weakened to produce acute shortages, growing inequality, increased poverty and the threat of hyper-inflation and mass unemployment. Centrifugal forces had become irresistible, and Moscow looked set to react with a return to the old authoritarianism, as the murders of Lithuanians in January 1991 demonstrated. *Marxism Today*, somewhat chastened since the days of the media mania about Gorbachev, carried articles belatedly recognising that the stuttering reform programme was itself the source of the deepening Soviet crisis while admitting that the leader himself could hardly save socialism as long as he remained a non-elected dictator.[50]

On 19 August 1991 Gorbachev fell victim to an apparent coup carried out by his former comrades-in-arms, who styled themselves the State Committee for the State of Emergency. This was conducted with such staggering ineptitude (testifying to the deep divisions within the CPSU) that Boris Yeltsin, head of the Russian republic and widely seen as the leading force for radical reform, was allowed to remain at liberty while state-controlled television stations reported his movements and those of the protest demonstrations mobilised around him. The three days during which this drama unfolded provided enough time for the various remnants of communism in Britain to declare their hand. *The Leninist*, billed as the central organ of the Provisional Central

49. R. Bellamy, M 'Crisis of Socialism', *Communist Review*, Summer 1990.

50. C. Leadbeater, 'Russian Roulette', *Marxism Today*, April 1990; J. Lloyd, 'Deep Freeze', *Marxism Today*, February 1991.

Committee of the CPGB, dwelt on the indecisiveness of the putschists, and a statement issued by the tiny faction on 19 August referred to the State Emergency Committee as representing an attempt to stay the hand of the counter-revolution. The New Communist Party also supported the forced removal of Gorbachev, with its journal *New Worker* observing that the General Secretary of the CPSU had 'unleashed counter-revolutionary forces' representing the interests of US imperialism which could now be overcome as Gorbachev's 'drive to capitalism' was reversed. Eric Trevett, the leader of the NCP, argued in a letter to the *Morning Star* that 'the emergence of a leadership dedicated to communist values deserves our full solidarity and support'. But the CPB had never opposed the Gorbachev reforms – despite the group's fondness for state socialism – and was able to oppose the coup on the grounds that democratisation and market reforms were the only answer to the USSR's problems. This did not prevent the group from warning, after the removal of the 'State Committee', about the dangers of a counter-coup, the persecution of Communists and the dangers of a Yeltsin dictatorship.[51]

There was never any danger that the CPGB would support the coup. Now styling itself the Communist Party in Transformation, it issued a statement on 19 August supporting 'all democratic forces in their resistance to the unconstitutional and undemocratic actions of the Deputy President and his supporters.'[52]

What is more interesting here is the CPGB's response to the measures taken in the immediate aftermath of the coup. For after an initial, half-hearted defence of the CPSU (whose official structures, incidentally, played no part in his removal), Gorbachev solemnly announced on 25 April his resignation as General Secretary and his departure from the party. By decree Communist journals were closed down and party offices sealed; certain republics banned the organisation altogether, and Gorbachev called upon the Central Committee of the CPSU to dissolve itself. Before the end of the month the atmosphere of a witch-hunt against Communists had been generated as the USSR was rapidly reformed out of existence and while the fortunes of a democratic alternative remained uncertain to say the least.

It was in this context that the CPGB leadership advised the dispersal of the CPSU membership on the grounds that the Soviet party had been 'deeply implicated' in the coup and thus emerged 'totally discredited'.

51. The responses to the Soviet coup of the New Communist Party, Communist Party of Britain, and CPGB were reported in the *Guardian* 26 August and 7 September 1991, and *Workers Power*, September 1991.

52. *Marxism Today*, September 1991. See also *Changes*, vol. 22, 31 August-13 September.

Gorbachev's own resignation was accordingly found to be an 'essential act in completing the victory of the democratic forces over the conservatives'. All that Nina Temple, General Secretary of the party since January 1990, wanted to add was that Gorbachev himself could be criticised for not having taken more radical measures earlier.[53]

Marxism Today offered a more sober judgement of the Soviet crisis, by Eric Hobsbawm, which pointed out that the Union was faced with economic, political and social disintegration which made, and continues to make, some form of authoritarian government likely. Within the USSR Gorbachev had become the man 'who destroyed a clumsy but operational economy and replaced it by a void, where there is no longer bread. *Perestroika* did not fail; it did not happen'.[54]

Conclusion

The CPGB's enthusiastic support for Gorbachev in the period 1985–90 was in some ways the last remnant of the old faith insofar as it put on display the party's lamentable ignorance of the massive scale of the USSR's problems and a corresponding naïveté about the party-state's capacity to deal with them. But as I have argued throughout this chapter, the dynamic of reform within the CPGB did not originate with the Gorbachev initiative, and it proceeded too far to be reversed or arrested by events in the Soviet Union. In his speech to the party's Forty-first Congress in November 1989, Martin Jacques described the Communist bloc as an historical 'blind alley' and announced the death of both Stalinism and the essential tenets of Leninism, such as the vanguard party, democratic centralism, its theory of the state and revolution. The delegates were enjoined, therefore, to 'consider all options' concerning the organisation's future, including merger, liquidation of the party, a change of name and a looser form of association. In 1991 the leadership recommended the adoption of the title 'Democratic Left' and a decentralised branch structure, which was endorsed by the membership at the Forty-second Congress in November of that year. While Jacques and the revisionists were long convinced that 'if we carry on in the old way we will be dead and buried', the process begun by Gorbachev accelerated the disintegration of the old faith and reinforced the collapse of membership which was begun by local factors.

53. *Guardian*, 26 August 1991.
54. *Marxism Today*, September 1991.

I have already observed that the process of rethinking socialism, as conducted by *Marxism Today*, did not involve the party in any serious attempt to salvage anything from the Marxist theoretical legacy or the practical heritage of the Communist tradition. The impact of the journal, which was the main driving force in setting the terms of party debate, was in these respects mostly destructive. Much of the opposition to this revisionist trend within the party derived from a deep though not always articulate disquiet about this apparent ditching of the whole tradition – rather that from a blind loyalty to the USSR. Thus the loss of members during the 1980s is attributable to demoralisation resulting from this failure to identify a positive and distinctive Marxist role for the party as well as to expulsions, splits, and forces beyond the organisation's control. This must also be considered one of the main explanations for the persistence of oppositional platforms and tendencies within the CPGB since the late 1970s. Even among members ready to regard the end of Soviet Communism as a 'cause not of regret but of celebration' there remains a conviction that there is a 'democratic communism' which should inform a new party of the Left in Britain.[55] Though the CPGB was down to just 4,600 members by 1991 none of the organisations of the Left in Britain can claim that the last decade has left them in a stronger position now than they occupied at the end of the 1970s. The possibility must exist then that some form of non-Leninist Marxism will emerge in the 1990s which will attract those radical Socialists who have been in retreat in Britain since the early 1980s; Gorbachev at any rate ensured that Soviet socialism would not continue to dazzle such people and thus prevent such a regroupment.

55. See D. Cook and P. Devine, 'Life in Death', *New Statesman and Society*, 6 September 1991.

–8–

The German Communists

Heinrich Bortfeldt and Wayne C. Thompson

The 1990s find German Communists in the throes of crisis. Only the Party of Democratic Socialism (PDS) is represented in parliament and it is burdened by its own history as the heir to the Socialist Unity Party of Germany (SED), which misruled the German Democratic Republic (GDR) for forty years. Its appeal is restricted to the eastern parts of reunified Germany and Berlin, and its future in German politics is not bright. The German Communist Party (DKP) in the western part of Germany remains as irrelevant as ever. It has been badly battered by the collapse of communism in the GDR (to which it was always uncritically servile); it has suffered great losses in membership and capacity for action; the cut-off of funds from the GDR has shattered its party organisation; its leaders no longer enjoy the confidence of the activists; and it has lost its theoretical bearings.

The SED and DKP both grew out of the Communist Party of Germany (*Kommunistische Partei Deutschlands* – KPD), which was founded 31 December 1918. After the Second World War the KPD toned down its revolutionary rhetoric and advocated an 'anti-Fascist democratic order' and a Popular Front. It sought to merge with the Social Democrats (SPD) as a unified German workers' party, something which happened in the Soviet zone on 22 April 1946, when the SED was formed. Because of bitter opposition to such a merger by leading Social Democrats in the western zones, no unification took place in the West. The SED took total power in the GDR in 1949.

In the first West German federal elections in 1949, the KPD polled 5.7 per cent of the votes and had fifteen members in the *Bundestag*, but in the next election in 1953 its vote plummeted to 2.2 per cent, far short of the 5 per cent threshold required for representation in the *Bundestag*. The Communists never again won seats, and their percentage of votes declined steadily, a weakening of support which merely increased their dependence upon foreign patron, the SED in East Germany. This dependence contributed to the Constitutional Court's outlawing of the KPD in August 1956. By the time the party was renamed the DKP and legalised in 1968, two important developments had occurred: first, the party's membership had shrunk to about 7,000; second, the tumultuous 1960s had produced in the FRG scores of radical and independent Communist or Radical Leftist groups to compete with the orthodox Communist Parties.

Party of Democratic Socialism (PDS)

The ideological challenge to the SED and its leadership stemmed from the Soviet policy of *perestroika* and *glasnost*. When Gorbachev came into power in March 1985, he attacked corruption and privilege within the party and advocated intraparty democracy, openness and the reconstruction of society. This indirect challenge to the SED's structure was enthusiastically welcomed by most SED members, above all by intellectuals, and split the party. But the party leadership, Secretary-General Erich Honecker and the Politburo, only welcomed Gorbachev's policies of arms reduction and improving relations with the US. When it was clear that Gorbachev would not use military force to support or rescue the SED regime and that he would no longer treat the GDR as a strategic ally, dramatic change became only a matter of time.

Lacking any appropriate response to Soviet policy, SED Politburo member Kurt Hager drew a now infamous moral from *perestroika*: you need not change your wallpaper merely because your neighbour does so. SED leaders were confident they could deaden the impact of *perestroika* in the GDR by disciplining party members, and Honecker himself in November 1988 banned the widely-read Soviet monthly digest *Sputnik*, which published frank articles on Stalinism (at that time Stalinism was not a matter of public discussion in the GDR). Since no explanation was given, many intellectuals believed that they had been humiliated and treated with arrogance. Open opposition within the SED was impossible, but in January 1989 it was revealed that in 1988 the party had disciplined about 23,000 members. In a total membership of 2.3 million that was slight, but it was the highest figure since 1971. In 1988 about 11,000 members were thrown out of the party, and by October 1989 the number had risen to 18,000. They were the ones who allegedly 'opposed the party's main strategy, denied the GDR's successes, constantly complained and grumbled, or else betrayed the party'. The SED was clearly in crisis.

Dissatisfaction amongst the population and party members grew steadily. From 1986 to 30 June 1989, the Central Committee received 148,364 letters complaining above all about social problems, living and working conditions and the lack of adequate services. The party leadership was unable to tackle all these problems and questions and responded by an even tighter censorship, falsified the local election results in May 1989 and backed the brutal military suppression of the Chinese students in Tiananmen Square in June 1989.[1] East Germans were dismayed, and when Hungary dismantled its security installations on the border on 2 May 1989, thousands of GDR citizens fled illegally through Austria to West Germany. In July and August 1989 alone, about 14,000 members left the party, and the SED had ceased to exist as a tightly-knit unit – a fact crucial for the 1989 peaceful revolution in the GDR.

The Fall of Honecker

Because Honecker had no intention of stepping down, he had to be forced to do so in what he later described as a 'conspiratorial' purge by his 'crown prince', Egon Krenz, and secret police chief Erich Mielke in a session of the Central Committee on October 18, 1989.[2] His successor, Krenz, was a typical *apparatchik* whose aim was to introduce cautious reforms within 'real existing socialism' to regain both the political initiative and control over East German society. He failed to notice he had no credibility and that the GDR was riven with dissatisfaction and was veering towards a revolution. Hundreds of thousands gathered at huge demonstrations throughout the country demanding: 'Let the *Stasi* [State Security] work in the factories!' and 'Down with the SED!' The party itself was faced with its first mass desertions: from January to early November 1989 about 66,000 members left the SED, three-quarters of them workers. The former 'leading party' was in a state of disarray: 'democratic centralism' broke down, and the SED was on its way to impotence. On 9 November the Berlin Wall came tumbling down. The new leadership had calculated that a people which was free to go would come back and hoped in this way to regain the initiative. In the first two days, one-sixth of the GDR's population went West for a visit, and almost all of them returned home. Germans, who for decades had suppressed displays of national feeling, experienced a deeply emotional outpouring, but suddenly German reunification was back on the agenda, and

1. Heinrich Bortfeldt, *Von der SED zur PDS – Aufbruch zu neuen Ufern?*, Berlin, Kommission Politische Bildung des Parteivorstandes der PDS, 1990, pp. 5–6. For a more comprehensive study of the transformation of the SED to the PDS, see H. Bortfeldt, *Von der SED zur PDS*, Bonn, Bouvier, 1992.

2. Reinhold Andert and Wolfgang Herzberg, *Der Sturz. Erich Honecker im Kreuzverhör* Berlin: Aufbauverlag, 1990, p. 45.

developments moved faster than the government's ability to react. The surge tide of reunification was a development for which the SED was not prepared.

At the same time, Honecker and many leading SED figures had been removed from office, arrested and charged with corruption. Socialism was further discredited as enraged East German citizens, long fed on exhortations to 'austerity', watched television images of the luxurious life-styles of the 'proletarian' leaders. Even worse were revelations of illegal arms sales to Third World countries, foreign currency manoeuvres and Swiss bank accounts. Said one rank-and-file SED member, 'We did not expect this of Communists and their creed of equality'.[3] Many party members felt betrayed and ashamed. Others went into action and forced the leadership to undertake decisive measures. Already on 8 November 1989, for the first time ever, a spontaneous mass demonstration of about 10,000 party members had taken place (in Berlin) while the SED Central Committee gathered for its tenth session. The crowds demanded an extraordinary party congress to elect a new leadership. In two months, from mid-October to mid-December 1989, a further 600,000 members left the SED. Hans Modrow, the former head of the Dresden party branch (one of the few leading Communists untainted by corruption) survived; he was elected Prime Minister on 13 November and with the 'Round Table' representing the new parties and movements in the GDR, he prevented the country from slipping into chaos.

On 1 December 1989, the SED was forced to strike the Communists' monopoly on power from the GDR's constitution. Two days later the entire discredited Politburo and Central Committee under Krenz's leadership stepped down. The SED's collapse marked the historical decline of a certain type of party. The state party's failure necessarily entailed the collapse of the whole system because socialism was based on it. The SED had been outpaced by Gorbachev's changes, could not handle the worsening situation and had to concede political liberty. Forty-eight days after Honecker's fall and five days after Krenz's resignation 2,753 SED delegates met in Berlin to decide the fate of their battered party. According to the assessment of Wolfgang Berghofer, Mayor of Dresden and one of the leading new figures in the SED at that time, the party was 'in a catastrophic state'.[4] At its December Congress there were no bold slogans on the walls proclaiming the triumph of socialism, no fraternal greetings, no fights for the delegates. Nothing was censored, and everybody was allowed to speak their mind.

3. *Time*, 18 December 1989, p. 17.
4. *Der Spiegel*, 11 December 1989.

During the first night of debate the atmosphere was so chaotic that it looked as if the Congress would fragment and fail. However, Modrow made a powerful speech and thanks to his authority a new leadership was elected. The new party Chairman was Gregor Gysi (who won 93.5 per cent of the votes), a lawyer who had made a name defending dissidents and the opposition New Forum and by heading the prosecution of former SED leaders accused of corruption. He recognised the need for a complete break with Stalinism and for a new form of socialism and that the SED bore responsibility for plunging the GDR into crisis. He represented a completely new type of party member: his behaviour was unconventional; he was a witty man with a sense of humour; and he stood for the rule of law. After the SED scandals, he seemed to be the right man at the right time. His leftist-inspired intellectual approach attracted the intelligentsia, though not the working class. The Vice-Chairmen were: Modrow, a unifying figure who attracted those who still believed in the idea of socialism; Wolfgang Berghofer, a pragmatist and man of action; and Wolfgang Pohl, a rather obscure party leader from Magdeburg. A new party executive with 101 members was elected (only four members of the former Central Committee belonged to it), and a new presidium was created. The Central Auditing Commission and the Central Party Control Commission were abolished, and a twenty-member Arbitration Commission was elected.

With a new leadership and a new constitution, the party then discussed a new programme. Most strategies were based on the assumption that the GDR would continue, but the party now accepted Germany as one nation culturally, although it strongly rejected a politically-united Germany, which it saw as a threat to Eastern Europe. Such views condemned the party to isolation during the unification process. A new economic strategy could not be found, but a market economy was rejected on moral grounds. Ideologically, the Congress hesitatingly moved away from Leninism. But such shifts were of interest only to intellectuals. Most party members had neither the time nor the inclination to discuss theoretical matters and looked for quick and practical solutions to the pressing problems they faced, such as unemployment. In conclusion, the Congress proclaimed a new party dominated by pragmatism: SED-PDS. This compromise between the old and the new was intended to prevent a split – SED-PDS was a mixture of continuity and renewal.

The Congress could not prevent the party's disintegration. In the last two weeks of December 1989, about a quarter of a million quit the party, leaving it with about 1,463,000 members. People held the SED responsible for forty years of prison-like existence. Demonstrators, who shouted 'Down with the SED!' and 'Expropriate the SED!', clearly did not believe in its capacity for renewal and wanted to remove it. In the absence of radical changes, most of the newly-founded 'Platform' groups within the SED-PDS no longer saw a positive function for their party, and other members were exhausted by personal attacks. Most, above all Modrow and Gysi, decided to keep the party going and introduce more decisive reforms. Although the party executive had rejected the demand for dissolution, the final collapse seemed to be only a matter of time. Berghofer left it and was joined by thirty-nine prominent members from Dresden; parallel to this a grass-roots movement emerged, involving what were called 'initiative groups', which demanded renewal and rescue of the party. But by the beginning of February 1990 the demand to shut it down had waned, and Gysi promised to further dismantle the old apparatus and remove discredited SED members. During the campaign for the 18 March 1990 elections, the PDS managed to consolidate itself.

The PDS and the First Free Elections in the GDR

The PDS held its pre-election Congress on 24–5 February 1990. Its membership had declined to under 700,000. Nevertheless, there was some optimism. It had cast off its discredited SED initials, as it had dropped its disgraced former leaders and claims. By calling itself the Party of Democratic Socialism (emphasising democratic socialism), it was bound to make hard-line Communists in Germany cringe. Its principal candidates were the popular Gysi and Modrow. Gysi was the outstanding attraction. PDS targeted three voting groups: the intelligentsia, those who felt emotionally tied to the GDR and the socially weak and disadvantaged.

In the East German elections of 18 March 1990 the PDS won 1.9 million votes (16.3 per cent of the total), more than expected, and emerged as the third strongest political force in the GDR. It had found its main support among intellectuals and the old administrative élites in the state bureaucracy, police, army and educational systems, and although only 10 per cent of the working class voted PDS, it had been backed by many voters worried about the social consequences of rapid reunification. It was stronger in the North than in the South, where social, environmental, housing and other problems were prominent, and it polled best in cities, winning 29.9 per cent in East Berlin, 25.8 per cent in Neubrandenburg, 27.2 per cent in Rostock and 22 per cent in Frankfurt-Oder. However, its 16 per cent of the votes left it far behind the opposition groupings, especially the conservative 'Alliance for Germany', which came within a whisker of winning an overall majority. As in 1949, Germans had turned to the Christian Democratic Union (CDU) as the party of prosperity and guaranteed democracy. Moreover, the election had been a vote for unity; the PDS was excluded from power and remained isolated in the march towards one Germany.

The Financial Scandal

The SED had been one of the richest parties in Europe. The party's wealth was such that it could not have come directly from membership fees alone. It must have come primarily from other, dubious sources, and the PDS relinquished SED property only under public pressure which cast doubts on the party's self-proclaimed renewal. In the summer and autumn of 1990 the PDS treasurer, Wolfgang Pohl, and his deputy, Wolfgang Langnitschke, had illegally transferred 107 million Deutschmarks abroad to rescue the money from what they saw as 'imminent confiscation' by the state. Both resigned and were imprisoned. Although Gysi and the party executive claimed to have known nothing about the deal, Gysi, as Chairman, had to take the political responsibility but did not resign. How was it possible that such an amount could be transferred without the party executive noticing and exercising its control? Moreover, the PDS had still given no clear and satisfactory account of the extent and whereabouts of the SED's wealth.[5]

The PDS and the First All-German Elections

PDS performance in the 2 December 1990 federal elections indicated that it was a political force only in Berlin and the former GDR. In Berlin *Land* elections on the same day, it captured 1.1 per cent of the votes in the western sector and 23.6 per cent in the eastern (9.2 per cent overall and twenty-three seats in the legislature).

The PDS cast itself as a party which had purged itself of Stalinism but not of socialism. In the electoral campaign it advocated a middle road between the discredited 'real existing socialism' in the East and capitalism in the West. Its slogan was *Lust auf links* (yearning for the

5. Johannes L. Kuppe, 'Die PDS-Finanzen – eine Skandalgeschichte', *Deutschland Archiv*, December 1990, pp. 1821–4; 'The Party's Not Quite Over', *Economist*, 10 November 1990; 'SED-Kohle retten', *Der Spiegel*, 13 May 1991.

left) and its leader Gysi (the only media star in a very mixed bag of Socialists) asserted: 'I was already defending political victims when your Kohls and Strausses gave Honecker billions in credits!' He tried to give the party a modern, 'with-it' image, and his followers wore buttons reading in English 'Take it easy, Gysi!' The party was noticeably well-funded and ran an extremely professional campaign. Gysi filled halls in the West with audiences of mainly young people who liked his unconventional and open style and his refusal to speak in 'Civil Service Mandarin'.[6]

As the senior partner of a 'Left List/PDS' electoral alliance (which was formed in late July 1990 but excluded the DKP), the PDS garnered only 0.3 per cent of the votes in the former West Germany and 11.1 per cent in the East, to give a total of 2.4 per cent nationwide and seventeen seats in the *Bundestag*. Party leader Gysi was directly elected for East Berlin's Hellersdorf-Marzahn (unusual for a small party candidate). Nevertheless, Gysi was not the party. The federal elections made it obvious that the downward trend, beginning with the March 1990 GDR elections, was continuing. About a half million former PDS voters did not vote in the federal elections. The PDS remains a regional political power, but in future *Bundestag* elections it will have to capture the usual 5 per cent of the votes nationwide to win seats, and it is highly unlikely that it will be able to do this.

The Second Party Congress

On 2–3 February 1991 the first all-German PDS Congress was held. It was overshadowed by the Gulf War. The delegates condemned the 'American aggression' as well as Saddam Hussein's occupation of Kuwait, and demanded an immediate end to the war. The PDS's presentation of itself as an antiwar party was part of its broader search for acceptance and a new identity within the peace movement.

The Congress re-elected Gysi as Chairman and two of his deputies: André Brie, a leading intellectual of the party, and Maries Denecke, who represents the women's group. A third deputy representing the western part failed to be elected following a fierce quarrel among the western delegates. A new seventy-member party executive was selected, among whom twenty-one came from the western PDS. A new post of party administrator was established, and the former DKP 'renewer' from Hamburg, Wolfgang Gehrcke, was named to it. His

6. Foreign Broadcast Information Service – Western Europe (FBIS-WEU), 3 October 1990.

appointment signalled the party's intention to expand to all of Germany. This was a significant achievement. But there was no consensus on a political statement. An assessment of the financial scandal did not feature in Gysi's report, and the analysis of the party's condition was superficial. The PDS leadership did not want to tax the rank and file with bad news.

On 21–3 June 1991 the Second Party Congress resumed: the first part had been devoted to electing the party's leading bodies, and major issues were tackled in the second part. Although Gysi claimed to detect some 'signs of stabilisation' in the PDS, he also criticised what he saw as a tendency towards self-destruction. He admitted that the attempt to expand the party's influence throughout western Germany had failed. After bitter debate, the delegates adopted a new statute, but their inability to agree on a new party programme demonstrated the absence of consensus on theoretical fundamentals, alternative strategies, how the party's history should be treated and whether the PDS should pursue a course of social reform or rigorous anti-capitalism.

PDS Reaction to the Coup in the Soviet Union

The PDS response to the unsuccessful attempt in late August 1991 (to depose Gorbachev and end reform) provided a measure of how little distance the party had come in its newly-professed adherence to democracy and freedom. In its initial reaction, the PDS leadership not only failed to condemn the action in a decisive manner, but it even expressed sympathy for the perpetrators and their alleged effort to re-establish 'law and order'. This show of sympathy was scarcely diminished by professions of 'great concern' about the momentous events and pleas to the putschists not to 'misuse' their power. This reaction was shameful for a party which claims to be democratic, and it widened the gulf between the hard-liners, whose influence was obviously rising, and reformers within the PDS; it brought the party one step closer to fragmentation. The failed coup weakened the hard-liners, but reformers also lost their way because they had viewed a reformed Soviet Communist Party leading the way to *perestroika* as the last hope for democratic socialism, and the coup left the CPSU in a shambles.[7]

It is unlikely that the PDS will be able to maintain its power in the new Germany. It relied too heavily on Gysi, without whom the party's

7. See 'In grosser Sorge über die Vorgänge in der Sowjetunion', 20 August 1991, and Heinz Jung, 'Der Moskauer Coup, der Gorbatschowismus und die Linke', 24–25 August 1991, both in *Neues Deutschland*.

visibility and attractiveness would fall rapidly, and it is burdened by being the heir to the discredited SED (99 per cent of PDS members were once in the SED). Its response to scandals which were uncovered and publicised by the press (not by the party's own leadership) showed that the PDS had dealt with its history too selectively. By 1991, the PDS had shrunk to 284,000 members, of whom only about 1,000 were from the West. The party faces an acute generation gap: 47.8 per cent of all members are pensioners, and only 8.9 per cent are under thirty years of age. Many members never adjusted to their new role in the opposition, never put aside their SED- and GDR-shaped thinking and never changed their opinion of capitalism. All these attitudes blocked their openness to what was new in Germany and prevented them from seeing anything valuable in German unity. Renewal within the party was sought only half-heartedly. Yet the negative sides of capitalism, such as the high unemployment rate and the dismantling of enterprises and institutions, have enabled a kind of nostalgia to emerge for the GDR, a country which no longer exists.[8]

Crisis within the DKP

On 5 January 1991 representatives of the PDS and DKP met in Berlin and agreed to remain separate and competing parties, with neither dominating the other, although occasional co-operation would be considered. However, after 1989 the DKP had entered a crisis from which it will never recover. The collapse of Communist power and ideology in the GDR and the Soviet Union's encouragement of reform in Eastern Europe devastated the DKP, which had always been servile to the SED and Soviet rulers. The DKP's leadership was incapable of responding to the 1989 revolution which brought the party to the brink of fragmentation and bankruptcy. Gorbachev's policies created a dilemma for the DKP: on the one hand, his calls for more democracy were avidly embraced by the DKP's rank and file, who had long been restless because of their lack of influence and participation. There were calls for the free election of cadres instead of their appointment by the party leadership. But the SED was cool towards Gorbachev's reforms and did not want to be exposed to the bacillus of *glasnost* from both West and East. Honecker knew that Gorbachev desired his downfall, so

8. Protocol of *PDS Parteitag*, 1. Tagung, Berlin, 26/27. January 1991, p. 25. Heinrich Bortfeldt, 'Die PDS und ihr Zweiter Parteitag', *Deutschland Archiv*, Cologne, 3/1991 and 'Hat die SED die PDS eingeholt?', *Disput*, Berlin, 2. Novemberheft 1990.

he ordered the DKP leaders to suppress reformist movements within the DKP at all costs.[9]

The DKP could not ignore these warnings from East Berlin, and its leaders tried to dampen the enthusiasm caused by the 'strong impulses' coming from Moscow. In the party's *Unsere Zeit* on 20 May 1987, a cautious Mies warned that in a capitalist country like the FRG 'there can be no imitation of the Soviet approach' and that the party must be careful 'not to throw the baby out with the bath water'. The DKP resorted to censorship to try to silence enthusiasm for the reform impulses from Moscow.

In 1988, the DKP faced its hitherto most serious crisis in two decades of existence. For the first time in fifteen years, its membership dipped to 38,000, and members' average age rose. Half those who left the party gave political and ideological reasons for leaving. By early 1988 Mies had to admit that for the first time in DKP history, there were, in fact, differences of opinion within it which were extremely difficult to reconcile. On 3–4 September he acknowledged that alongside a majority wing of *Bewahrer* ('maintainers'), there was a minority of *Erneuer* ('renewers') and that 'A break with essential principles of democratic centralism is appearing in outline.'[10]

The DKP tried to cope with this challenge in two ways: first, by permitting open discussion within the party and by allowing the party news organs to report those disagreements. Never before had there been so much frankness in the party's publications, discussions and gatherings. At the September 1988 Presidium meeting, two opposed discussion papers were allowed for the first time; eighteen out of ninety-four members did not agree with the top party leadership, and therefore no agreement could be reached on a common text. At the same time, the DKP tried to limit discussions, declaring that although they may show a diversity of opinion, they could 'not lead to political confrontation or to splintering of forces'. They must always serve 'the conscious unity and strengthening of the fighting power of the party'.[11] That is, criticism had to remain subordinate to the principles and goals of the party. The second way of trying to erect a dam against the flood of demands for more 'democratisation' and a more public party was to discipline those 'renewers' who crossed the vague line which the top leaders had tried to draw between permissible and impermissible criticism.

The DKP leadership could have no illusions that the Ninth Party Congress, which took place in Frankfurt am Main 6–9 January 1989,

9. *Der Spiegel*, 7 September 1987; *Die Zeit*, 16 October 1987.
10. FBIS, 15 September 1988; *Stern*, July 1988.
11. *Die Welt*, 23 June 1988.

would be one like no other before it. One third of the delegates came to make things difficult for the conservatives, whom they called 'concrete heads'. Citing the DKP's political impotence and lack of electoral success, the 'renewers' mounted an unprecedented challenge against the leaders and explicitly invoked the reform spirit of Gorbachev. Many observers asked what had ever happened to comradely solidarity. But the intra-party perils which the DKP faced at its 1989 party Congress pale in comparison with those brought on by the political earthquake which hit the DKP's exalted models – the GDR and SED – in the second half of 1989: the events, 'shock us!'[12]

It is an understatement to say that the DKP was overwhelmed by the peaceful revolution in the GDR and by unification. A few die-hards asserted that it was a 'betrayal of the working class' and 'democracy flim-flam' when the 'class enemy' was given free rein to eject Communists from power through elections. The minority wing seized the opportunity to convene a 'Renewal Congress' in Frankfurt am Main in October 1989 to discuss the divisions. The 'renewers' decided to create their own structures which would enable them to prepare separately for the DKP's future congresses. Yet, although the 'renewers' had shaken the DKP to the roots, they were unable to take control of it because of some serious tactical errors. What little unity they had came from their rejection of the leadership style of DKP bosses who had dominated since the 1950s. By DKP standards, the renewers' Frankfurt Congress in October 1989 was a daring move, but they adjourned without offering their comrades an organisational alternative to what had existed for decades. Moreover, although their numbers within the DKP grew by the day, they were the first to leave the party in disgust. Forty per cent of all DKP members left in the wake of communism's collapse in the GDR, but by the end of 1989, 95 per cent of the 'renewers' had gone, either joining the PDS or other leftist groups or leaving politics altogether.[13]

Disaster struck the DKP in late November 1989: the SED informed it that all foreign currency support (which despite DKP denials had amounted to an estimated DM50-70 million annually sent through conspiratorial channels) would be terminated. SED subsidies had always been essential to financing the high costs of maintaining party headquarters in Düsselforf, an office in Bonn and more than two hundred local offices, the production and distribution of propaganda materials, mass rallies and election campaigns and subsidies to DKP affiliated or influenced organisations. DKP functionaries were kept on

12. FBIS-WEU, 21 November 1989.

13 FBIS-WEU, 3 and 21 November 1989, and *Neues Deutschland*, 24 November 1989.

the payrolls of Communist firms and travel agencies directed by the SED. The DKP had few other financial resources.

After 1989 the DKP had to operate completely on its own. Contributions dried up, and the split in the party prompted many members to leave or to stop making their contributions. In consequence, almost all of the party's bloated bureaucracy was dismissed – about five hundred people in all. In February 1990 the PDS paid 'damages' amounting to DM6 million to the DKP to alleviate the 'social costs' of those functionaries who had lost their jobs. However, the DKP used the money to build a new party apparatus of about fifty persons, rather than to distribute it among the unemployed comrades. What small funds remained were in the hands of the apparatus; the 'renewers' got nothing. The party's publications were severely affected: the daily organ, *Unsere Zeit*, was converted to a weekly, and some other party publications were terminated; the DKP's news agency, Progress Presse-Agentur (PPA) and publishing house, Paul-Rugenstein-Verlag, were shut down. The latter's bankruptcy eliminated the vital prop for the DKP's most important publication aimed at domestic alliance partners: *Volkszeitung*. East German advertising in DKP publications disappeared.[14]

The DKP was further embarrassed by revelations in January 1990 that *Stasi* had trained up to three hundred DKP members in secret camps inside the GDR in the use of weapons and explosives to serve in a secret military organisation within the FRG. Support for terrorists had reportedly been a pet project of Honecker himself.[15]

It was a shattered, demoralised DKP which assembled in Dortmund the end of March 1990 for its Tenth Party Congress. Few 'renewers' remained among the 311 delegates, so there was no confrontation, although a pluralism of opinions was manifest. Many delegates noted that in order for the party to renovate, it had to recognise the reasons for its difficulties: its leaders' false calculations and the uncritical idealisation of conditions in Socialist countries. The orthodox former Vice-Chair, Ellen Weber, spoke of blindness towards the reality of 'real existing socialism'. In the presence of a visiting delegation from the PDS, a greeting from its Chairman, Gregor Gysi, was read, in which he apologised in the name of the PDS for the old SED-leadership's share in the blame for the DKP's deep crisis.

If there was much talk of renewal, almost no steps were taken to bring it about. The DKP made a few cosmetic changes. The single chair was replaced by a collective leadership of four: Heinze Stehr,

14. FBIS-WEU 30 November 1989; *Der Spiegel*, 4 December 1989, pp. 89–92.
15. FBIS-WE, 4 January 1990, p. 5; Wilke, 'Krise', p. 37; Horchem, 'Verfall', p. 54.

Anne Frohnweiler, Helga Rosenberg and Rolf Priemer (all fundamentalists). The party leadership was reduced to forty-six, half of whom were women; all were orthodox Communists who had opposed the 'renewers'. The party's statutes were temporarily changed to allow DKP members to criticise the party's leaders or policies internally in lower party echelons, but public criticism remained forbidden. The delegates' most important decision was not to seek union with the PDS. Ellen Weber proclaimed the end of West German Communists' dependence upon East Berlin. This was a great relief for the ambitious PDS, which could only be hurt by being associated with the orthodox DKP; the heir to the SED had enough image problems as it was, and a linkage with the DKP would be a kiss of death at election time. The PDS created an electoral party of its own at the end of July, called the 'Left List PDS', which excluded the DKP.

The influence of the 'renewers' within the DKP ended once and for all. When the PDS opened four regional offices in the West in July, it relied for logistics on former 'renewer' Wolfgang Gehrcke, whose team was almost completely composed of ex-DKP reformers. A few weeks later it created party organisations in the ten western *Länder*, whose leaders were former Greens and DKP 'renewers'. Although the DKP attacked these 'PDS revisionists', it had no alternative to supporting them in the December elections. In a rare flash of realism, it was admitted at the DKP's Executive Committee session in Essen 22–3 September 1990 that hopes that the 'PDS, the DKP, and other Leftist-Socialist and Communist forces may eventually arrive at a common position . . . will require a long time' to realise.[16]

A party which has never polled more than 0.3 per cent of the votes in federal elections has an obvious problem. The DKP tried to break out of its isolation by forming electoral alliances. It jumped on the bandwagon of extra-parliamentary movements, whose momentum comes from dealing with issues of broad concern in the FRG. Looking back on *Land* and local elections in 1990, the party saw nothing but dismal failures. Thus, facing the 2 December 1990 *Bundestag* elections, it decided to spare its members further embarrassment and instead to support the Left List PDS, which won 0.3 per cent of the votes in former East Germany.

16. *Neues Deutschland*, 28 March 1990, p. 3; FBIS-SOV, 30 March 1990, pp. 28–9; FBIS-WEU, 2 October 1990, p. 10.

DKP Domestic Policies

The DKP vehemently demands an end to the 'bar to occupations' against those deemed to be risks to the state, and hence a new recruit must be prepared for a possible sacrifice of his livelihood.[17] The DKP still tries to appeal to workers, a steadily-declining class in the FRG's modern economy. It orders its members to take an active role in trade unions, with the goal of persuading unionists that workers' interests are only served by class struggle. It places great value on its 'educational work', particularly for the union youth organisations. Even though few DKP members have risen to leading positions in the unions, three-quarters of them belong to unions, and they exercise influence in some, particularly those of printers, journalists and mass media. (Communists are especially strong in the Mass Media Trade Union, which was set up in 1985.)

Despite potential dangers, the party hopes for the formation of broad alliances. These can be the 'working class unity of actions', namely DKP co-operation with trade unionists, workers not affiliated with any party, Christian workers and Social Democrats. Such alliances can also be with intellectuals and the bourgeoisie, and these 'coalitions of reason' can seek broader objectives. DKP members need not occupy the leading offices, and they can show 'political flexibility' while maintaining 'ideological conviction'. That is, co-operation should be based on common interests and should not be brought about through compromises with reformist positions.

The DKP leadership believed it saw the wall breaking down between Social Democrats and Communists, a wall which has existed since the foundation of the KPD in 1918, and which was strengthened by the effort of the KPD to absorb the SPD after the Second World War. Serious disagreement continues to exist between the two parties on 'the system question': what kind of regime and economic order is best for the FRG. It has long sought to eliminate or lessen the 'fears of contact' (*Berührungsängste*) which has made most groups in the FRG disinclined to deal with Communists. In 1988 the DKP had adopted the slogan: 'Continue on this path: towards Social Democrats – for unity of action!' It led nowhere. (The SPD also observes a hands-off policy towards the PDS.)[18]

17. *Der Spiegel*, 19 October 1987; *Neues Deutschland*, 2 February 1989. *Berufsverbot* is the term used by those who oppose this law. The official title is *Radikalenerlass* – Radicals' Decree.
18. Bundesminister des Innern, *Verfassungsschutzbericht 1987*, Bonn, hereafter VSB.

Perhaps most important in the party's efforts to reach out to other groups was its participation in the peace movement. Operating within the peace movement was particularly comfortable for the DKP because it was thereby able to devote its energies to supporting a key Soviet and GDR security objective, although neither the DKP nor the many Communist splinter parties were ever the initiators or string-pullers of the peace movement groups within the peace movement often accepted logistical support, which was the Communists' greatest contribution to the movement. The DKP and its affiliated organisations had a disproportionally large representation in many of the movement's operational co-ordinating committees. Nevertheless, the Greens and other non-Communist activists in the peace movement intensified efforts to distance themselves from Communists. Clearly, the peace movement in the 1980s and during the 1991 Gulf War was far too large and heterogeneous to be controlled by outside powers or the DKP. The party failed to capitalise on its support of the peace effort in the early 1980s; five thousand newly-won members from the movement left the DKP within two years.

Communists have no reason to be happy about their attempts to work together with the badly-divided Greens, whose decline was underscored by the fact that West German Greens failed to win 5 per cent in the 1990 federal elections and were therefore ejected from the *Bundestag*. Although there are former Communists within the Greens, they are from the militant Communist splinter parties which tend to be hostile or unco-operative towards the DKP. The Greens never discussed coalitions with the Communists, even though the DKP agreed with the fundamentalist Greens' (so-called 'Fundis', who on 12–13 May 1991 founded their own party, the 'Ecological Left') position on violence in demonstrations: that there should be an end to the state's 'monopoly on the use of force'. An exasperated Robert Steigerwald of the DKP noted that 'most of the Greens keep aloof from the working class, asserting that it is unable to bring about a revolutionary transformation of society. Marxism is dismissed as a nineteenth-century theory; political economy is replaced with ecology. Marxists and those who worship economic development are equally presented as prisoners of an obsession with economic growth and consumption.'[19]

19. *World Marxist Review*, September 1987; *Neues Deutschland*, 1 February 1988; Innere Sicherheit, 15 May 1987; Moreau, 'Krisen', in *Das Parlament*, 9 November 1990, p. 47; *Christian Science Monitor*, 24 November 1987; Steigerwald quote in *World Marxist Review*, November 1986.

Berlin

Since 1990 the minuscule Socialist Initiative (SI) has been heir to the defunct Socialist Unity Party of West Berlin (SEW). SI publishes a quarterly magazine *Konsequent* ('Consistent'), with a circulation of 2,500. The dramatic changes which occurred in the GDR and the rest of Europe in the autumn of 1989 surprised and overwhelmed the SEW, which had historically been totally servile to and dependent upon the discredited SED. Before folding almost immediately, its *Neue Zeitung* ('New Newspaper', earlier *Die Wahrheit*) asserted in October 1989 that 'the times today call for new thinking, new acting – nothing remains static'. In the wake of the political hurricane which blew down the Berlin Wall on 9 November, 40 per cent of the SEW members stormed out of the party, and its entire Politburo and Secretariat resigned. An SEW resolution acknowledged that massive pressure by the GDR's population had forced a renewal of socialism. One of its leaders, Klaus-Dieter Heiser, emphasised that 'the process of renewal within the SEW was accelerated by the development in the GDR'. He admitted that in the past, the SEW had idealised the achievements and situation in the GDR and had therefore been blind to the growing alienation between the people and the leaders of the SED and the state. 'We had believed that the collective rights were to be valued more highly than individual human rights, such as freedom of movement, which had been fought for in the bourgeois revolution.'[20]

The SEW has had to struggle to survive in a city which has become very different. Under chaotic circumstances, a party Congress on 28–9 April 1990 sealed the SEW's fate. The 250 elected or self-appointed delegates, representing no more than 1,600 total party members, of whom only about a thousand are dues-payers, transformed the SEW into SI, whose ideological manifesto parroted that of the PDS. However, the SI was unable to establish a durable alliance with the PDS, which decided to expand its own organisation into West Berlin and the rest of the FRG. The SI was able neither to field its own candidates in the first all-Berlin elections on 2 December 1990, nor to help enlarge the vote of the PDS in the western part of Berlin. There the PDS won only 1.1 per cent of the votes, which together with the 23.6 per cent it won in the eastern part of the city, amounted to 9.2 per cent for the PDS in all of Berlin. The PDS will be the major Communist political force in Berlin for several years into the 1990s, while the SI will remain irrelevant.

20. *Frankfurter Allgemeine Zeitung*, 16 October 1989; Moreau, 'Krisen'; *VSB 89*; Heiser quotes: *Neues Deutschland*, 15, 21 and 28 November 1989.

on

ͅsm is a spent force in Germany, condemned to political irrelevance. Although the PDS will be represented in the *Bundestag* until 1994, when it will almost certainly fall short of the 5 per cent electoral minimum and be evicted from Parliament, its influence is steadily decreasing. It lacks acceptance because it is burdened by its own history, and all attempts at renewal have remained half-hearted. The PDS survives as a purely regional political force, fixated on the former GDR. Its efforts to broaden its appeal to western Germany failed. It is split between a faction which regards the past critically and favours progressive Socialist reforms and one which expresses strong anti-capitalist views and evokes a sort of old-time Socialist nostalgia. It remains to be seen whether such a pluralist PDS can survive. Membership is declining steadily: in autumn 1991 it dipped below 200,000, and young people in particular have left it. (As a result, pensioners predominate in the rank and file.) To make matters worse, the other parties seek its demise, and they exclude it from political decision-making. All these internal and external threats to the PDS prevent any form of resurgence.

The DKP is, as always, impotent and irrelevant. In May 1991 its membership stood at a dismal 8,500. In its former stronghold, Hamburg, the party garnered an unimpressive 680 votes in the June 1991 *Land* elections, behind virtually all other left-wing parties and groupings. Discredited by its complete dependence on the former SED, and incapable of drawing any useful lessons from the collapse of East German socialism, the DKP feels itself to be increasingly isolated. Despite *perestroika* it clings to the tattered Leninist concepts of the party and socialism. It is shunned by a PDS which is concentrating on its own survival and does not want to tarnish its fragile public image by associating with the orthodox DKP, which has, for all practical purposes, become a mere political sect.

The remaining Marxist-Leninist, Trotskyite, anarchist and autonomist sects are impotent at election time. Nevertheless, they are poised to try to take advantage of the many problems stemming from uncertainties growing out of the German unification process. All in all, following the collapse of communism in the Soviet Union and Eastern Europe, including Germany, the outlook for these groups is extremely bleak. They are in deep shock and are searching in vain for stable new ground.

Premature *Perestroika*: The Dutch Communist Party and Gorbachev

Gerrit Voerman

The reaction of the Communist Party of the Netherlands (CPN) to *glasnost* and *perestroika*, the reforms with which Soviet party Secretary Mikhail Gorbachev surprised the world after his coming to power in 1985, was in essence *déjà vu*. Basically, the CPN believed that it had itself gone through a process of reconstruction in the early eighties in a way which anticipated the reforms initiated in the Soviet Union, although, of course, the scale and setting were completely different. Because of its premature renovation, the CPN assigned itself a position in the modernising *avant garde* of the international Communist movement.

In this chapter, the response of the CPN to Gorbachev will be described. Some attention, however, has to be paid first to the metamorphosis the CPN underwent at the beginning of the 1980s, especially with reference to its international standpoint and its reappraisal of Leninism and 'really existing socialism'. The changes which came about in this area determined the attitude the CPN adopted later. In addition, the somewhat ambivalent reactions to the downfall of Eastern European socialism within the CPN will be discussed. Although the Dutch Communists had already decided in principle on co-operation with the Radical Party (PPR) and the Pacifist-Socialist Party (PSP) within the framework of a new environmental political formation called 'Green Left' (*Groen Links*), the tearing down of the 'iron curtain' certainly contributed to the decision to merge completely with PPR and PSP in Green Left and to dissolve the CPN in June 1991. Hence before describing the modernised CPN of the eighties, its existence as an orthodox Communist Party and in particular its less orthodox relation to the Soviet Union must be examined. From the early sixties to the middle of the seventies, the CPN was one of the byways of the international Communist movement. During this period, the CPN distanced itself from Moscow's leading role within world Communism (although it did not dissociate itself from Soviet theory and practice). Later on the CPN would boast of this 'autonomous' position and describe itself as 'pioneering'.

The Orthodox CPN

The history of the CPN stretches back to before the Russian Revolution. In the Netherlands, the split between reformists and revolutionaries within the labour movement had already taken place in 1909. This gave the CPN a certain independence when the Communist International was set up. However, Moscow quickly gained control of the Dutch Communists, and like every other party it was 'bolshevised' by the mid-1920s.

After the Second World War, the CPN returned to legality as the political satellite of the Soviet Union, and during the Cold War, the party completely identified itself with Moscow. In international affairs, the CPN espoused the so-called 'theory of the two camps', and accused the capitalist camp, led by the United States, of preparing a third World War. Only through the efforts of the (by nature) peaceful Socialist camp headed by Moscow, said the CPN, could this be avoided. In this 'battle for peace' the CPN took part 'in indissoluble solidarity with the Soviet Union.' Not only because of its international role, but also because of its social system the Soviet Union was held to be a radiant example. The CPN assured its adherents that the victory of socialism in the Soviet Union was attended 'with the birth of a new type of human being . . . namely Socialist man, who as a priority believes the welfare of the community to be a precondition of his personal welfare'. All these triumphs were attributed to Stalin, who was praised in the constitution of the CPN as 'the greatest reformer of society, teacher and statesman, who has ever led progressive humanity'.[1]

Destalinisation, which was started in 1956 by Khrushchev's secret speech, shocked the Dutch Communists. The CPN executive reacted by conceding that Stalin had made some mistakes, but was still very favourable about its Soviet mentor. Yet the party leadership regretted that it had defended the personality cult to the Dutch public, and stated that it would never again support actions in other countries if these fell outside of its area of knowledge.[2] Non-interference in other parties (confirmed by the Eighteenth Congress of the CPN in October 1956)

1. *De weg naar socialistisch Nederland*, Amsterdam, Brochurehandel der CPN, 1952, pp. 10, 19, 24.
2. See 'Resolutie over het twintigste congres van de CPSU', *Politiek en Cultuur*, vol.15, 1956, pp. 309–11.

was a prelude to the concept of 'autonomy' to which the CPN was converted in the sixties. Togliatti's concept of 'polycentrism', however, was strongly criticised by the CPN: the leading role of the Soviet Union was not in question. In fact, the CPN was *plus royaliste que le roi*. The introduction of the idea of 'noninterference' seemed to be dictated only by repugnance at Khrushchev's unmasking of Stalin and was an excuse for the party not to have to face the problem of destalinisation.

The CPN as International Misfit

In the sixties, the CPN was estranged from the Soviet Union because of the conflict between Moscow and Peking. In 1963, after the breakdown of the negotiations between the two Communist powers, Party secretary De Groot suddenly declared the 'autonomy' of the CPN within the international Communist movement. The impulse behind this came from the potential rupture of the special relations between the Dutch Communists and the pro-Chinese Indonesian Communist Party which could come about because of the Sino-Soviet dispute. These parties had engaged in a common struggle against the Dutch colonial system. On the ideological disputes between Khrushchev and Mao, De Groot stated that the conflict was essentially 'about economic issues, about the balance of power within the Socialist camp and within the International Communist movement'. From then on, the CPN would be 'responsible only to the working population of the Netherlands . . . Our international activities are only useful if they are made subservient to our primary tasks.'[3]

Nevertheless, the CPN stuck to its view that the Socialist countries as such – including the Soviet Union – were the only nations promoting global peace and declared therefore that 'the expansion of the Soviet sphere of influence was an historical step forward'.[4] Moreover, the CPN did not turn pro-Chinese; the emerging Maoist tendency within the party was expelled overnight, as was a small pro-Soviet group. Moscow was held responsible for the rupture in the international movement and in consequence, relations with the Soviet Union worsened: International Communist meetings were attended either by a low-ranking delegation or not at all. In 1967, the CPN did not celebrate the sixtieth anniversary of the Russian Revolution and,

3. A.A. de Jonge, *Het communisme in Nederland: de geschiedenis van een politieke partij*, Den Haag, Kruseman, 1972, pp. 145–6.
4. D. Hellema, 'De dilemma's van Jalta', *Politiek en Cultuur*, vol. 45, 1985, p. 203.

one year later, the armed intervention of the Warsaw Pact in Czechoslovakia was strongly condemned as a 'violation of Leninist principles'.

The Eurocommunist Curse

After a short period of *détente* with Moscow around 1970, Dutch Communists' xenophobia continued: the CPN isolated itself and was viligant against 'hostile interventions'.[5] But it kept aloof not just from orthodox parties, but also from the 'Eurocommunist' Italian, French and Spanish parties which were trying to modernise. The CPN perceived in this European framework a new (Italian) 'centre', which was regarded as a threat to its 'autonomous' position. However, the CPN boasted that it had introduced the concept of 'autonomy' into the international Communist movement, long before 'Eurocommunists' were claiming a greater degree of independence from Moscow.

In the middle of the 1970s, this position of self-chosen isolation started to change: slowly but surely the CPN made its entry onto the international scene. In June 1976 it took part in the conference of European Communist Parties in East Berlin and supported the resolution in which the 'autonomy' and 'independence' of all parties was defended.[6] The importance the conference attached to the concept of 'autonomy' as one of the basic rules of mutual relations within the international Communist movement was regarded as a victory by the CPN. Sticking to its principles, it refused to take a stand in the dispute between the Eurocommunist parties on the one hand and the Moscow-orientated orthodox ones on the other. In reality, the Dutch Communists praised the 'international peace-loving policy' of the Soviet Union and condemned 'reactionary interference in the internal affairs of the Socialist countries'.[7]

Renewal of the CPN

This temporary public courtship of the CPN with the CPSU did not bring electoral good fortune. In May 1977, the CPN lost five out of

---

5. 'Resolutie van het 24ste congres van de CPN' *Politiek en Cultuur*, vol. 32, 1972, p. 333.

6. 'Voor vrede, veiligheid, samenwerking en sociale vooruitgang in Europa', *Politiek en Cultuur*, vol. 36, 1976, pp. 186–205.

7. 'Delegaties CPN-CPSU spraken over gevaren bewapeningswedloop', *Politiek en Cultuur*, vol. 37, 1977, pp. 139–41.

seven seats and instead of participation in government, which the party had demanded, Dutch Communism became politically marginal. This electoral defeat, however, ushered in a period of profound ideological change. First the party shook off its Stalinist coat and then went on to renounce its Leninist heritage: 'Leninism' was abolished both as a theory and as an organisational model. At the same time, the new social movements managed a hold on the CPN, and during the eighties an entirely new party made its appearance, which merged into a new political formation called 'Green Left' at the end of the decade. In this landslide, the traditional view of the Socialist countries changed profoundly, and the principle of the 'two camps' also perished.

The CPN's metamorphosis was preceded by a change in the social composition of its membership.[8] Within the Communist membership industrial workers were replaced by members of the 'new middle class', who were promoting new, 'post-materialist' demands like protection of the environment and democratisation, and were less attached to the Soviet Union. The newcomers conformed to the rules and traditions of the Stalinist party at first, but after the disastrous parliamentary elections in 1977, intellectuals and (later) feminists rebelled against the Stalinist cadres and demanded more freedom of discussion and ideological renewal.[9] The strife between the orthodox wing and the renovators ended in a victory for the latter. Under the pressure of the combined opposition of intellectuals and feminist members, Leninist ideology was thrown overboard in 1984; the abolition of the Leninist principle of democratic centralism followed five years later.

The new era was ushered in at the Twenty-sixth Congress of January 1978. Here the strategic concept of the 'coalition formation' was unfolded. Communists, Socialists, Progressive Christians and others were urged to link up to form an alternative to the centre-right coalition. Apart from parties, all kinds of social organisations were invited to contribute to this so-called 'democratic power formation'. Apart from these strategic changes a new ideological programme was announced in which the CPN would map out the 'Dutch road to socialism'.

Though the CPN seemed to adopt a different tone, it initially remained Marxist-Leninist: something which became manifest in its attitude towards the Socialist countries. In accordance with its

8. See G. Voerman, 'Een anatomische les: de congressen van de CPN ontleed', *Tijdschrift voor sociale Geschiedenis*, vol. 16, 1990, pp. 182–99.

9. See M. Fennema, 'The End of Dutch Communism? The Communist Party of the Nederlands', in M. Waller and M. Fennema (eds.), *Communist Parties in Western Europe: Decline or Adaption?*, Oxford, Basil Blackwell, 1988, pp. 158–78.

'autonomous position', the CPN did not defend everything happening in Eastern Europe, but it condemned 'the reactionary interference in the internal affairs of the Socialist countries'. It admitted that there were 'unsolved problems', 'contradictions in the internal development' and 'common difficulties' in the Eastern bloc, but at the same time it stated that 'no party had the right to interfere in another party's affairs'.[10]

The CPN remained committed to the orthodox 'theory of the two camps', in which the United States was escalating the arms race whereas the Soviet Union was pursuing a policy of *détente*, and was the power supporting the masses struggling for peace. Hence, 'the Socialist countries are indispensable allies of the Dutch working class in the struggle against the dangers of the arms race'.[11] At the beginning of the eighties, this Moscow-dominated stand was still predominant within the CPN: the bracketing of the Soviet Union with the United States as jointly responsible for the arms race was then rejected. Any analysis which put the Soviet Union and the United States on a par ignored all distinctions between 'bellicose' capitalism and 'peace-loving' socialism, according to the CPN.[12]

Changes in International Policy

Within a few years, however, the CPN had changed this 'theory of the two camps' for the traditionally-abused 'theory of the superpowers'. Though this volte-face in its international position was a part of the general metamorphosis the CPN was experiencing, two factors in particular played a role. In the first place were events which took place in the early eighties such as the Soviet invasion of Afghanistan, the military coup in Poland and the war between Vietnam and China. Then there was the success of the Netherlands peace movement, which the CPN had initiated, and which led to a kind of merger with the broader, less radical peace movement. At the same time, the CPN itself was drawn in a more 'neutral' direction.

In August 1977, the CPN had started a campaign against the introduction of the neutron bomb which, apart from its direct aim, was also intended to improve the morale of the Communist rank and file after the electoral disaster. The campaign proved to be a success; within nine months the Communists had collected more than a million

10. Stellingen van het partijbestuur van de CPN voor het 26ste congres (Amsterdam, Pegasus 1977), pp. 34–35.

11. Ibid., pp. 35–36.

12. M. Bakker, Spanning en verantwoordelijkheid', *Politiek en Cultuur*, vol 40 (1980), 45.

signatures. The campaign improved the prestige of the CPN within the international Communist movement and contributed to the breaking of its isolation. Moreover, the Dutch Parliament was against the N-bomb, and the Communist leadership decided to extend the campaign to the arms race as a whole; the Twenty-seventh Congress of the CPN of June 1980 made the 'struggle for peace' a priority. The 'Stop the N-bomb, stop the arms race' committee took part in the developing broader peace movement in the early eighties and campaigned against the stationing of American Pershing II's and cruise missiles in the Netherlands, although the Soviet SS-20's were also criticised. Of course the leadership of 'Stop the N-bomb' could not do less without isolating itself and losing its gains; hence it made concessions to the peace movement.

Criticism of Soviet nuclear armament was facilitated by the change of international policy. The unshakable faith in the 'peaceableness of the Socialist forces' was damaged firstly by the Soviet invasion of Afghanistan. The invasion was indirectly denounced after some weeks of silence. The Communist Member of Parliament (and *éminence grise*) M. Bakker described the 'one-sided military' Soviet way of acting as 'an ill-fated decision', though in the last resort the United States was held responsible. The credibility of 'really existing socialism' received another blow from the military *coup d'état* in Poland. Immediately after Jaruzelski had seized power in December 1981, the coup and the subsequent repression of Solidarity were condemned by the CPN 'unconditionally and unequivocally'.[13] The involvement of the CPSU in a neighbouring country was also rejected as 'an intervention in Polish affairs'. In an elaboration the director of the scientific bureau of the CPN repudiated the argument that the Polish military had to intervene in order to protect the safety of the Warsaw Pact as a whole. The CPN rejected the idea that 'the interests of the blocs – and within these those of the strongest powers – are decisive'.[14]

Thus in the early eighties, the CPN gradually abandoned the dogma of the Socialist bloc as its natural ally in the 'anti-imperialist' struggle. In fact, socialism as a mobilising theme was replaced by the peace movement. This simultaneous emancipation and revaluation was partly the result of the relative success of the Communist campaign against the N-bomb and the rise of the broader peace movement. The CPN argued that the maintenance of the balance of power between both superpowers had not resulted in a lasting peace; henceforth the mass struggle for peace in the capitalist world was held to be decisive. However, the view

13. 'Verklaring van het partijbestuur', *Politiek en Cultuur*, Vol. 42 (1982), p. 78.
14. Jaap Wolff, 'Tragedie in Polen', *Politiek en Cultuur*, Vol. 42 (1982) pp. 43–46.

of both the Soviet Union and the United States as joint instigators of the arms race and dominators of their 'blocs' was contested within the CPN. The orthodox argued that the ideological disorientation of the CPN had resulted in the merger of 'Stop the N-bomb' into the 'pacifist, neutralist, and classless' peace movement; only a return to class-consciousness in international affairs could open a new perspective, and the positive anti-imperialist contribution of the Soviet Union and the partition of the world into two camps had to be accepted.[15] However, at the Twenty-eighth Congress of the CPN in November 1982, the orthodox wing suffered a heavy defeat. The Congress did not endorse the Soviet Union as an 'automatic and natural ally in the struggle against the arms race'.[16] The party recognised that the existence of both hostile political-military blocs, one under the leadership of the United States and the other headed by the Soviet Union, had induced the arms spiral (although the CPN still saw the United States as the engine of the arms race). In order to halt escalation, both blocs, NATO and the Warsaw Pact, had to be dissolved.

Building on the Congress resolution which had put the peace struggle at the top of the agenda, the CPN started a diplomatic offensive within the International Communist and left-wing movement. This policy was consistent with its domestic coalition strategy: the CPN had contacts not only with ecologist movements elsewhere and with Polish Solidarity, but also with the CPSU and other orthodox Communist Parties. Moscow in its turn was interested in the CPN because of the hesitations the Dutch government manifested about stationing American missiles in the Netherlands. To their Soviet interlocutors the Dutch Communists made no secret of their disgust with the concept of equal military parity between East and West, and the CPN advocated the dissolution of the blocs. In discussions with the CPSU, the Dutch party stated that it 'did not believe the SS-20's to be a contribution to Dutch safety'.[17] Despite the change of line, some members of the renovating wing in the CPN believed that the party was too Moscow-minded and broke away (like Member of Parliament G. Schreuders).

Criticism of the One-party System

The emancipation of the CPN from international Soviet policy was accompanied by a dissociation from the socio-political system. This

15. J. de Leeuwe, 'Een kritiek op hoofdlijnen van het ontwerpprogram van de CPN' *Politiek en Cultuur*, Vol. 42 (1982), p. 233.

16. 'Resolutie CPN-congres', *Politiek en Cultuur*, Vol. 43 (1983), p. 42.

17. E. Izeboud, 'Een open debat is nodig', *CPN-ledenkrant*, February 1985, p. 2; see also T. van Hoek, 'Den Haag-Moskou-balans?, in *CPN-ledenkrant*, November 1985, p. 2.

criticism of the one-party system was also a part of the CPN's transformation. In this process of detachment, the Polish military *coup d'état* by General Jaruzelski was again a catalyst. The intervention of the Polish military had, it said, demonstrated the 'bankruptcy of the authoritarian statist model of socialism'.[18] According to the CPN in its denunciation, the Polish Communist Party had blocked a real renovating popular movement and had in this way demonstrated the failure of the one-party system. In the eyes of the Dutch Communists, democracy started from power sharing and coalitions. Restoration of all democratic rights in Poland was demanded, including the freedom of trade unions.

In the wake of the Polish events, the monolithic and totalitarian structures in Eastern Europe became increasingly the subject of criticism, which focussed on the monopoly of power by a small group within the apparatus of party and state. At the same time, the CPN attached greater value to the unfolding new social movements in the Netherlands such as the women's liberation, environmental, anti-nuclear and peace movements as partners within the hoped-for coalitions. Correspondingly, the dissident political groups in Eastern Europe which took a stand against the Socialist regimes came into its view – not only as possible alternatives to the one-party state, but also as possible allies against the division of Europe into two blocs. This development culminated in the Twenty-eighth Party Congress of the CPN in November 1982, when the CPN expressed its sympathy with 'the democratic opposition movements in Eastern European countries' and decided 'not to maintain relations with the Polish and Czechoslovakian Communist Party in the circumstances'.[19]

The New 'Marxist-Feminist' Party Programme of 1984

The criticism of the international position of the Soviet Union by the CPN and its related verdict on the domestic affairs in the 'Socialist motherland' were laid down in an entirely new declaration of principles which was ratified by the extraordinary congress of February 1984. In this declaration Leninism was exchanged for feminism as one of the 'sources of inspiration' of the CPN. Though Marxism survived, the idea of 'class-struggle' as the sole motor of history was abandoned. Instead of the sole clash between capital and labour, the declaration

18. A. Benschop, 'Bonapartistisch socialisme? Stellingen over de gemilitariseerde partijdictatuur in Polen', *Komma: tijdschrift voor Politiek en Sociaal Onderzoek*, Vol. 3 (1) (1982) pp. 119–149.

19. 'Resolutie CPN-Congres', p. 43.

recognised the existence of various other 'contradictions', such as the ones between the genders, between man and nature, between North and South and between hetero- and homosexuality. The CPN declared that it was opposed to the mixing of the policy of the state with religion or a specific ideology and rejected the identification of state with party. It supported the multi-party system as 'essential to a democratic way of decision-making. Within socialism, constitutional rights . . . have to be guaranteed to every party, whatever their social views.'[20]

In the new declaration of principles, there was no lauditory reference to the Soviet Union. The CPN accepted the clash between West and East, but it did not side with one of the protagonists. Instead it committed itself to a 'new Socialist internationalism', which was aimed at the dissolution of the international blocs. In the CPN's programme, Moscow and Washington were again held jointly responsible for the arms race, although it was thrust upon the Socialist countries, which had 'overestimated the role of military force within international relations too and underestimated the consequences of military might on the attractiveness and development of socialism'.[21] Renovating movements within 'real existing socialism' were pressured by the authorities who were manipulating the perception of an imperialist threat. The CPN expressed its support for these dissident democratic groups in Eastern Europe.

Immediately after the CPN Congress, the conservative wing proceeded to found the League of Communists of the Netherlands (*Verbond van Communisten in Nederland*: VCN). An orthodox manifesto was drawn up, based on rigid Marxist-Leninist principles such as the leading role of the Communist Party, a positive view of 'real existing socialism' and unconditional loyalty to the Soviet Union as the 'fortress of peace and progress'.[22] The CPN was charged with 'revisionism and defeatism', because it had underestimated the power of the Socialist countries in the 'anti-imperialist battle'. The VCN asserted that by denying the class character of the struggle for peace and seeing Moscow and Washington as similar superpowers, the CPN had slid down to 'neutralism, anti-Sovietism and opportunism'.[23] Hence, as a result of the CPN's politics, the position of the United States and NATO was objectively strengthened.

20. *Machtsvorming voor een socialistisch Nederland: partijprogram van de CPN*, Amsterdam, CPN-brochurehandel, 1984, pp. 32, 12 and 72.

21. *Ibid.*, p. 22.

22. R. Dammen, 'Hereniging van communisten op basis van Marxisme-Leninisme', *Manifest*, 2 June 1987, pp. 4–5.

23. R. Dammen and L. Meertens, 'De Lange Mars naar het Winterpaleis', *Manifest* October 1983, p. 1.

Perestroika before the Word

By the middle of the eighties, the CPN had been transformed. Its traditional concept of the Communist *avant garde* had been abandoned, the multiparty system had been embraced, democratic centralism had been repudiated and the party had been remodelled into a 'democratic and feminist organisation'[24] in which pluralism, respect for minority opinions and open decision-making processes were guaranteed. It was not so surprising that the Gorbachev reforms were well received within the CPN. In the following years, both the changes in the international policy of the Soviet Union and the domestic process of renovation, in which rigid bureaucratic centralism apparently made way for more democracy, were welcomed. After a period in which the orthodox Communist Parties were scornful of the renewal of the CPN, the Dutch Communists saw prospects for their rehabilitation. Former Chairman H. Hoekstra, for instance, recalled the scepticism when talking to Eastern European officials about the transformation of the CPN in the early eighties. Now he was justified. 'It cannot be denied that issues that we have put on the agenda were very relevant and are nowadays central problems everywhere – in the CPSU and other Communist Parties'.[25] According to Hoekstra, the CPN had made the running in the international Communist movement by putting these vexing questions on the agenda.

Apart from this somewhat pretentious notion of having been one of the pioneers of the modern international Communist movement, the CPN claimed to have exercised an influence on Gorbachev's change of the Soviet Union's international policy, especially the abandonment of its objective of nuclear-strategic parity with the United States. With his strategy of de-escalation, Gorbachev had rejected the search for parity of military power between the two superpowers, at least as the CPN saw it. This renunciation of the reliance on increasing armaments in order to maintain peace was regarded as a '"Copernican revolution" in the political-military way of thinking' of a superpower.[26] Now Gorbachev had tried to stop the war of attrition by offering fundamental concessions in order to reduce arms, despite American efforts to step up the race again by announcing the deployment of Euromissiles and the Strategic Defense Initiative.

When the arms race ended, the CPN considered itself one of the pacemakers in the Communist world. It took it for granted that

24. *Machtsvorming*, p. 16.
25. H. Hoekstra, 'Diepgaande veranderingen vanuit hun eigen visie beoordelen', *Politiek en Cultuur*, Vol. 47 (1987), p. 204.
26. L. Molenaar, 'De kernbom en het "nieuwe denken"', *Politiek en Cultuur*, Vol. 48 (1988) p. 426: see also H. Hoekstra op. cit. p. 206.

conversations which were held with the CPSU in previous years had contributed to this change of direction. The official representative of the CPN at the Twenty-seventh Congress of the CPSU argued that 'the discussions, the sometimes critical dialogue which the CPN had with the CPSU, have had a positive influence'.[27] In the CPN's view, the underlying factor in Moscow's transformation of foreign policy was the growing awareness within the Soviet leadership that the 'imperialist' United States could not be stopped without the support of the peace movement of the capitalist countries. The Kremlin's analysis was believed to be a recognition of the stand which the CPN had taken for years: in order to establish a strong peace movement, Dutch Communists had not been willing to subordinate the struggle for peace to the 'class struggle' and had criticised the Western and Eastern contribution to the nuclear arms race. By exceeding narrow class bounds, the coalitions for peace could be broadened to the full.

Downfall of Socialism in Eastern Europe

Despite the renovation of the CPN, its distance from the Soviet Union and the subsequent departure or the orthodox wing, traditional affinity with Moscow still had not disappeared within the party. In welcoming Gorbachev, some within the CPN nourished hopes that Soviet communism might be able to renew itself. Members of the old guard especially cherished these expectations. Bakker asked himself whether 'communism might again become a fascinating ideal . . . because of this large Socialist state, the Soviet Union?'[28] Others also hoped that Gorbachev's efforts to add democracy to the 'really existing socialist system' might increase the political appeal of Socialist ideology. Remarkably, opinion about the Soviet Union became more positive again within the party as a whole even though Moscow seemed to have been definitively 'eradicated as a source of inspiration within the CPN' in previous years.[29]

The main reason for a revaluation of the USSR was that despite all the criticisms, the CPN still believed the Soviet socio-economic system to be essentially Socialist. An open-minded, fundamental and critical analysis of the socio-political structure of the 'really existing socialist' countries had never really been undertaken, despite the party's

27. Jaap Wolff, 'Indrukken van het CPSU-congres: versnelling en vernieuwing vereist', *Politiek en Cultuur*, Vol. 46 (1987), p. 194.

28. M. Bakker, 'Idealen', *Politiek en Cultuur*, Vol. 47 (1986), p. 125.

29. D. Hellema, '*Internationale politiek en de crisis van links*', *Politiek en Cultuur*, Vol. 48 (1988), p. 54.

ideological renovation. Its traditional outlook on the Soviet Union in this sense was demonstrated very clearly at the Seventieth celebration of the October Revolution in 1987. A special issue of the theoretical magazine of the CPN was dedicated to the 'first successful Socialist revolution'. Moreover, at the international celebration in Moscow in November, the CPN wished 'much success in the building of socialism'.[30] Soviet society was 'Socialist', for better or for worse; for the CPN the formal possession of the means of production by the state was apparently a sufficient basis for socialism.

The CPN between VCN and Green Left

Partly as a consequence of this second but partial revaluation of the Soviet Union within the CPN, a rapprochement appeared to be under way between the renovating and orthodox currents in Dutch communism. The CPN believed that Gorbachev's policy was in line with its own policy in the early eighties. The VCN, which had followed the Soviet Union slavishly, hailed the political changes under Gorbachev as a proof of the renovating capacities of Leninism. Yet despite its insistence, the CPN (not represented in the Second Chamber since the elections of 1986) was not willing even to consider a reunion. Instead of merging with the orthodox Communists, the CPN entered in an electoral coalition with the Radicals (PPR) and Pacifists (PSP).[31] Under the banner 'Green Left' these parties – together with a small Progressive Christian party and the representatives of new social movements – took six out of 150 seats, three more than the component parts had acquired separately in the previous elections. Dutch Communists re-entered the Second Chamber after an absence of three years. After the elections, the organisational development of Green Left was continued at the expense of the independence of the participating parties and in November 1990, a new party, Green Left, was officially founded. This party tried to combine ecological, 'green' demands aimed at environmental protection with traditional left-wing, 'red' issues such as a more egalitarian distribution of incomes. The 'old' parties all dissolved themselves in 1991, including the CPN (on 15 June).

30. 'Begroeting en discussiebijdrage', *Politiek en Cultuur* Vol. 48 (1988), p. 54.
31. On the foundation of the Green Left see G. Voerman, 'Le retour du communisme au sein du parlement Neerlandais', in *Communisme* No. 24. (1990) pp. 109–113.

Gerrit Voerman

Disintegration of Eastern European Communism in 1989

Partly because of the hopes which were entertained for the possible appearance of a revitalised socialism of high moral standing as the result of *glasnost* and *perestroika*, the revolutions behind the Iron Curtain at the end of 1989 were a cold shower for the CPN. Of course the Dutch Communists were pleased with the disintegration of the first of the two political blocs in Europe, which was consistent with their international objective. At last the spirit of peace came down on earth, but at the same time the Last Judgement was passed on 'real existing socialism'. The events which led to the breaking up of the Warsaw Pact shed a harsh light on the way socialism had operated in practice. And because the CPN had stuck (from its early days) to the dogma that Eastern European societies were still Socialist in some way, the party was hit very hard by the destruction of the Iron Curtain. In general, the reaction was one of disillusionment. I. Brouwer, the last Chair of the Communist parliamentary group in the Second Chamber, wrote shortly after the events in February 1990: 'What do you mean, Socialism? Just a short time ago, the October Revolution of 1917 produced a worthy successor in the Revolution of 1989, which deposed the ruling Communist Parties or compelled them to abdicate.'[32] Socialism turned out not to have been a guarantee against unemployment, poverty, environmental destruction and so on, but appeared to have been morally corrupt and bankrupt. Of course this was not unsuspected, but the bare truth which was revealed went far beyond what had been imagined.

Within the CPN a debate started in 1990 about the practice of socialism, in which fundamental questions were not evaded. The concept of the 'Communist vanguard' in particular was identified behind the Eastern European abuses and the besmirching of elevated Socialist ideals. Yet the CPN's affinity with the Eastern European systems (despite all its criticisms) was not questioned during these discussions. Avoiding this painful self-analysis, the CPN turned away from the Eastern European Socialist variant – losing an illusion but not abandoning its ideals, as the party executive made clear at the beginning of 1991, a few months before the Congress was going to decide about the dissociation of the CPN:

> The objective of the CPN was the accomplishment of a Socialist Netherlands by the democratisation of power. This aspiration was seriously hampered in the course of time by errors and abuses in the countries which called themselves Socialist . . . The fact that systems have existed in the

32. I. Brouwer, 'Het socialisme als poldermodel?', in *Politiek en Cultuur*, Vol. 50 (1990) p. 19.

world which called themselves Socialist and which are bankrupt politically and morally, is no reason the CPN to abandon its ideals . . . , although it has to be recognised that the crisis within the Eastern European countries was far deeper than assumed in the past and that the support for Socialist ideas has been narrowed considerably because of this crisis.[33]

The End of Dutch Communism

The history of relations between the CPN and the Soviet Union is paradoxical. In the 'autonomous' phase in the sixties and early seventies, the CPN had hardly any contacts with Moscow but followed in the ideological tracks of the CPSU. In the 'eighties, the CPN gave up Marxist-Leninist orthodoxy and drifted away from the Soviet Union, but at the same time, however, contacts became more frequent than in the period after the Cold War. The traditional concept of socialism as a peace-loving global force could not withstand the drive to renovation after 1980. Yet the idea that the societies behind the Iron Curtain were in essence Socialist though in a rudimentary form survived the transformation and formed the link between the orthodox and the modernist phase in the relations with Moscow.

The fraternal thread was cut by the *Götterdämmerung* in Eastern Europe in 1989. Just before, the affinity with the Soviet Union had become larger again because of Gorbachev's reforms, in which the CPN recognised some of its own ideas. The impending end of the party-state and the new era of *détente* gave rise to hopes of a Socialist renaissance. After the downfall of Eastern European socialism, the party could not sustain the myth of 'really existing socialism' any longer and turned away.

Thus in 1991, the CPN dissolved itself and merged into Green Left. Its route to this new political formation, however, was traced out some time before 1989, though the speed of the merger – and the corresponding dissolution of the party – was accelerated by it. As in the beginning when the CPN was not the consequence of the Russian Revolution of 1917 (the existing revolutionary Marxist Party merely changed its name), so in the end, the death of the party was not caused by the Eastern European revolution of 1989 alone. Above all, the dissolution of the CPN was the product of an 'autonomous' development, which – viewed in retrospect – was ushered in by the 'premature *perestroika*' Dutch communism went through in the early eighties.

33. 'Discussienota over de wijze van voortbestaan van de CNP' in *CPN-Ledenkrant*, March 1991, p. 3.

Conclusion: The Communist International and the Future of Communism

Santiago Carrillo, when Secretary-General of the Spanish Communist Party, stated that the dissolution of the Communist International (in 1943) had transformed relations with the CPSU and that subsequently no decisions were taken with prior consultations – the leadership of the Soviet party was informed only after the fact.[1] Semprùn, however, is clear that policy was decided by Stalin (to whom the Spanish leadership went for advice).[2] There is no reason to believe that other Western parties were any different and much indicates that their closeness to the PCSU continued in most respects into the 1980s. There were, however, changes in the international movement after the Second World War and there was a slow but steady disintegration (starting with the Yugoslav split and then the Sino-Soviet split). The key point in the process was 1956.

After the Kominform was dissolved in 1956, as a domonstration of the desire for 'peaceful coexistence', the CPSU International Department (probably set up before the dissolution of Komintern in 1943) acted as the principal agent of Soviet influence and control. The International Department was organised into sections for different areas of the world and had 'country specialists' who would visit the parties concerned and often appeared as embassy staff. The International Department's representatives also held the principal positions of power in the fronts and co-ordinated the activities. As directive control began to weaken, the International Department had to see what different parties could achieve and what the CPSU could do with the movement.

The Talleyrand-like survivor at the head of the International Department from 1955–86 was Boris Ponomarev (who probably entered in 1937), and his subordinate at the 'Latin desk' from 1960–86 was Vadim Zagladin. After 1988 the CPSU's International Department was run by Valentin M. Falin, who took over from Anatolii Dobrynin. The first deputy head of the International Department from 1975–88, Vadim Zagladin, moved up to become Chair of the Supreme Soviet and was seen as a 'moderate' Gorbachev supporter. The French party

1. S. Carrillo, *'Eurocommunism' and the State*, London, Pinter, 1986, p. 173.
2. J. Semprùn, *The Autobiography of Frederico Sanchez*, Brighton, Harvester, 1979, p. 60–2.

fell into the same section as 'Latin parties' (hence the frequent appearance of Zagladin at Italian meetings), but the CPGB and the CP-USA came under a different section (headed by Chernyayev for many years).

The Italian Communist Togliatti translated Khrushchev's attitude to the world movement as 'polycentrism', the autonomy of each party in fraternal co-operation – unity in diversity. There never was a 'polycentrism' in Togliatti's sense, but the obligation to follow Soviet orders was replaced with a tactical accomodation to domestic conditions – that was national roads to power in the West. The CPSU would not abandon its leading role, but it would cease to lay down the tactical details for each individual party, though parties would work within a common strategy defined by the CPSU, which was the head of the 'anti-imperialist forces'. Khrushchev intended the strategy to be established by world and regional conferences under CPSU tutelage and with binding resolutions: this is what started to happen (with the world conferences of 1957 and 1960). Yet Khrushchev had started a slow emancipation of the Communist Parties, and the Chinese party broke ranks followed by several minor parties. Khrushchev had wanted to develop local party autonomy but also to determine strategy from the perspective of the Soviet state and the Eastern bloc. These were not compatible objectives and before long the effect of the tension was felt. One example was the revelation of Stalin's crimes and the condemnation of the cult of personality, which was made for Khrushchev's own reasons but which had a devastating impact on local parties which had not been prepared or consulted (they had, as under Stalin, been informed).

Hence after Khrushchev had taken full power in Moscow the differentiation of the Communist movement started and became irreversible: although the process did not find favour with the old-fashioned French party it did with the Italians and eventually with many others. The world conference of 1960 was conflictual, and it was not until 1969 that a third world conference was held and, despite a series of initiatives, that was the last one. However, the Khrushchev experiment in transformation was short-lived, and the Brezhnev regime returned to the old values which demanded full-hearted support for the Soviet Union and a co-ordinated world movement following a centrally-defined strategy. The leadership of Brezhnev's USSR developed a two-speed internationalism which put the 'socialist internationalism' of the Eastern bloc in a superior position to the 'proletarian internationalism' which united nonruling parties. The French party was later to object to this ranking of relations between parties, but the idea of limited sovereignty (the 'Brezhnev doctrine') was not acceptable to most local parties, which were asserting the right to choose their own leaderships.

The CPSU's grip on the international movement continued to weaken and the bringing together a world conference in 1969 was done at the price of concessions to the minor parties. As a result of these difficulties the Soviets moved to the device of holding regional rather than world conferences, and the references to the CPSU's directing or leading role were watered down. The 1970s were the decade of regional conferences: for Europe these were in 1974 and 1976. These meetings disguised the lack of total agreement with wide participation (though even there some parties were absent). In 1967 a pan-European meeting had been held (in Poland) because it proved impossible to hold a world meeting, and this tactic was repeated with the European conferences of 1974 and 1976. The last of these ended without a final resolution, although the 1969 world meeting had ended with a final document (only partially endorsed by the CPGB, PCI and PCE). Direct Soviet co-ordination then moved from uncontrollable regional meetings to bilateral meetings – usually ending with a ritualistic communiqué. A new conception of internationalism began to be developed in which the French party initially participated. This new idea depended on the mutual obligations of parties and the opening of relations to non-Communist movements. The Italians, in particular, wanted to make contact with Second International Parties, although the French were less keen and, after 1977, hostile to any such dilution.

As noted, the increasing difficulties the CPSU had in mobilising the Communist movement was reflected in the diminishing number of parties prepared to support Moscow's positions and in the abandonment of regional conferences for conferences around specific objectives (such as opposition to the 'Euromissiles'). The disarray of the world movement was exemplified by the diversity of positions on the invasion of Afghanistan and on the coup by General Jaruzelski in Poland.

Gorbachev's ascent to power signalled a brief offensive phase in Communist international relations. Foreign initiatives were redoubled in order to stave off the final crisis of the Soviet system by, for example, following the Italian method of making contacts with Social Democratic parties. Gerardo Iglesias, the leader of the Spanish party, wrote that it was 'important to develop an alternative Left on the Continent, which could modify the relationship of forces and trends throughout Western Europe . . . unity with the social democrats on condition that they evolve leftwards'.[3] The strategy was much the same as that outlined in the early 1980s: to carry out campaigns on issues

3. F. Thom, *The Gorbachev Phenomenon*, London, Pinter, 1986, p. 107.

such as feminism, the environment, the Third World and peace which would mobilise broad fronts around Communist objectives. There were hopes for a world meeting again at this time.

The problem faced by Gorbachev was that Reagan's 'Star Wars' (SDI) programme threatened to bankrupt the Soviet Union, which could not follow suit. The limited ability of the Western Communists to move public opinion was a constraint, and the campaigns went ahead with narrow foreign policy objectives. Communist Parties then took up the Soviet standpoints, in proposing a denuclearised world by the year 2000, for example, proposing 'nuclear-free zones', reduced military expenditure and so on.[4] The anti-American, anti-nuclear campaigns had some success and seriously disrupted the joint NATO front to the Soviet Union in the mid-1980s, but it was not enough; the Euromissiles, SDI and NATO solidarity survived with the result that the offensive to 'decouple' the USA from Western Europe was abandoned.

Gorbachev made a number of concessions which were significant in Communist ideology. In the report to the Twenty-seventh Congress (February 1986), Gorbachev did not claim that Moscow remained the centre of orthodoxy in world Communism[5] and conceded that 'the Communists of each country [may] analyse and estimate the situation for themselves; independently determine their strategic course and their policy'.[6] The equality of fraternal parties was being accepted and the flexibility of the system was increased: the efforts, which had gone on under successive leaders since the early 1970s, to convene a new world conference were abandoned.[7] It is significant that the Socialist Parties were represented at the Twenty-seventh CPSU Congress and were given privileged access to the Soviet leaders which, the Italian party excepted, the other Western European Communists were not.

If at the Twenty-seventh CPSU Congress there was a Communist world movement, by 1992 there no longer was. The dramatic events of 1989, symbolised by the collapse of the Berlin Wall, meant that the Socialist state leadership had almost entirely disappeared. The Soviet Union relinquished its hold on Eastern Europe, and the Eastern bloc, predictably, ceased to exist. Gorbachev continued to make spectacular foreign policy proposals (arms control and in support of the 'common European home'), but domestic problems with minority nationalism and a collapsing economy undermined his authority and capacity for

4. Ibid., p. 108.
5. H. Timmermann, *The Decline of the World Communist Movement*, London, Westview, 1987, p. 61.
6. Ibid., p. 60.
7. Ibid., p. 63.

manoeuvre while they increased his need for Western assistance. Events in 1989 were clearly moving beyond the USSR's control; Gorbachev even conceded that the USA was a 'natural part' of the European structure.

The world movement under Gorbachev had uncertain contours because of the Sino-Soviet split, and because of the increasing independence of its affiliates, but it retained an importance as a political resource which legitimised the Soviet regime. However, an elaborate hierarchy had developed: the 'Socialist camp' (the USSR and the Eastern bloc) came first, led by the CPSU; followed by Communist Parties in the West and the Third World (the 'Revolutionary movement'); then National Liberation Movements (Third World Nationalists); and finally sympathisers (usually left-wing Social Democrats and disarmers). The non-ruling parties were also distinguished by the degree to which they were pro-Moscow (some, like the Maoists, were in fact hostile), and this led to a finely-graded status structure visible in the ranking of parties at CPSU Congresses and Communist events such as funerals or celebrations.

The Communist Fronts

A number of world-wide Communist fronts was run by the CPSU, and although the emphasis was on the Third World for most purposes, the Western parties were active participants in the fronts – staffed by English, Italian, Finnish and sometimes other European nationals. The size of a Communist Party was, it would seem, less important than the politically apposite personnel (a European was of no use to preside at a Third World-oriented front, for example). The staff of the various fronts had to be politically reliable, but in any case the control by Moscow was thorough and bureaucratic. The purpose had been twofold. The first was to mobilise around the CPSU's objectives. In the eighties these were almost exclusively attacks on NATO ('peace and disarmament') and action against the USA's Star Wars programme – SDI. The second objective was propaganda and disinformation which, despite Gorbachev's arrival in power, continued on a massive scale (it is virtually impossible to trace in detail).[8]

The principal means of indirect Soviet control had become the *World Marxist Review* (WMR) – published in forty different languages in 145 countries. *The World Marxist Review* (WMR-started as

---

8. See C. Rose, *The Soviet Propaganda Network*, London, Pinter, 1988.

Problems of Peace and Socialism) was a resolutely pro-Soviet theoretical journal, (the Chinese withdrew in 1963) but the local parties had the right to determine the contents of 'their' edition and, for example, a critical article by Ponomarev was pulled from the French edition of June 1974. The *World Marxist Review* was based in Prague but run by the CPSU's International Department, and the main purpose of the massive 'editorial board' was to 'help coordinate the activities of the international Communist movement through its conferences'.[9] Before its collapse in June 1990 the journal had an 'editorial board' of sixty-eight Communist Parties, but it was run by the Soviet editor-in-chief (Aleksandr Subbotin), the managing editor was also Soviet (Sergei Tsukasov, who died in 1989) and the staff were also Soviets. There were 'editorial' conferences attended by high ranking party members in December 1978 (sixty-nine attended), October 1980 (seventy-eight attended), in 1981 (eighty-one participants) and in December 1984 (ninety-one attended).

The *World Marxist Review* conferences testified to the Soviet efforts put into the anti-Euromissile and anti-SDI campaigns and the consequently increased effort against 'anti-Sovietism', but there was only a minimum agreement on the need to reinforce the anti-imperialist struggle. When Gorbachev took power the WMR was revamped and, in keeping with the new strategy of wooing non-Communist forces, included social Democrats, Greens, disarmers and so on. The idea seems to have been less political than to develop a Gramscian cultural 'hegemony' on a world scale, but Gorbachev had also abandoned the traditional aim of encouraging rifts in the West. (Of course Gorbachev still believed in the superiority of socialism). In 1989 subsidies from the Eastern states ceased and the WMR folded in June 1990 ('for reasons outside of our control'). The last feeble co-ordinating centre of world Communism slipped unnoticed out of existence.

After the *World Marxist Review* in importance came the fronts themselves. Fronts were intended to draw in sympathisers with Communist campaigns, but Soviet heavy-handed authoritarian management often undercut this aim. There was also a hierarchy of fronts. The most important front was the World Peace Council, which organised campaigns around Soviet objectives and which seems to have included representatives from other fronts, presumably to co-ordinate activities. The World Peace Council based in Helsinki was formed in 1950. In 1984 the French Communist Jacques Denis was one of the thirty-nine Vice-Presidents, and Daniel Cirera one of the fifteen

---

9. R.F. Staar (ed.), *Yearbook of International Communist Affairs*, Hoover, Stanford, 1989.

Executive Secretaries. In the early part of the 1980s the main concern was to prevent the installation of Euromissiles by the USA, but after 1984 its campaign objective was tactically changed to a call for the weapons of both superpowers to be dismantled, although it continued to emphasise that the USA was the immediate danger. The change of emphasis enabled a much more flexible approach to the issue, and in particular enabled alliances with other Western peach movements. The World Peace Council probably went out of existence in the year 1990-1, but the WPC;s campaigns could have served to delay the deployment of NATO Euromissiles in the 1980s.

The second most important front, and the only significant one left after the collapse of the Eastern bloc in 1989, was the World Federation of Trade Unions. The French were important here because they were (after the Italian CGIL became semi-detached in 1976) the only important Western unions affiliated. However, even the WFTU had as a campaign objective in the 1980s the promotion of the CPSU's peace and disarmament campaigns which, like other fronts, it linked to development on the grounds that the money spent in the West on arms could be diverted to the Third World. The theme of the 'New International Order' (often wrongly assumed to be French) is important here. The fronts repeated the Communist claim that the West – via multinationals in particular – despoiled the planet and created a debt crisis which deprived the Third World of the control of its own resources. Nuclear-free zones in various regions were another theme, though not one taken up by the French party's fronts, which were in a weak position on this issue.

The French were also strong in the professional international unions set up by the WFTU for specific trades. The World Federation of Scientific Workers was based in London and claimed 740,000 members. Its president was Jean-Marie Legay, Pierre Biquard was one of its five Vice-Presidents and M. A. Jaegel was its Deputy Secretary-General. The English Secretary-General, John Dutton, was assisted by a Russian and a French national (G. Durrafourg). The WFSW recently publicised the 'New International Scientific Order' in counterpoint to the 'New International Economic Order', to encourage a transfer of technology to the Third World. The World Federation of Teachers' Unions had a French Secretary-General – Daniel Retureau in 1986, and in 1989 one of the seven Vice-Presidents was Michèle Baracat and the General Secretary was Gérard Montant.

The WFTU was invited to quit its headquarters in Prague after the collapse of communism, and it held its 1990 conference in Moscow. However, the bulk of its 190 million 'members' were in the Soviet state unions (compromised in the August 1991 coup), and deprived of that support (and in particular the funds) the capacity to survive based on the Polish Communist Unions, the Cypriots and the French must be doubtful. In particular the notion of Leninist revolutionary syndicalism must have been given a heavy blow by the end of communism in the Soviet Union.

Next in line was the World Federation of Democratic Youth, which became a Communist front in 1949 when the Western representatives withdrew. It had an associate, the International Union of Students. The International Union of Students had a high-level French input. The Pyongyang World Youth Festival was co-ordinated by Thierry Angles, who became IUS Secretary in 1989. There was symbolic French Communist (or sympathiser) presence in 'dignified posts' in some other fronts (for example Gérard Gatinot was one of the twenty-three Vice-Presidents of the International Organisation of Journalists). However, there was relatively little top-level Western European presence in the Christian Peace Conference, the International Federation of Resistance Movements or the Women's International Democratic Federation. These organised 'youth festivals' in Communist bloc countries – like the one in Pyongyang in 1989 – and had some success. Amongst other surviving fronts in 1991 was the International Association of Democratic Lawyers, which had the indefatigable publicist Joë Nordmann as its president and Pierre Lavigne as one of its fourteen secretaries. It was based in Brussels and claimed 25,000 members in 1990.

Despite French, Portuguese and other Communist attempts to keep the Communist movement alive and their contributions to the fronts, there was very little left of world communism after 1991. The hierarchical and centralised nature of the world Communist movement means that it cannot survive without the resources of the co-ordinating offices of the CPSU, which gave it direction and purpose. The isolated meetings of hard-liners representing nongoverning parties (like the Greek, Portuguese and French) and the remaining regimes like Cuba and North Korea do not amount to a new movement and it is difficult to see how they could be anything more than a meeting of sympathisers along the lines of the Second International.

Appendix: Statistical Information on Western European Communism

Finland

The *Suomen Kommunistien Puolue* (SKP)
Finnish Communist Party
Membership: 12,500 (claimed)
Leadership: Claes Andersson (Chairman)
                Matti Viialainen (Secretary)

Vasemmistoliitto (LA) Leftist Alliance replaced the SKP, which was dissolved in April 1990.
Membership: c. 32,000
election results: March 1991 274,000 (10.07 per cent)
                    (19 seats).
Auxiliary organisations: Most were disbanded in April 1990.

Electoral Results: General Election (SKDL)

Year	% Vote	*Eduskunta* Seats*
1945	23.5	49
1948	20.0	38
1951	21.6	43
1954	21.6	43
1958	23.2	50
1962	22.0	47
1966	21.2	41
1970	16.6	36
1972	17.0	37
1975	19.0	40
1979	17.9	35
1983	13.4	26
1987**	9.4	16
1991***	10.1	19

* There are 200 seats in the unicameral *Eduskunta*.
** In 1987, the hard-line umbrella organisation, the Democratic Alternative (DEVA) gained 4.3% of the vote and 4 parliamentary seats.
*** The 1991 result is for the Leftist Alliance.

Publications: Newspapers sympathetic to the Finnish party (not run by it).
Kansan Uutiset (daily; Helsinki; circulation 43,454)
Hameen Yhteistyö (daily; Tampere; circulation 11,155)
Kansan Sana (daily; Kuopio; circulation 8,843)
Kansan Tahto (daily; Oulu; circulation 16,015)
Satakunnan Tyo (daily, Pori; circulation 10,175)
Ny Tid (daily; Helsingfors; circulation 1,500)

France

Parti Communiste Français (PCF) French Communist Party
Membership: 585,661 (1990 claim). Depending on the definition of a 'member', the real figure could be between 75,000 and 200,000.
Leadership: Georges Marchais (General Secretary)
Last Congress: Twenty-seventh PCF Congress (December 1990)
Electoral Results:
Legislative   (1988)   11.28%   (2,765,761 votes)   27 seats
European   (1989)   7.71%   (1,401,171 votes)   7 seats
Auxiliary Organisation: CGT
Publications:
L'Humanité   (daily; circulation c. 50,000)
La Marseillaise   (daily; Marseilles)
Liberté   (daily; Lille)
L'Echo du centre   (daily; Limoges)
L'Humanité – Dimanche   (weekly)

Germany

Partei des Demokratischen Sozialismus (PDS)
Party of Democratic Socialism; formerly *Sozialistische Einheitspartei Deutschland* (SED) Socialist Unity Party
Membership: c. 280,000
Leadership: Gregor Gysi
Electoral Results: (2 December 1990) 2.4% (17 seats)
Publication: *Neues Deutschland*

Deutsche Kommunistische Partei (DKP) German Communist Party
Founded: 1968
Membership: c. 20,000 (1990 claim). Some party delegates estimated membership in 1990 to be only 10,000, of which 7,000 were dues-payers.
Leadership: Collective leadership of four spokespersons: Heinz Stehr, Anne Frohnweiler, Helga Rosenberg, Rolf Priemer.
Governing Board: 46 members, half of whom are women.
Last congress: Tenth Congress in Dortmund (March 1990)
Electoral Results: (1990) DKP fielded no candidates in the December federal elections, but supported Left List/PDS, which won 2.4% of the votes (11.1% in former East Germany) and 17 seats in the *Bundestag*.
Publications: *Unsere Zeit* (Our Time), Düsseldorf. Because of party

financial crisis, weekly since late 1989. Its circulation is in a state of flux at the present time.

Auxiliary Organisations: *Sozialistische Deutsche Arbeiter Jugend* (SDAJ) Socialist German Workers' Youth; *Marxistischer Studentenbund-Spartakus (MSB-Spartakus)* Student Union-Spartakus; *Junge Pioniere* (JP) Young Pioneers;

Great Britain

The Communist Party of Great Britain (CPGB) (Secretary-general Nina Temple) transformed itself into the Democratic Left in 1991, but a number of splinter groups remain.

Communist Party of Britain (CPB)
Membership: 1,000 (est.)
Leadership: Mike Hicks (General Secretary)
Publication: *Morning Star* (daily; circulation c. 10,000)

New Communist Party (NCP)
Membership: 500 (est.)
Leadership: Eric Trevett (General Secretary)
Publication: *New Worker* (weekly)

Greece

Kommunistiko Komma Elladas (KKE) Greek Communist Party
Membership: c. 40,000 (1991)
Leadership: Aleka Papariga (General Secretary)
Last Congress: December 1991 (Fourteenth)
Electoral Results:
April 1990:   10.28%   (677,059 votes)   in coalition   19 seats
Publications:
Rizospastis   (daily; circulation c. 20,000)
Kommounistiki Epitheorisi   (monthly theoretical)

Italy

Partito Democratico della Sinistra (PDS) Democratic Party of the Left;
formerly *Partito Comunista Italiano* (PCI) Italian Communist Party
Membership: 1.3 million (claimed)
Leadership: (1991) 177 deputies; 84 senators; 225 regional
councillors. In large cities the PCI holds the position of mayor only in
Bologna. Sr Nilde Jotti is currently Speaker of the Chamber of
Deputies.

Full-time Party employees: Piero Fassino, the Organisation Secretary,
stated in *L'Unità* (4 October 1988, p.3) that at that time the PCI had
2,500 full-time employees, and that it was planned to reduce this
number to 1,700 in reply to a charge by Corriere della Sera that the PCI
had 25,000 functionaries.

Electoral Results:
European

1972	1976	1979	1979	1983	1984	1987	1989
27.1%	34.4%	30.4%	29.6%	29.9%	33.3%	26.6%	27.6%

Regional

1979	1975	1980	1985
27.9%	33.4%	31.5%	30.2%

Rinascita closed in Spring 1990 and although *L'Unità* sold 400,000
daily in the 1950's and 250,000 in the mid-1970's, it sold only
180,000-200,000 in the late 1980's.

Sweden

Vänsterpartiet Kommnisterna (VKP) Swedish Communist Party/Vänsterpartiet (VpK) Left Party
Electoral Results:

Year	% Vote	*Riksdag* Seats*
1970**	4.8	17
1973	5.3	19
1976	4.8	17
1979	5.6	20
1982	5.6	20
1985	5.4	19
1988	5.8	21
1991***	4.5	16

*There are 349 seats in the *Riksdag*.
** 1970 was the year of the shift to unicameralism.
*** Contested by the Left Party.

Portugal

Partido Communista Português (PCP) Portuguese Communist Party
Membership: 120,000 (May 1990 claim)
Electoral Results (in coalition)
Legislative

(1985)	15.5%	893,216 votes	(38 deputies)
(1987)	12.2%	(685,109 votes)	31 deputies

Presidential (1991) 12%
Local

1975	1979	1982	1985
18.1%	20.9%	20.9%	19.4%

Publications: *Avante!* (weekly)
O Militante (theoretical)
O Diário (daily; circulation c. 40,000; closed in July 1990)
Auxiliary organisation:
Confederação General de Trabalhadores Portugueses (CGTP) General Confederation of Portuguese Workers, controlled by the party, claims to have one million members.

Scandinavia

The Radical left in the Nordic Parliaments, 1992

Country	Party	% Vote	Seats	Total Seats
Denmark	Socialist People's	8.4	15	175
Iceland	People's Alliance	14.4	9	63
Finland	Leftist Alliance	10.1	19	200
Norway	Socialist Left	10.1	17	165
Sweden	Leftist Party	4.5	16	349

Spain

Partido Communista de España (PCE) (Spanish Communist Party)
Membership: 55,000 (uncorroborated figure)
Leadership: Julio Anguita González (General Secretary)
Last Congress: held in Madrid (December 1991)
Electoral Results (as part of *Izquierda Unida*)

European Parliament	(June 1989)	6.2%	(961,742 votes)	4 seats
General Election	(October 1989)	9.05%	(1,851,080 votes)	17 seats
Regional				
Catalonia	(May 1988)	2.88%	(38,214 votes)	0 seats
Andalusia	(June 1990)	12.67%	(349,591 votes)	11 seats
Basque Country	(October 1990)	1.41%	(14,440 votes)	0 seats

Publications:
Mundo Obrero (monthly; edited by Miguel Bilbatúa; claimed circulation 24,000)
Neustra Bandera (quarterly; edited by Armando López Salinas)
Colecctión Debate (series of monographs published at irregular intervals)

Notes on Contributors

José Amodia is a Senior Lecturer in the Department of Modern Languages at the University of Bradford. He teaches Spanish Language and Politics and is the author of *Franco's Political Legacy* as well as a number of articles on Spanish politics.

David Arter is Professor of European Integration at Leeds Polytechnic and the author of numerous works on Scandinavian and Finnish politics including *The Nordic Parliaments: a Comparative Analysis* (London), Charles Hurst 1984, and *Bumpkin Against Bigwig* (Tampere 1978).

David S. Bell is a Lecturer in Politics at the University of Leeds.

Heinrich Bortfeldt was a student at the Martin Luther University Halle-Wittenberg, a Research Assistant in the Institute of History, Academy of Social Sciences, in Berlin and completed a doctorate on American and German historiographical views of post-war Germany.

John Callaghan is Professor of Politics at Wolverhampton Polytechnic. He has published on British communism and the British Left as well as on British politics generally.

Stephen Gundle is a Fellow in Politics at University College, Oxford, and his recent publications include chapters on cinema, politics and society in Z. Baranski and R. Lumley (eds.), *Culture and Conflict in Postwar Italy* (London, Macmillan, 1990). He is the author of a full-length study of the Italian Communist Party to be published by Cambridge University Press in 1992.

Maria Teresa Patricio is a Professor of Sociology in the Instituto Superior de Ciências do Trabalho e da Empresa, Lisbon. She is the author of numerous books and articles on Portuguese politics and society.

Ole L. Smith is Professor in the Classics Department of Greek at the University of Gothenburg, Sweden. In addition to extensive writings about the history of the Greek Communist Party he has also written about modern Greek politics.

Alan D. Stoleroff is Associate Professor at the Instituto Superior de Ciências do Trabalho e da Empresa, Lisbon. He has written and published extensively on labour and trade union issues in Portugal and is currently directing a research project on the industrial relations system in Portugal.

Wayne C. Thompson is Professor of Political Science in the Virginia Military Institute. He has studied and researched for many years in West and East Germany and is the author of many books and articles including, *In the Eye of the Storm* (University of Town Press, 1980) and most recently, *Western Europe 1990* and The Political Odyssey of Herbert Wehner.

Gerrit Voerman is an historian and is the director of the Centre of Documentation on Dutch Political Parties of the State University of Groningen (Netherlands). He has published frequently on Political parties and is a member of the Research Group on Western European Communism. He is preparing a theses on the CPN.

Index

Index

Index

Morán, G. 104
Morning Star 13, 123, 134, 136
Movement for a New Left (Greece) 88
multipartism 167
Munich 61
municipal elections
    1985 (Italy) 16
    1989 (Italy) 25
    (Spain) 106
    1987 (Spain) 107–108
Mussolini 1

Nagono Karabakh 132
Nagy, I. 26
Napolitano, G. 17, 28
Natta, A. 17, 18, 19, 20, 62
National Front (French) 65, 67
national liberation movements 94
nationalisation 71, 110
nationalism 131
NATO 12, 36, 53, 54, 60, 105, 107, 110, 114, 160, 175, 177
Nazi/Soviet pact 1, 12
Netherlands Communist Party (CPN), 1, 2, 3, 7, 10, 11, 13, 32, 158–171
    Twenty-seventh Congress 163, 168
    Twenty-eighth Congress 164, 165
    dissolution 169
neutron bomb campaign 162–63
Neu Zeitung 155
New Communist Party (UK) 13, 122, 130, 136
New Democracy (Sweden) 50
New Forum (GDR) 143
new middle class 161
New Right 38, 42, 50
new socialist internationalism 166
New State (Portugal) 70, 71
New Worker 136
Nicaragua 110
Nilsen, K.A. 33
non-interference 159, 162

Nordic Council 46
Nordgren, E. 41
North Korea 11, 60, 77, 180
North-South divide 48, 166
Norwegian Communist Party (NKP) 3, 57
Norway 37
nuclear arms 163, 168
nuclear deterrent (French) 60
nuclear free zone 48, 176, 179
nuclear weapons 110

Occhetto, A. 15, 23–4, 25, 26, 27–28, 29, 30, 62, 112
oil crisis 4
one party state 165
OPZZ unions (Poland) 63
organization of party 80
Ostellino, P. 23

Papachristodoulou, K. 97
Papariga, A. 89, 95, 96n
parliamentary democracy 72
Partido del Trabajo de España 117
Partido Carlista (Spain) 106
Partido Humanista (Spain) 106
Party of Democratic Socialism (PDS – Germany) 139, 143, 144, 145, 146, 147, 148, 150, 151, 152, 153, 155, 156,
    Second Congress 147
    financial scandal 145, 147
    response to August coup 147–148
PASOC (Socialist Action Party – Spain) 106, 115
PaSoK 4, 8, 88
Pacifist Socialist Party (PSP – Neth) 157, 169
Pasquino, G. 15
Paul-Rugenstein-Verlag 151
peace policy 74
peace movement 6, 57, 58, 60, 105, 110, 154, 162, 163, 164, 168
peace offensive 58

Index